Jamaica's Dogsled Team

by John Firth

To Anne + Ed.

Love Eve + Bob too

One Mush: Jamaica's Dogsled Team
Publisher: John Firth/Jamaica Dogsled Team
Whitehorse, YT, Canada

Printed in Canada by Friesens

ISBN: 978-0-9867603-0-3

Cover Design and Dogsled Rigging Illustration – Schramm Design, Ucluelet, BC

Cover Photos – *Front:* Chris McLennan www.cmphoto.co.nz (photo of Newton Marshall), HarryKern.com (Focus, Focus, Focus – Quest Start), Eppo Eerkes (mountain backdrop). *Back:* Eppo Eerkes (Newton and Marbles, Jamaica Dogsled Team at Iditarod)

Interior Design and Layout – Reber Creative Design & Communications, Victoria, BC

Editing and Project Management – Erin McMullan, Ucluelet, BC http://freshhorses.ca/

See page 313 for a complete list of photo credits.

Tricia Ruddock
48 Bonnechere Crescent
Toronto, ON M1K 4Z3
Tel: 416-266-9225
Email: truddock@chukkacaribbean.com
Website: www.jamaicadogsled.com

One Love...One Heart...One Mush

One: One Love, the signature Reggae classic from the late Bob Marley, is the unofficial national anthem of Jamaica. The first half of the opening line of the song "One Love" is a common greeting or good-bye between Jamaicans. The second half of the opening line is "One Heart." The national motto for Jamaica is "Out of many, one people."

Mush: believed to be from the French word "Marche!" meaning "Go!" in English. It was thought to be the command used to get a dogsled team started pulling, but it isn't actually used any more. The sport of driving dog teams is called Mushing.

YUKON
QUEST

Foreword

by Rachel Manley
Governor General's Award winning author and daughter of former Jamaican Prime Minister Michael Manley

What a humbling, inspiring work.

I am blown away by this story. It's not just moving and well-told. It manages to break ranks with the normal history or travel or sports story by combining all three, without ever compromising each part. This story, told through the extraordinary Quest of Newton Marshall, Jamaican musher, shrinks many diverse cultures into a common parable of determination overcoming hardship, courage overcoming challenge and danger, perseverance overcoming the handicaps and hurdles of poverty and its every setback. Most of all, it is the determination of mindset over every obstacle and hurdle, the golden quest of a spirit that triumphs to mend the human heart.

In this fine book, expertly crafted by a writer who knows not just his craft but his subject, and has researched each changing landscape, each nook and cranny, and enchantingly vivified it, one learns so much about what is universal in even the most far-flung cultures from rugged Alaska and the Yukon, and freezing First World Minnesota, to the sunny, Third World Caribbean island of Jamaica. It also teaches us what is universal in the navigation of the earth we share as its creatures; how both dogs and man can be each other's salvation if we could only learn to love and trust each other as we face the plights we share, each using their special gifts.

And what a gift of hope this is. How utterly unexpected and uplifting. It makes me want to start all over again at the very beginning and try this thing called living one more time...and get it better.

Caribbean Sea
Montego Bay
Runaway Bay
Chukka Cove
Saint Ann's Bay
Ocho Rios
HANOVER
SAINT JAMES
TRELAWNY
Negril
WESTMORELAND
SAINT ANN
SAINT MARY
Annotto Bay
Port Antonio
SAINT ELIZABETH
CLARENDON
SAINT CATHERINE
SAINT ANDREW
PORTLAND
Bluefields Bay
Black River Bay
MANCHESTER
Kingston
SAINT THOMAS
Long Bay
Portland Bight
Caribbean Sea
Jamaica
National Capital
Roads
Rivers
0
10 KM
20 KM
0
10 Miles
20 Miles

Preface

Jammin'

September 28-30, 2007

At some point during the festivity at Chukka Cove, Dick Watts noticed the lonely figure lingering by the front gate.

It's not unusual in Jamaica to see people hanging around a gate or door in the towns and cities but not here at Chukka Cove, located midway between two north coast towns, St. Ann's Bay and Runaway Bay, especially on this day when it seemed the whole world was welcome to owner Danny Melville's 60th birthday party.

While close enough for the Chukka Caribbean employees to commute to work, it was too distant and isolated for people to travel just to hang around the gate. The private road on the east side of the Polo field, that gave the adventure tourism center its name, is treated like a public access to the ocean but not heavily traveled.

Occasionally, a dreadlocked fisherman would be seen strolling up the road in the mornings carrying a small bucket, in which he had bait and a hand line or two coiled up. Or going back down in the late afternoon heat with the day's catch dangling.

Danny had originally built Chukka in 1983 as a Polo field and equestrian riding ground and the main event of his three-day bash featured a friendly polo match on Saturday afternoon. His family had a longstanding love of horses and a three-generation history of competing in the "King of Games." His sons contended in the Saturday game. Saturday's crowd was approximately 350 guests, almost half from Europe, other Caribbean islands, Canada and the United States, and included government dignitaries, businessmen, acting and performing celebrities, academics and what Carole Melville, Danny's wife, called the "gathering of the rich young stallions" – a number of friends and polo-playing colleagues of his three sons, Alexander, Marc and Daniel Jr. A collection of sports cars and sport utility vehicles plugged the driveways and the road in front of the villas and around the Polo field.

The Melvilles in polo gear (L to R) Daniel Jr., Alexander, Danny's mother Janet, Marc, Danny.

Two teams, each consisting of four horse and rider combinations used mallets, hammer-shaped clubs with very long handles, to pass or shoot a small wooden ball until they drove it into their opponents' goal on the opposite end of the field. It had rained steadily since Friday evening and kept up through Saturday morning, so the game was contested in an atmosphere of mud and torn turf flying into the air from the horse's hoofs. Players and spectators could hardly tell who played for which side as mud obscured their uniform colors and smeared over their goggles.

The crowd huddled under their umbrellas, not caring who they were cheering for, encouraging both sides equally. Although one of the oldest organized sports on earth, for some of this crowd, it was their first time witnessing it.

A polo game is four, six, or eight periods of playing time, each about seven minutes long, which are called "chukkas." The length of each game depends on how serious the match is intended to be. When the game ended so did the rain, allowing the Chukka staff time to wipe down tables and chairs set up in the large fenced paddock called the dog arena, because it was where the Jamaica Dogsled Team (JDT) ran their tours.

The humid air sizzled to the beat of "Chalice" – a major Jamaican band of the 1980s and early 1990s – keeping the crowd dancing until dawn on Sunday morning.

Reggae isn't just music to comfort, distract and entertain – it's the Jamaican people's universal voice. An ideology. The measure by which one can judge the nation's inhabitants. It defines the island, giving voice to their history of slavery and colonization, political corruption and civil disorder, while celebrating the joys of life on a tropical island, the hopes and dreams of a people struggling to find their destiny.

When Jamaica dances, everything moves and it moves to an erotic rhythm. It is organic therapy. A therapeutic means of dancing out despair, dancing in denial, using overtly sexual body language. The undulating bump and grind frees the dancers from inhibitions. They can lose themselves in pleasure and, on this night, they did.

The arena was fragrant with the rich, smoky flavors of "Jerk" pork and chicken slow-cooking over simmering fires. Humming with voices limbered up and unleashed by the drinks flowing freely from the open-air bars. Danny rubbed shoulders easily with the wealthy and renowned. He was old Jamaican money and an integral builder of its future. A man easy to become friends with. And he knew how to throw a party.

Like most things that Danny invested his time in, even his birthday bash had a charitable twist. In lieu of gifts his guests were asked to bring donations for the Jamaican Society for the Prevention of Cruelty to Animals (JSPCA). Five thousand dollars had been raised.

"A once in a lifetime party," sighed a hungover but happy Danny from behind his rimless prescription sunglasses on Sunday morning as he watched some of his guests straggle out of the front gate. "Once and never again!"

Some visitors stayed for the "recovery party," a quiet family time by the swimming pool in front of the villas at the north end of the Polo field. Among them was Dick Watts, an optometrist from Whitehorse, Yukon, Canada, who owned the villa next door to Danny.

While the music and dance had hypnotic lure, it was the moment Dick had glanced away from the party and caught sight of that lonely figure down by the gate that stuck in his mind. It seemed so out of place, he decided he needed to know more.

On Monday Dick walked to the office for Chukka Caribbean Adventures, near the horse stables, seeking operations manager Devon Anderson. "Who's that hanging around the front gate?" he asked.

The stocky Jamaican, usually brimming with confidence and purpose, looked sadly for a long moment down the driveway toward the entry. "That's

Newton," he responded quietly. "He was banned from the property and doesn't feel comfortable coming up this way."

Dick was familiar with the name. Newton Marshall had once been an employee of Chukka, working with the dogsled team, but there had been some problems a year or so earlier. He hadn't heard the details but knew it involved two of Danny's neighbors, Shelley and Brian Kennedy, and resulted in Newton being dismissed from his job. Devon was hesitant to talk further about it.

When Dick asked others they reluctantly answered. Each time with a sense of deep disappointment and profound personal betrayal. Every day until he had to return home Dick watched the gate, but Newton never reappeared.

Dick wasn't the only Whitehorse resident at Chukka Cove that weekend. Hans Gatt and his partner Susie Rogan also made the trip for the birthday party. Hans, one of the world's top professional dog drivers, has a passion for sleddogs. While he's happy to stop and chat with people, he gives the impression of not being complete or totally at ease unless he's socializing with a dog or standing on the back end of a sled. It is a characteristic common to professional champions such as horse racing jockeys, dog mushers, polo players and equestrian riders – athletes involved in a sport where an animal is an equal partner with a human.

He was making daily walks to the kennel to visit with the dogs and give advice to the Jamaica Dogsled Team trainer and tour guide Damion Robb. One morning he encountered a young Jamaican he hadn't seen before. Robb was doing one of his daily chores – working his way through the kennel with a shovel cleaning up behind the dogs. However, this new man was simply visiting. Knowing how Jamaicans feel about dogs, that fact alone piqued Hans' interest.

He found himself impressed by the way the man talked to the dogs, rubbing their bellies or ears and playing with them. He apparently enjoyed the dogs – something rare among Jamaicans. The dogs obviously loved and trusted him in return – something equally rare in Jamaican dogs. Some people are natural-born dog men, he thought. Hans hadn't witnessed that kind of relationship with any of the other employees including Devon and Robb.

"He was very good with the dogs," said Hans. "He has something about him that just makes him good without really trying."

Hans walked through the kennel, visiting the dogs, talking to them, unconsciously doing what a professional dog man will do – checking paws for damage, pulling on the top of the head to test for dehydration, bending legs and wrists to see if there were any strains or stresses. Occasionally he would talk to Robb, suggesting that he keep a close watch on certain dogs or proposing possible changes in routine for specific animals.

The other Jamaican, in turn, kept an intrigued eye on Hans. He knew that a man from the Yukon was at Chukka Cove and that he was one of the world's top dog mushers. He assumed this slender Austrian was him. Being at the kennel was an exception to his ban from the property.

"At first they told me I couldn't even come on the property to go to Mrs. Kennedy's class," he said. "When they let me come to the classes I asked Devon if I could visit the dogs and he said 'okay' but that was it. I couldn't go anywhere else or do anything else at Chukka. Just visit the dogs."

The kennels were not so big that two people could keep any distance between them for any period of time. Finally, when they passed close to each other, the Jamaican turned and introduced himself.

"I'm Newton," he said. "I used to work here. I just like the dogs so I come back to visit."

Like Dick's memory of the lonely figure by the gate, it was that moment that became Hans' most memorable recollection of Danny's party.

One Love. JDT team member Chance with Newton.

Counting down to Newton's Yukon Quest.

Mush Mon!

Whitehorse, Yukon, Canada

February 14, 2009

"Stay focused," Hans Gatt reminded Newton Marshall before they left the dogyard that morning. "Don't make any last minute changes. Making changes at this point sets you up to make mistakes. There's going to be a lot of people there. Cameras and media. Don't get distracted. Double-check everything to make sure you don't leave anything behind. Once the race starts what is left behind stays behind. You can't get it later."

Now, with the *Gatt Sled* Dodge truck parked just a few meters from the Start line and the crowds milling around, Newton checked the thermometer on the back of his sled. -31°C.

"Minus 30," he muttered to himself, "Nobody jammin' at minus 30." Then his grin returned and he glanced up at his handlers, Rick and Annette "Nettie" Johnson. "Not too bad. It's warming up."

His voice was almost drowned out by the cacophony of hundreds of spectators, 29 Gortex-wrapped mushers and their handlers packing sleds, and over 400 barking dogs bounding into the air, whimpering and howling their desire to get going.

No matter where you were in the city of Whitehorse, you couldn't help but hear the dogs. There were still a couple of hours to the start. The sun was just starting to make its appearance above the southern horizon. As it will when the weather is cold, chimney smoke rose straight up into the motionless air. When people breathed or a dog barked visible clouds of moisture billowed out of their mouths. Moustaches and beards were thick with icicles and frost rimmed the edge of winter hats.

At first the pace of preparation was fairly relaxed. A "Mush Mon" Jamaica Dogsled Team banner was draped across the front of the truck, in case anyone missed the Jamaican flag on the sled bag or the "Jamaica" stitched across Newton's back. Hans and Newton pulled the sled down from the top of the dog box and stretched the gangline out in front of it.

Newton started unloading the bags and packing dog food, extra dog coats, cooker fuel, human food and mandatory gear – axe, sleeping bag, extra dog booties, snowshoes, veterinary records for the dogs, a functional "cooker" or stove and a Yukon Quest promotional package – into the sled.

He posed for pictures with several of the people crowded around his area. They wished him luck. Some just wanted to touch him or shake his hand. They introduced their children to him. The idea of having the Jamaica Dogsled Team (JDT) in the race obviously intrigued not only Yukon residents but also visitors from Europe and the United States, exploring the streets where the teams were marshaled.

What Newton was about to start had been attempted by fewer people than attended Danny Melville's sixtieth birthday party. Only 340 mushers had started the Yukon Quest over its 26-year history. Only 238 completed it.

The steady parade of people stopping outside Newton's roped area fired a constant stream of questions at him, which he mostly fended off with single-line answers. Courteous, cooperative, yet conveying the message that there were things he still needed to do to get ready and a long chat wasn't one of them:

"I'm the first Black man and first Jamaican in the Quest and I'm quite proud of that.

Young JDT fans.

"I will just work off the schedule and hopefully it will get me to the Finish line.

"My goal is just to finish. Once I finish, I will have won.

"I could be at home. Warm.

"These dogs can go forever. My dogs in Jamaica? They can go like that for maybe a mile."

He posed for a photo with a cardboard cutout of a human figure called "Flat Stanley" – a character sent to the Yukon by a Grade Two elementary school class in Ontario. Flat Stanley would be photographed at most checkpoints with different mushers each time. The school class used Stanley to follow the race from start to finish on the Internet.

Danny Melville hovered nervously around the truck, trying to stay out of the way but wanting desperately to be involved in the action. The Jamaica Dogsled Team was his dream and the thrill he felt at seeing it turn into reality was almost too much for him to bear. "I'm so excited. So anxious I can't even eat," Danny said. "He's very brave to do this."

As the clock ticked down and departure time got closer, Newton started to display some nerves, anxiously going through his checklist again and again with Rick and Nettie. For veterans this was a practice of muscle memory. They knew the routine intimately and performed almost unconsciously, never missing a step.

For rookies like Newton it was overwhelming. So much depended upon not making a single mistake before you even got on the trail. Even small errors had the capability of turning into big problems in the extreme environment of the Quest.

The first team was to leave at 11 a.m. with the others following at three-minute intervals. Newton would be leaving in seventh place. The Johnsons helped him "drop the dogs," which involved removing the dogs from their cubicles in the dog box, a canine hotel mounted in the back of a truck. Then

Newton interviewed by reporters before the race.

Newton stood astride each dog and slipped harnesses over their heads. Some, the ones with thinner coats of hair, he put dog coats on to keep warm.

When each dog was dressed, the Johnsons clipped them to chains attached to the side of the truck. Even as their musher went through his steps, the dogs had their own rituals. Some sat silently. Others bounded into the air, barking hysterically. A few crawled under the truck and curled up as if for a nap. Most rubbernecked, their heads turning in every conceivable direction to take in the activity around them.

As his starting time ticked ever closer, Newton removed them from the truck chains and clipped them into place with tuglines attached to the gangline in front of his sled. When hooked into place, the dogs, previously so sociable, friendly and curious about everything and everyone, suddenly became very businesslike. Ignoring the excitement and distractions around them, they tuned in exclusively on Newton. Their eyes following his every move. They responded to his presence as he double-checked their lines, bent down and shoehorned their paws into dog booties or simply stopped to rub them between the ears. All the time Newton chatted gently with each dog in soft, lilting Jamaican patois.

"Hey McKinley."

"Redford nice no rass (Redford's the best)!"

"Wha Gwan Newman (what's going on Newman)?"

Bootying up the team.

After initially helping him set up the sled and get his bags off the truck, Hans and Susie would occasionally wander over to check his progress and provide assistance. They were also getting Hans ready to run so were trying to prepare two teams to go. Hans was scheduled to leave in 16th place, a half hour behind Newton.

Around Newton his fellow competitors, rookies and veterans alike, were feeling pre-race jitters. There were 23 men and eight women racing. Newton was one of 14 rookies. Alaskan mushers formed almost half the field with 13 teams. Yukon teams were next with five. There was one each from Colorado, New Hampshire, Quebec, British Columbia, the Northwest Territories, France, Britain, Austria, Japan, Jamaica and Germany.

Their starting positions had been determined by random draw during a banquet on Thursday night. Today they had to be ready to go when their time came. If a team wasn't ready to go they would have to wait until all the other teams had left before being allowed to depart, but their elapsed time for the race would be calculated from their scheduled start.

"This is the most stressful time," said Marie-Claude Dufresme, partner and handler for veteran Jean-Denis Britten, from Dawson City. "It's all about time and not having enough to get ready."

Even veteran mushers were apprehensive about the race ahead. No matter how experienced the musher or how prepared, they tended to look at what should have been better and fretted about potential, unanticipated adversity. They planned as perfectionists but race disasters could rise up like ghosts. The longer the race, the more time they had to think about what could go wrong and worry. The more opportunity for setbacks existed. The Quest was almost 1,000 miles long.

"Don't think about how long the race is," Hans advised Newton, "when you get on the trail don't think about Fairbanks. Think about Braeburn, the first official checkpoint, just 100 miles away. Then think about Carmacks. Worry only about the part of the trail you're traveling on and don't think past that until you get there. One mile at a time. One hour at a time."

"You better get nervous," one of the pre-race favorites, veteran Jon Little from Kasilof, Alaska, had a different approach to the race. "If you don't, you shouldn't be here. It's the trail and the task ahead – to get to Fairbanks – that makes me nervous. This is not a 100-mile race. It's a matter of keeping the team together and trying to keep them slowed down for the first 500 (miles). The first time you do something like this you hear all the stories about the things that are coming up and you don't know what to expect. You don't know what's around the next corner."

Rookie Colleen Robertia, also from Kasilof, was apprehensive about what she might find just past the start chute. "The biggest fear is the unknown. The name (Yukon Quest) says it all – it's a quest on so many levels. One, a personal level. How will I cope emotionally with all of this?

"It really is a Quest and you got to have those in your life. Mine is right now. There will be others, but this is the one for me right now. It's an emotional journey as much as a physical journey. That in itself, it changes you or it changes me.

"My dogs have never done such a long race. I've gone through some tough things in my life so I know I'm tough. But I'm also caring for 14 animals who love me unconditionally and trust me. I want to make sure we finish, not as a team, but as a family."

Every rookie dealt with uncertainty in their own way. Newton said a prayer to himself that morning while sitting in the outhouse (an outbuilding with an unheated toilet and without running water, and, if you're lucky, it has a door and a padded seat).

The first team to leave was British musher and first-time Quester Mark Sleightholme. It's the least favorite starting position since it means you're "breaking trail" – there's nobody traveling in front of you for the early part of the race. It gives the other teams someone to chase for a while. Everybody passes you at some point during the race and you have to wait until they've gone by before you can pass anyone at all. If you take a wrong turn there's nobody else to blame, but everybody who followed you on that wrong turn will blame you.

Scheduled to leave almost 90 minutes behind Sleightholme and over an hour after Newton, another rookie, Quebec musher Normand Casavant, would be the final team to pull out. With extra time to prepare himself he was unfazed by the commotion around him.

"I'm always happy. I do the 'danse de Saint Guy.' It's the happy dance. I'm happy that Mother Nature created the type of country we need to run our dogs. And it's fantastic starting last. I have 28 teams to pass!" Normand babbled excitedly.

Newton sensed the dogs' barking and howling increase in volume as the anticipation built. His own dogs started pulling at their lines, yelping and howling, "Let's go!" and leaping into the air. The first teams finally headed toward the Start line. Then he could hear the spectators clapping, cheering and whistling as the dogs slingshot their musher and sled down the start chute, snow and booties flying into the air in every direction.

A group of race officials found their way through the crowd of dogs, sleds and mushers to Newton. "You're team number seven?" one asked.

"Yeh Mon."

"You ready?"

"Yeh Mon."

"Good. We need to check your mandatory gear, then we'll get you to the line."

Rick and Nettie, along with a few other volunteers who arrived with the officials, took hold of the tuglines connecting the dogs to the gangline. When the officials signed off on his gear, Newton unhooked the sled from the front of the truck. The handlers were now the only thing preventing the team from charging out and down the trail.

Newton prepares the sled.

They moved forward onto First Avenue where the start chute was located, the dogs straining at their tuglines, dragging the handlers toward their "on-deck"

Photographers angle for a good photo.

position behind the banner marking the Start line. Newton could stop them by stepping on the brake, but only just.

Colleen Robertia was temporarily ahead of him, waiting for her time. Then the handlers jumped back and her dogs, finally free to run, took off.

Now, for the first time, Newton could see clearly down the start chute. The cloud of snow that marked Colleen's passage directly ahead of him. The snow fencing covered with sponsors' banners and flags. The crowd packed in behind the fence and on bleachers waving, cheering, clapping, and stretching down the street as far as his eye could see.

Journalists by the dozen lay or knelt in the snow to either side of him for some distance down the chute, trying to get photos from a low angle. Others were in lift buckets, suspended over the middle of the trail, trying to shoot from a high angle.

One official waved him forward until the brush bow on the front of the sled was under the start banner. Extra handlers stepped forward to help hold the dogs. Another official stepped up beside him to wish him luck and shake his hand. Newton gave him a big grin but couldn't remember what was said. Susie stepped in behind him, patted him on the shoulder and talked at him, but he couldn't listen.

The true impact of what he was about to start suddenly hit him. His grin faltered, looking more like clenched teeth than a smile. His knees

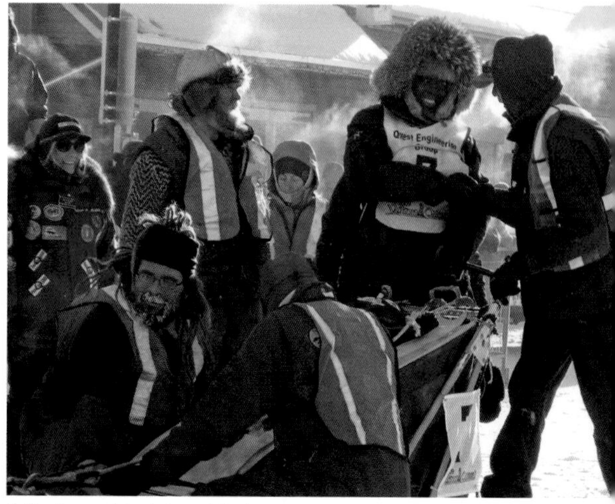

A final good-luck handshake . . .

almost buckled. His hands got clammy cold. His eyes grew wide and he found it hard to draw a breath. “It was intense,” Newton said later.

The Start line announcer unintentionally helped pull him back into focus with his lame chatter. “Thirty seconds,” he declared, and then added, “You stay warm out there now. Keep a Reggae tune in your head for us.”

Newton heeded the advice. He started singing a Reggae tune to himself – a song he’d made up and used before when he or the dogs seemed out of sorts.

“Ten seconds,” said the announcer, “Eight, seven, six….”

He gripped the driving bow like a departing lover, seemingly unsure whether he should hold on or let go.

At the word “Go!” the handlers stepped back, the dogs stopped barking, leaned into their harnesses, dug into the snow.

. . . and GO!

on Ques
TIONAL SLED DOG R

26th Running
Whitehorse to Fairban
Proud 2009 Sponso
OUTSIDEtheCUBE
TransCanada
In business to deliver
2009
LOTTERIES
YUKON
NORCAN
TALS • LEASING

Lifting his foot off the brake, Newton pushed into the snow behind him, and then stepped onto the drag mat, a heavy piece of rubber meant to slow teams down when they get too excited and want to run too fast. His grin looked more like a grin again. He could breathe freely once more.

Down the chute a rooster tail of snow billowed up around him. Further down the street, as the crowd thinned, he started waving to them. The trail twisted clear of the final buildings, left the road and ran through a long park next to the Yukon River. They loped past groups of people who called his name and shouted "Jamaica Mon" into the frozen air. He weaved through a batch of willows, blinked in surprise at a few photographers who leaned out of the bushes to take quick pictures and then dropped over a slight bank onto the river ice.

Most rookies falter because they never gain the confidence to believe they can finish. His moment at the Start line apart, Newton never seemed to doubt his ability to go the distance. Confidence was never the aspect of the race that messed with his head.

"The cold don't bother me," he said just before the race, "just as long as there's no open water. Open water that don't freeze proper. Those are the worst. The most scary."

Although he lived on an island surrounded by the golden warm waters of the Caribbean Sea, Newton had never learned how to swim.

Water still flowed freely under the river ice and occasionally the trail passed close to open leads, or holes in the ice.

For the moment, the fact that he was traveling on ice didn't occur to him, although just behind him was a massive, wide, open lead in the ice. Finally, Newton and the dogs were away from the crowds and had a packed trail to follow. The team settled into a steady loping rhythm. He kept singing, now more from pleasure than nerves.

It's a hard road to travel
And a mighty long way to go
Stony and the blessed leaders
Is gonna lead me by the way I go.
Many a lonesome valley
Where many few wants to go
It's a hard road to travel
And a mighty long way to go.

"And a mighty long way to go."

Alan Stewart and Devon Anderson on a dryland dogsled cart.

Epiphany

All great schemes are crazy. That's what makes them great.

Unknown

May, 2005

"How do you do that (start a dogsled team) in Jamaica?" Danny Melville wondered.

"You make a dogsled team the same way you make a bobsled team. That may not sound very original but it would enable us to take advantage of the publicity that came ahead of us.

"I could say, 'dogsled team.' People would say, 'You mean bobsled don't you?' 'No. I don't mean bobsled, I mean dogsled...' Bobsled. Dogsled. Bobsled. Dogsled...."

Danny and his wife, Carole, were visiting his mother in Victoria, British Columbia, in May, 2005. His sons, Alexander, Marc and Daniel Jr. back in

Kingston, were shopping for dune buggies for use in the Turks and Caicos. There was one interesting prospect, Badland Buggies, in Edmonton, Alberta, but they had no one in western Canada who could go and check the product out – except Danny.

So they called, "Dad, can you jump on a plane and go check out this guy's operation? He looks like a good source and we're interested in buying some."

A couple of days later he met with Bruce Hodder, Badland Buggies' owner, designer and metalworker. An engineer who designed drill rigs for oil exploration companies, building buggies was his passion. He started by creating kits for people to build their own but it didn't take long for him to move into manufacturing. However, he didn't construct production line buggies. Bruce's sons liked big, heavy 500-pound dune buggies with 250-horsepower motors that would literally fly off the sides of the sand dunes, so that's what he built.

After reviewing the specifications, Bruce wasn't sure that he was building what Chukka was looking for but he took Danny into the workshop anyway so he could form his own opinion.

As they walked through the shop, cluttered with various vehicles in assorted stages of construction, Danny's attention was caught by an odd-looking contraption that appeared to be a mix between a snow machine and a sled, with two seats in the front and a riding platform at the back. What struck him about it was the fact that it was on wheels, had no visible means of power and the chassis was mounted on shock absorbers.

"What is that?" He wandered over to the vehicle, looking curiously at the wheels and the front end, which actually was made from the front end of a snow machine.

"A dryland dogsled," responded Bruce.

"A what?!"

"A dryland dogsled."

When Danny starts to get excited about something his voice goes up about two octaves. "Dryland! You mean no snow? I've never heard of such a thing! Who's it for?"

"I'm building it for a guy who lives in the Cairngorm Mountains in Scotland. He's a dog musher and they don't have much snow there."

"Scotland! They do dryland dogsledding in Scotland?"

"All over the world actually. Europe. Australia. California."

The idea hit Danny and he just knew it had to be good. "I knew what dogsledding was about, but it was a winter thing. Never had I heard of dryland dogsledding. I didn't know it was a sport. I knew nothing of dogsledding's history in Alaska and the Yukon. And I didn't know it had become a sport all across North America and in Europe.

"I didn't realize what I was getting into. I just thought this was something I could use in Jamaica. It hit me as being outrageous for a tourist to come off a cruise ship or out of a hotel and go back home with a photograph and tell everyone, 'I went dogsledding in Jamaica.' I looked at that sled and thought, 'If you can run a dogsled on wheels we can do this. Jamaica has lots of dogs. Somebody must do this.'

"But we couldn't be just outrageous. We had to be outrageous and be good at it."

"Give me the name of the guy," Danny demanded. Every innovator fantasizes about finding that one crazy offbeat experience that will persist in memory long after the financial results, whether good or bad, have been forgotten. They all hope to recognize it when it happens because such opportunities only happen once in a lifetime. Danny had the feeling this idea was on the verge of visionary greatness. It would be good for Jamaica. What was good for Jamaica was good for business.

"Alan Stewart," replied Bruce.

Danny left the workshop promising to be back in a few minutes with his camera. While he was gone Bruce phoned Alan in Scotland.

"I've got a Daniel Melville here. He's a Jamaican adventure tour operator and is looking for some off-road buggies for a project on one of the Caribbean islands. He saw your dogcart and wants to talk to you. Interested?"

"That's fine," responded Alan, "tell him he would be better off using my email than calling."

Danny returned, photographed the sled and departed again, this time with Alan Stewart's phone number and email address.

He had already resolved what he was going to do. He had even determined how he would go about doing it.

When the idea of Jamaicans in winter sports is mentioned the Jamaican Bobsled team, the "Hottest Thing on Ice," is the first to come to mind. The team was born when two American businessmen noted the similarity of a pushcart derby they watched in Kingston with the sport of bobsledding.

The team rose to world prominence when they first qualified for the Winter Olympic Games in Calgary in 1988 and four successive Olympics after that. The novelty of having a team from an island that has never seen snow, compete in winter sports at the highest level inspired a book and a movie by the same name, *Cool Runnings.*

3-dog race.

They still remain a major draw for winter sports fans and media even though it has been almost a decade since they competed in the Olympics.

A lesser-known example was the Ice Room at the Coral Cliff Hotel in Montego Bay, Jamaica. It was an insulated space in the middle of the hotel with the insides of the walls lined with ice blocks. In the center of the room was a carved ice table with champagne goblets. People would pay $20 each to put on a winter parka and go in for a shot of vodka. Jamaicans and tourists alike lined up for their drink. When the Canadian owner of the hotel lost interest in the Ice Room, so did the public. And it was eventually dismantled, the space used as part of the hotel's casino.

From Edmonton, Danny flew to Toronto and started putting himself through what he called "Dogsledding 101."

What he discovered was that dogs have a natural instinct for pulling. Put a harness on a dog, attach weight to the other end and, without encouragement or training, the vast majority of dogs will lean into the traces and pull against the weight.

Dog mushing is the general term used to describe both the practical and sporting use of transport powered by dogs. While it most specifically implies the use of dogs to pull a sled on snow, it does include carting, pulling pulkas, scootering, sleddog racing, skijoring, freighting, bikejoring and weight pulling.

The earliest record of dogs being used as draft animals was by the ancient Greeks employing them to haul plunder from their conquests almost 3,000 years ago. While the Roman Empire held sway Swiss Mountain Dogs were used as cart-pullers to transport milk and cheese to market. Norway's Oseberg Ship Burial, which dates from 834 CE and was discovered in 1904, provided evidence that Vikings used canine carts. European tapestries and manuscripts from the 13th and 14th centuries document their role at all levels of society. Dogs were used by the Blackfoot Indians in the North American Midwest to transport goods on an A-shaped sled called a travois.

In 1850 naturalist philosopher Henry D. Thoreau wrote about Canadian dogcarts and the "extensive use made of these animals (dogs) for drawing, not only milk, but groceries, wood and ice."

At the start of the 20th century dogs were still in common use as a means of transportation. A 1905 newspaper ad promoted a Studebaker Junior Wagon pulled by dogs for children. Sulkies, usually pulled by horses, were raced with dogs. Postcards printed in the first half of the century showed dogs hauling cargo, beer kegs, firewood and pulling calèches, a formal carriage in which ladies and gentlemen traveled.

But the day of the dog-drawn carriage was coming to an end. Automobiles replaced them, just as they did horses. So they became dogs of war.

The French first used a canine corps to pull machine guns and ammunition wagons during the First World War. Here Danny ran across the name of a Scottish-born musher, "Scotty" Allan, who trained 450 dogs for the French military. The United States Army saw the value of his work and contracted with Allan for dogs to haul supplies over the mountain passes between France and Germany. Several of the dogs were decorated for valor by these two governments.

By the end of the Second World War the use of dogs as a means of dryland transportation and for military purposes had...dried up. However, people still loved to own dogs and dogs still loved to pull. The use of dog-powered transportation became more of a recreational activity than a necessity.

Backcountry adventurers used dogs as pack animals or to pull pulkas, small sleds designed to be pulled by a person or animal, in winter. People hitched them up to scooters (scootering). Someone invented a harness that enabled bikers and skiers to hitch up a dog (bikejoring and skijoring). Then they started hooking them up to people who used their own two feet to run cross-country (canicross). The dryland versions of the sport spread worldwide: Western Europe, Australia, New Zealand, South Africa, Korea, Mongolia, the Scandinavian countries, Canada, Japan, Argentina, Chile, Peru, Columbia, Alaska, and the lower 48 of the United States.

The governing bodies of dog mushing, the International Federation of Sleddog Sports (IFSS) and the International Sled Dog Racing Association

(ISDRA), started organizing the various forms of dryland dog driving in the 1980s since it was, and still is, the fastest growing aspect of the sport.

Estimates of dryland and snow mushers around the world were made by ISDRA in 1997 as being in excess of 20,000 – with only 6,000 of those in North America. Most North American dog drivers lived in the central U.S., central Canada, the Yukon and Alaska. By 2009 the number of mushers in North America had, according to ISDRA, dropped to 3,000 – with 1,200 of those in Alaska where mushing is the state sport. However, the total number of mushers in the world remained constant. In the winter of 1999-2000, there were 302 sanctioned races, on dryland and snow, with total prize money of just over $384,000.

Dog mushing has twice been a demonstration sport at the Winter Olympics. Olympic rules permit the addition of two sports that aren't part of the medal program to each Games. One sport has to be native to the host country. In 1932, the United States claimed dog mushing as their native sport for the third Winter Olympiad in Lake Placid, New York. In 1988, Canada did the same in Calgary – the same Games where the Jamaican Bobsled team made its debut.

What interested Danny most was the mix of Canadian and American corporate sponsors for the sport, which included international banks, oil companies, hotel chains, information technology providers and suppliers of dog food. The other item he looked for was media coverage. Canada's TSN sports network, the American Outdoor Life Network (OLN), regional television, radio and print media outlets reached a potential audience estimated to be in excess of 10 million viewers – mostly in the United States and Europe.

At the end of one of the Internet pages he was reading he noticed a reference to two events called the Yukon Quest and the Iditarod, but didn't pursue either. They were long distance races and at this point he was just interested in touring. Racing was something he had already started to think was a necessary component of the tour, but was still a secondary goal at this point.

Danny knew it wouldn't be an easy sell to his sons and business colleagues. They would openly start to wonder what he had been smoking. He could already hear them – "Dad, you've really lost it this time" or "You're crazy. No we don't need another tour. We don't want another tour. Especially not one like this!" There was no time to waste.

He emailed Alan Stewart:

"Jamaica is known for Bob Marley and the Bobsled team Alan. Also known for other things, which overshadow many good things. I want to start the Jamaican sleddog team, not just to take people out as a tour business, but like the Bobsled team they can train in Jamaica on wheels, then travel abroad to compete. I want a museum (for the JDT) and if possible, a number of dogs we can start to train. Can you help?"

"I want to do this," he said to Alan in a subsequent phone call. "We have a guy, Devon Anderson, that I think can do this and I'm thinking about developing this as a tour that would be unique to Jamaica. Would you take Devon and train him?"

Alan proved to be as crazy as Danny. "Sure," he responded, "Send him off."

Damion Robb demonstrates correct dogsled team lineup.

The JDT version of Alan Stewart's cart: (L to R) Rick Johnson, Nettie Johnson, Danny, Devon Anderson, and Damion Robb.

Danny

None but ourselves can free our minds.

Bob Marley

Being a visionary isn't everything it's made out to be. Most of the time people are questioning your reason. Sometimes they question your sanity. More often they just simply laugh at you. For 25 years people have laughed at Danny Melville, no more so than because of the Jamaica Dogsled Team, and he's proud of it. He wears mirth as a badge of honor.

For him, it is the price of passion. The kind of passion that made him one of Jamaica's most interesting entrepreneurs of his generation. A fervor that has some people calling him the "Walt Disney" of Jamaica as the biggest adventure tour player in the biggest industry in the Caribbean Sea.

In adventure tourism, you need to be a visionary because it's the one area of business where if people tell you it won't work, then you probably have a winning idea.

It depends upon knowing your competitors, getting the necessary financing, winning customers from someone else and enduring tough times until some sustainable level of success is reached.

It takes a strong advocate who is willing, above all, to make decisions that aren't always sound by the standards of the business-school textbook. An inexact science where the odds are that challenging risk will succeed more frequently than counting beans precisely.

"I had no specific business plan," said Danny when talking about Chukka Caribbean Adventures. "I just felt this thing could be made into a success. It's not like we sat down and did a detailed business model and had all the projections and the numbers. We did have an idea of how many tours were needed to break even and a rule that each tour had to eventually be self-supporting, but that was it.

"I started talking about one idea with my son and he looked at me and he said, 'Dad, you're nuts. This thing is not going to work. We're going to go broke doing it.' Not every idea has been right. Lots of time I bomb. But then something else comes along. It's all gut feeling and I've done that a lot of times. And thinking large isn't enough by itself. You also have to think lucky. It's that Jamaican thing. We believe we can do it, so we do."

Danny and his brothers were the latest of generations of Jamaican Melvilles dating back to the 1700s. Born in 1947, he was the youngest of four brothers. His father John Melville, a gentleman farmer, lived on his inheritance from Danny's American grandmother, Bernice Briggs. She was one of two daughters of Thomas Briggs – founder of the Boston Wire Stitcher Company, later renamed Bostitch.

Shortly after Danny's birth his father bought a farm named Arthur's Seat, 500 acres in the hills above St. Ann's Bay with little running water and soil so full of rocks it was a challenge to grow weeds. Danny grew up in the mountains, developing an understanding of the land and the people who farmed it. He nurtured a love of horses because of his father.

"My dad was a smooth (polo) player and an excellent rider. He was passionate about polo. Of the four brothers, two of us, Bryan (the oldest) and Andrew (second youngest), were like my mother. Not active, outdoor type people. My second oldest brother, Christopher and I were more like my Dad. Christopher played polo and was a good player but had a terrible accident at age 20. He had brain damage, was in a coma for three weeks and in hospital for three months. He was never able to play again. I played polo for 33 years."

The younger Melvilles could have continued on as gentlemen farmers but John had a different future in mind for them. While he appreciated the lifestyle his inheritance had given him, he determined that his children were going to get an education and learn how to be businessmen. His sons attended some of Jamaica's best private boarding schools, Jamaica College in Kingston and Munro College in St. Elizabeth.

"When I left high school I went to work on a large estate, Worthy Park," explained Danny. "They grew sugar cane and I was hired on as a junior overseer. They also raised cattle and had a feedlot. That's when I thought I wanted to raise cattle."

John Melville purchased a company called Tropical Battery in 1967, the same year Danny traveled to the United States to study agriculture at Eastern Oklahoma State College in Wilburton, Oklahoma. Danny soon realized that being a cattle rancher wasn't what he wanted after all.

Bryan, Christopher and Andrew had become partners in Tropical Battery and Danny decided it was time he got his own career started. Real estate development looked interesting so he started learning it while buying land in and around the mostly undeveloped, small, north coast town of Ocho Rios. In 1973, he constructed a small strip mall called Coconut Grove where Chukka Caribbean Adventures and the Jamaica Dogsled Team have an office.

Before independence (August 6, 1962), Jamaica had the fastest growing economy for a developing country in the world. Of the two nations who achieved independence from Britain that year, Singapore and Jamaica, the Caribbean nation was considered to be the one most likely to succeed. That first decade of independence had seen that economic promise fulfilled.

The British provided Jamaica with a lot of good things. What appeared to be a solid government structure. An extensive and reliable infrastructure – roads and railways to enable the agricultural industry to get product to the coast for export. However, the superficial prosperity gave a treacherous reading. Paradise had a problem.

If there was a blemish in the legacy left by the British, it was the traditional flaw of the colonial master. They did nothing to educate their subjects in preparation for the day they became independent. Even into the 1970s, few Jamaicans held management positions in their own government.

In the early 1970s, the late Michael Manley, then Prime Minister, started implementing policies with the goal of turning Jamaica into a socialist state.

A cornerstone of his foreign affairs program was flirting with Fidel Castro's communist regime in Cuba.

"He was trying to change the social order," recalled Danny. "And there were a lot of things that needed changing in Jamaica but he was impatient. Trying to change too quickly and he scared people. The kind of change he was looking for wouldn't come without the fiscal discipline to accomplish it. People panicked about socialism, communism and the whole thing about nationalizing industry and property. They felt he was throwing the baby out with the bathwater."

When the business establishment and middle class protested Manley responded, "Jamaica has no room for millionaires. For anyone who wants to become a millionaire we have five flights a day to Miami." The millionaires, including Danny's parents and brothers, took him up on his offer.

"People just left," Danny said. "You'd see a guy one week. The next week he'd packed up his belongings and was gone. People moved families to the United States then would commute to run their business.

"It was a crazy time. There was a huge brain drain. We started into a cycle of devaluation. That destroyed the civil service who were relying on pensions to take care of them in old age. There was a history of mismanagement. The experienced bureaucrats left and there was no one to take their place. Then more mismanagement and mistakes because of the panic and because of a lack of understanding."

Crime skyrocketed and political violence was widespread. As old money fled offshore to Canada and the United States, new money redirected itself to anywhere but Jamaica and the entire middle class followed the money. When the flood of migration finally slowed down to an annual trickle there were few left capable of running a country or any industry.

"We went from one Jamaican dollar being worth more than a U.S. dollar in 1969 to being worth less than two cents. Jamaica changed. To the point where Jamaica is this wonderful vibrant country on one hand with high tech wonderful people. And on the other hand, there is a lot of coarseness. People who have not been socialized or educated. Who moved up to occupy what would be considered the middle class and have the responsibility of running the country."

When Danny's family moved to Canada in 1974, they encouraged him to come with them. "I said, 'I'm not going anywhere.' And I stayed. We went through some rough times, but also there came opportunities to develop business."

In Ocho Rios he took his first steps into the tourism market. His real estate development company took over the management of villas for ex-patriates who had fled the turmoil. The owners would enjoy them for a month in the winter, and Danny's company rented them out to tourists for the rest of the year. Then personal security became an issue as unemployment and crime rates in Jamaica continued to climb.

It was impossible to offer protection to tourists staying in villas so people stopped renting. All-inclusive resorts started to make their appearance along the north coast and visitors, fearing for their safety, found they could, for a set amount of money, come to Jamaica and never have to set foot outside of their hotel. High convenience. High security.

Danny's first venture into tourism was over but he had developed a taste for it. It appealed to his creative side. It provided a vehicle to channel his passion for Jamaica. But before he could do anything else about it, there was another job that needed to be done. Tropical Battery was in chaos.

In 1978 Danny moved to Kingston, bought out his brother's shares and took over management of the business. The company was a manufacturer of batteries of all types, an industry protected by government industrial policies dating from the 1950s and designed to create jobs for Jamaicans by building a protective wall of tariffs on imported goods. Tropical Battery was no longer cost-effective and Danny could see full liberalization of the tariff barriers was due to come, rendering the manufacturing of batteries in Jamaica obsolete.

He started the transformation of the company from a manufacturer to an importer-distributor. Briefly, he considered getting into the auto retail business but decided, "don't sell the car. Sell the stuff that keeps the car on the road. We didn't sell anything that you didn't really need every day. Ninety-five percent of everything we sold was stuff you needed every day."

Dressed not in business suits but in shorts and T-shirts, he slowly and laboriously rebuilt the company. His workdays started early in the morning and went on until long after dark each evening. He developed a reputation as an entrepreneur who initiated change almost solely by sheer will power.

His sons were introduced to the no-nonsense idea of hard work and long hours early in their lives. While in high school they would work weekends on the assembly lines at Tropical Battery, making sales trips for Tropical and grooming horses at Chukka Cove. Even in later years they were never coddled by their father. When ultimately brought into the family business they were given menial jobs at the lowest unskilled labor level. They had to learn the business from the bottom up.

"Each one of the boys got one aspect of his abilities," Carole Melville summarized. "Marc is good with operations and organizing people. Zander (Alexander) is good with numbers. Daniel Jr. has good people skills. But none of them got the vision. They're incredibly hardworking boys but they can't quite see what he sees."

In 1982, Danny decided it was time to follow his heart rather than his reason. He bought a 50-acre sugar plantation on the north coast between St. Ann's Bay and Runaway Bay, considered by many to have little potential. The next year construction started on the Polo field, equestrian riding paddocks and villas for visitors to stay in at the newly christened Chukka Cove.

His ambition was to build a center that would offer an alternative destination for wealthy horse owners in the United States and Britain. In the late 1970s the center of the equestrian and polo worlds was shared between Argentina, the United States and the United Kingdom.

For the first time his vision failed him. Danny had miscalculated the market.

"I brought polo in Jamaica to levels it hadn't been in years. And equestrian. Bringing in international players and riders. Getting recognition everywhere in the horse world." But it wasn't enough. "People just didn't

The Polo field at Chukka Cove.

see Jamaica as an equestrian destination," Danny said. The business faltered, lost money in its first decade of operation and by 1990, was in jeopardy of ending up on the bank's foreclosure alert list.

Tropical Battery was also in crisis again. His foresight had faltered. The final removal of tariff barriers outpaced the conversion of the company from an unwieldy manufacturer to a streamlined distributor. The national economy continued to sputter aimlessly. Tropical's market share started to fall rapidly and high interest rates were battering the bottom line. Danny considered all his options. In the end he called his sons Marc and Alexander, who were attending university in Florida and Daniel Jr., still in Jamaica, to make them an offer. Equal shares in the business but they would have to earn it.

"We could sell it all or they could come home and we could make a run at making it work. I don't like failure. I have to be positive and have passion because I have to, to make it work," he said.

Applying the work ethic learned from their father, Danny's sons began the process of turning Melville Enterprises, owner of Tropical Battery, into the Jamaican business success story of the late 20th and early 21st centuries. From a company with only 40 employees hawking wares from the back of pickup trucks in 1990, it grew to become an economic force on the island. In 2009 sales exceeded $2 billion, the company had 550 employees and included investments in the gaming industry as well as increased diversity in consumer goods.

Rebranding Chukka Cove was part of the new plan. It was also the perfect place for Danny to allow his imagination to run, for the most part, unchecked.

Because of his early investments in Ocho Rios he was developing contacts within the cruise ship industry and his interest in tourism made Danny the best fit as the executive in charge of Melville Enterprises' new company, Chukka Caribbean Adventures. He considered the features that gave an element of the exotic to Jamaica and studied what everyone else was selling. He noted the increasing number of hotels and all-inclusive resorts

No beaches at Chukka Cove so getting into the water was adventuresome.

in the Ocho Rios area and the growing popularity of cruise ships. When he traveled abroad he was aware of the effect "Jamaica" had on people. It was, he quickly concluded, one of the most recognizable names in the world. Even if they didn't know much about the country itself, people everywhere could name at least one Jamaican – usually Bob Marley. In the absence of any other developing industries in Jamaica, the potential for tourism on the north coast was becoming increasingly apparent.

White crystalline sand beaches that stretched forever. Tropical winds – the "Doctor Breeze" from the sea by day and the "Undertaker" from the mountains at night. The unhurried "soon come" island life. The idea that there was something special about this place that you couldn't find anywhere else. The belief that all those heavenly properties were in the very air itself.

Its dazzling power drew almost three million visitors a year from across the globe to experience by taste, by smell, by touch its laid-back vibrations and exciting rhythm. A paradise for those who wish to lethargically soak up the sun or dance wantonly under the stars.

"It's as if your body has suddenly arrived where your mind has always been," according to a former owner of one of Negril's world-renowned landmarks on the west shore.

But while Chukka Cove was on the coast, it didn't have what the average tourist was looking for. The shoreline in front of the Polo field was a series of sheer cliffs rising from the water. To go swimming you had to jump off the rocks 15 or 20 feet into the water and use ladders to climb out. There were a couple of beaches on neighboring estates but if Chukka was going to be paradise for its visitors, Danny would have to find a less traditional way to accomplish it.

He looked inland because there is more than the climate and the beaches to Jamaica. The coastal plain is quite narrow. From the shore you can see with the unaided eye the rugged interior mountain ranges, which actually form most of the landmass of the nation. This is an island where a person could live their entire life 1,000 meters above sea level, just 30 kilometers from the coast and never once see the water.

The hills are coated with verdant, lush rainforests abundant with dazzling flora. Marvelous tropical trees, orchids, fern, hibiscus, bougainvillea, oleander, poinsettia, palm trees, fichus and trees hanging with ackee, bananas, pimento, naseberries, breadfruit and Bombay mangoes, which don't thrive elsewhere in the western hemisphere. Whistling frogs, cicadas,

The office at Chukka Cove Farm.

mongoose, hummingbirds and glorious-plumed doctor birds populate the undergrowth and branches.

Waterfalls, springs, rivers and streams drop down through the narrow valleys.

In the central regions one passes through fruit groves and fields of vegetables. In the higher elevations, near the island's tallest peak of Blue Mountain (2,437 meters), coffee beans thrive. Sugar cane plantations cover massive areas near the southwest coast.

Danny understood the value of the open nature of the people. Jamaicans have a tremendous sense of joy, fun and music. If you are open and friendly to them, prepared to smile without being asked, the returning smiles on their faces are as bright as any you will find on earth. They're not afraid to engage – to talk, to laugh with a total stranger. The people are attractive, for the most part very courteous and want the tourists to be happy while visiting their home.

If you are looking for something, they'll not only tell you how to get to where you're going – they'll go out of their way to show you.

Jamaica is music. Music is Jamaica. No matter where you are on the island there's a stereo that could deliver Reggae to the entire island, someone is tuned into a small radio or they're singing. As reliably as the sun rises, people sing and dance in front of their red, green, blue or unpainted thatched huts, hanging with bananas, fruit or vegetables, on the side of any road.

"There is something special about Jamaica," Danny Melville waves his hand towards the inland. "This is the most beautiful island in the Caribbean. It has a vibe. A soul. What Jimmy (Buffett) calls the 'Spirit of Life.' The people have passion. More so than the other islands in the Caribbean and I think this is what draws people here.

"You know how strong 'Brand Jamaica' is? Internationally the best-known Jamaican, far and above all else, is Bob Marley. Jamaica has given many great things to the world. Reggae. Jimmy Cliff. The bobsled team. Sprinters Usain Bolt and Shirley Fraser. Marcus Garvey and his work in Jamaica and the United States, setting the groundwork for the NAACP (National Association for the Advancement of Colored People) and Martin Luther King. Appleton Rum. Blue Mountain Coffee. Red Stripe Beer. Bananas. Sugar. Bauxite. A romantic destination in a beautiful country. A nation is what it gives to the world."

Chukka Caribbean started with proven sellers borrowed from other tourism destinations and made good use of one resource they had left over from the equestrian days – horses. Chukka provided trail rides on horseback in the mountains above St. Ann's Bay and further down the coast at White River, ranging in length from one hour to three or four days. Bicycle tours from mountaintops to seashore. River tubing on the White River. Jeep safaris through the towns in the interior of the island. Treetop zip line tours. All Terrain Vehicle (ATV) journeys through the rain forests. Dune buggy rides along beaches on the neighboring estates.

The company spread its wings, offering tours in other north coast cities, Montego Bay and Negril, and offshore in Barbados, the Turks and Caicos, the Bahamas and Belize – becoming the premiere soft adventure tour company in the Caribbean.

While running the polo and equestrian center Danny enjoyed leading the other players down to the beach on Sunday afternoons, where horse and rider went for a swim together in the Caribbean Sea. He proposed a tour that took visitors for a trail ride to a small beach where they would go for a swim while still mounted. Not only had no one ever done it, nobody had even thought of it before. It became the top-selling tour the company had.

Its main rival in popularity was another wild idea and a good example of how a visionary's mind works.

"One morning I woke up and I just said we're going to do Zion Bus. I thought it couldn't possibly miss. My sons were skeptical. A lot of people

Zion Bus takes tourists to Nine Mile, birthplace of Bob Marley.

were skeptical. But I just knew it would sell. We did the research into Bob's life because it had to be authentic. It had to be real.

"The music was going to make them do it. The story was going to make them do it. The bus was going to make them do it. The day I rolled that bus down to the cruise ship, people just looked at us like we were crazy. They couldn't believe it. They wanted to buy the coconuts off the roof."

The Zion Bus Line takes tourists to the town of Nine Mile, the birth and final resting place of Reggae legend Bob Marley. The interior of the bright multihued buses are covered with photographs of Marley and his band, the Wailers, and pumped full of the superstar's music. They used to be topped with a luggage carrier full of fiberglass coconuts, which were so realistic even the locals thought they were real. Over the years low-hanging tree branches have knocked them off so now they carry just a few. It's a new bus, dressed up to look old, that rattles its way over battered roads into the mountains, giving visitors a short glimpse into the heartland of the island while dining on traditional Jamaican food and sipping on a "Belly Wash" lemonade. The buses were designed by Danny's third wife, Carole.

At some point during his years of struggling with Tropical Battery, Danny and Winsome Bowen, his first wife and mother of his three sons, simply grew apart and divorced amicably. He married a second time, a "rebound relationship" he calls it, but that ended after three or four years.

One evening in 1992 he was clearing messages off his home answering service when he heard one from Rachel Manley – the daughter of Michael Manley. Rachel was an old friend he didn't hear from very often since she had moved to Toronto several years earlier to teach and write.

"I'm in Jamaica visiting Douglas (her uncle)," the message said. "Give me a call." So he did in typical Danny fashion – when he was able to fit it into his schedule two days later.

"Danny," said Rachel, "I have someone here. She wants to say hello." She handed the phone over to the "someone."

"Hello," she said.

There was a long pause at the other end of the phone then Danny tentatively asked, "Carole?"

Danny and Carole Melville.

"Yes," she responded. He turned up at the front door 15 minutes later.

"The moment he walked through the door that was it," recalls Carole. "Rachel didn't see me again during those four weeks. From then till now we've been together."

Danny and Carole had known each other as teenagers when Carole had lived at the home of Rachel's grandfather, Norman Manley, while attending school. "I was in love with her," Danny remembers, "but she wasn't in love with me."

"It was a good thing that long separation," Carole said. "He had a lot of growing up to do. When I arrived in Jamaica to visit Rachel she showed me the newspaper and said, 'Guess who's on the front page today?' I hadn't seen Danny in 28 years. I remembered this skinny person with jet-black hair, no beard, no moustache. I looked at the picture and I thought, 'It's the same face, but now he's this grey-haired guy.'"

They married in 1994.

"We not only have our marriage," said Carole, "We also have old memories. We have a history."

Her pragmatism – she was the conservative partner in a small retail outlet in Barbados – keeps Danny grounded. Her artistic nature – she's also a photographer – feeds his imagination.

Governments, national and parish, have occasionally called upon Danny's talents. It was a photo of him as chair of the national lottery that had caught Rachel's eye the day Carole came to town. As the chair of the St. Ann Development Corporation he made improvements to one of Jamaica's biggest tourist venues, Dunn's River Falls, helping to make it profitable. He also headed the Tourism Products Development Corporation, which established standards, product development and licensing within the industry for "Made in Jamaica" products.

The government-run Caymanas Park racetrack was heading towards bankruptcy so they recruited Danny to turn its fortunes around.

"He had the vision. He brought people back," Carole described. "He changed their way of doing business. Improved the technology and stepped down when the racetrack started turning huge profits."

In 2001 he shocked an entire nation when he resigned his seat in Parliament, after representing St. Ann's for three years. When originally asked to run, he thought it an opportunity to turn his business acumen to the benefit of the country. Instead he found himself an idealist relegated to being a backbencher.

"Pretty quickly I got disillusioned. I could not accept that my role – after having been in business for 30 years – my job was to attend funerals. To hand out plywood (siding for people to build the shacks they live in) and zinc (corrugated metal roofing material). A backbencher has no voice in Jamaica. They had asked me to run because they wanted new blood and new ideas and when elected, they didn't want new blood or ideas any more.

"So I resigned my seat three years into a five-year term. I was the first Member of Parliament to ever resign. If a person gets discontented with their role they usually just don't run in the next election. But resigning your seat! That doesn't happen in Jamaica. Nobody breaks party lines. I simply stated what I felt was wrong with the system and left."

The resignation coincided with a decision to take more time off. An old leg injury from his polo days was making it difficult for him to move around the way he used to. He would still be involved with the business, reviewing financials and talking with his sons every day, and he would sort-of run Chukka Cove. Just not from an office. He established a workstation on the dining room table in his villa.

The plan was that he and Carole would start traveling more. Visiting her five children from her first marriage, scattered between Canada and Australia. Staying in their condo in Barbados or visiting his brothers and mother in Canada. It almost worked.

Danny's new venture

Spectators at Takhini River Bridge.

Newton's Schedule

Whitehorse to Carmacks

177 miles, 33 hours

Newton Marshall and the Yukon Quest weren't made for each other but they needed each other in 2009.

Newton was an unlikely dog musher because he never thought of himself as a dog man. He was a poor kid from the wrong side of the road whose first instinct was survival in a dysfunctional tropical world. If he had just been an ordinary poor kid in Jamaica he wouldn't have ever been viewed as something more.

However, his affinity for animals and his ambition to elevate himself above the cycle of poverty set him apart. The community that raised him placed little value in him. It could have turned him to the anger and aggression prevalent in communities bereft of hope. He chose not to be a part of it, risking instead becoming a social pariah in his own home. Rejecting what it stood for was excellent emotional preparation for the alien dog mushing world he eventually found himself in.

He had a natural athleticism beyond the average person. Dick Watts once watched him hurdle a five-foot high gate in Jamaica with a minimum of effort.

"A couple of the dogs started to mix it up in the arena and Newton was doing something by the kennel. He ran from the kennel, jumped to the top of the gate, put one foot on it and pushed himself over the fence. I couldn't believe it. He jumped over a gate that's almost as tall as I am and did it like he did it every day."

Newton recognized that dog mushing was his route out of the cycle of poverty, "Don't want to go back to that rough life."

"Because everyone expects him to finish," Hans made it clear so everyone understood there was more than just a race at stake. "If he doesn't finish then he just goes back to Jamaica and everyone's forgotten about him in no time."

It took people like Devon Anderson, Hans Gatt, Rick Johnson and Danny Melville to look at him and know exactly what he had been born for. He was uniquely suited for the type of harebrained scheme that only Danny could come up with.

At 985 miles the Yukon Quest International Sled Dog Race is the world's longest non-mechanized race. It's older, richer and better-known Alaskan cousin, the Iditarod, runs 908 miles from Anchorage to Nome via the northern route, and just over 960 by the southern. The Quest, as it's called by its adherents, is the only major North American race to cross the boundary between Canada and the United States.

Each February it runs through the heart of Alaska and the Yukon, a forbidding frozen subarctic landscape of rivers, mountain passes and forests larger than the entire island of Jamaica. Most of the race is run in the dark shadows of night. In winter this close to the Arctic Circle there are only four or five hours of light each day. Temperatures range from plus five to minus 60. Wind gusts blow as hard as 60 miles per hour.

There are only eight official checkpoints and a few cabins along the way where the teams can stop to rest. It's essential the musher know how to care for his team in the wilderness. The longest single stretch between official checkpoints is 202 miles, from Pelly Crossing to Dawson City. The shortest, from Carmacks to Pelly Crossing, a mere 73 miles. There are four mountain summits to climb and a couple hundred miles of jumble river ice to negotiate. It is appropriately titled, and recognized by the mushing and ultra-endurance sports world as "The Toughest Race on Earth."

Yet each year it continues to struggle for survival and recognition in the shadow of the Iditarod. Canadian media, when it bothers to include it in news and sports coverage at all, frequently calls it by the wrong name. American media virtually ignores it. Sponsors look at it and then head elsewhere with their money.

The problem is that major news and sports media outlets in the United States were already committed to the Iditarod by the time the Quest came into existence. Those were also the years that the world was caught up in the charisma of Alaskan Susan Butcher who won four Iditarod titles and became an international celebrity for gender equality in sport.

The media didn't see the Quest as being anything new or different – to them a dog race was a dog race. No matter how good an event it was – the Quest was never able to break into the big time. North American sponsors liked what they saw but most wouldn't commit to it. It did get extensive television coverage in Europe in the late 1990s where it was called "the Tour de France of winter" and was widely popular.

The Yukon Quest required that kind of magical moment that would turn the heads of the world press. It desired the Jamaica Dogsled Team. It needed Newton Marshall.

It took a lot of beer to come up with an idea as crazy as the Quest – and two men with foresight to make it a reality.

It was a casual comment made while three mushers and one dog handler were having a few post-race beers in the Bull's Eye Saloon in April, 1983. The three mushers, Leroy Shank, Ron Rosser and Willie Libb, had just finished a middle distance race called the Angel Creek – Bull's Eye Saloon. The handler, Roger Williams, had no idea why he was there at all. He really didn't like dogs but he did like his co-worker at the *Fairbanks Daily News Miner,* Leroy, who had talked him into helping him with this race.

Someone, none of them recall for sure which one it was, suggested that the Angel Creek – Bull's Eye race was so much fun it should be longer. It started with just a short addition, a few miles up the valley to Chena Hot Springs. Then it turned north (another jug of beer please), crossed the mountains to Circle Hot Springs and finally to Circle City on the banks of the Yukon River.

It might have stopped there but Roger, a chemical engineer by education and historian by interest, saw the significance of continuing. This was, he realized, a race with history that people could actually touch. The trails being used were the same ones blazed over a hundred years earlier that had opened up the northern frontier. In the summers it was the rivers that were used as highways. In winter, it was the dogsled trails.

"Once we got to the Yukon River, I thought, 'Well shit. We're at the Yukon River, there's a trail there all the way into the Yukon. We could run a race, an international race and it also follows a historical trail. We could really do something that makes a statement.'" (And since we're still racing, we'll need some more beer.)

The race eventually reached Los Angeles, California, that night and like most beer-fueled conversations it would normally have been dismissed as a flight of inebriated fantasy. And likely would have, except for Leroy and Roger.

Leroy was a two-time finisher of the Iditarod, at the time the world's only long distance dogsled race, and felt the race had departed from its original ideals. He felt the race now catered to the elite racers, the big-name competitors and that recreational mushers like him were treated like second-class citizens. There was a need for something where a winner didn't need

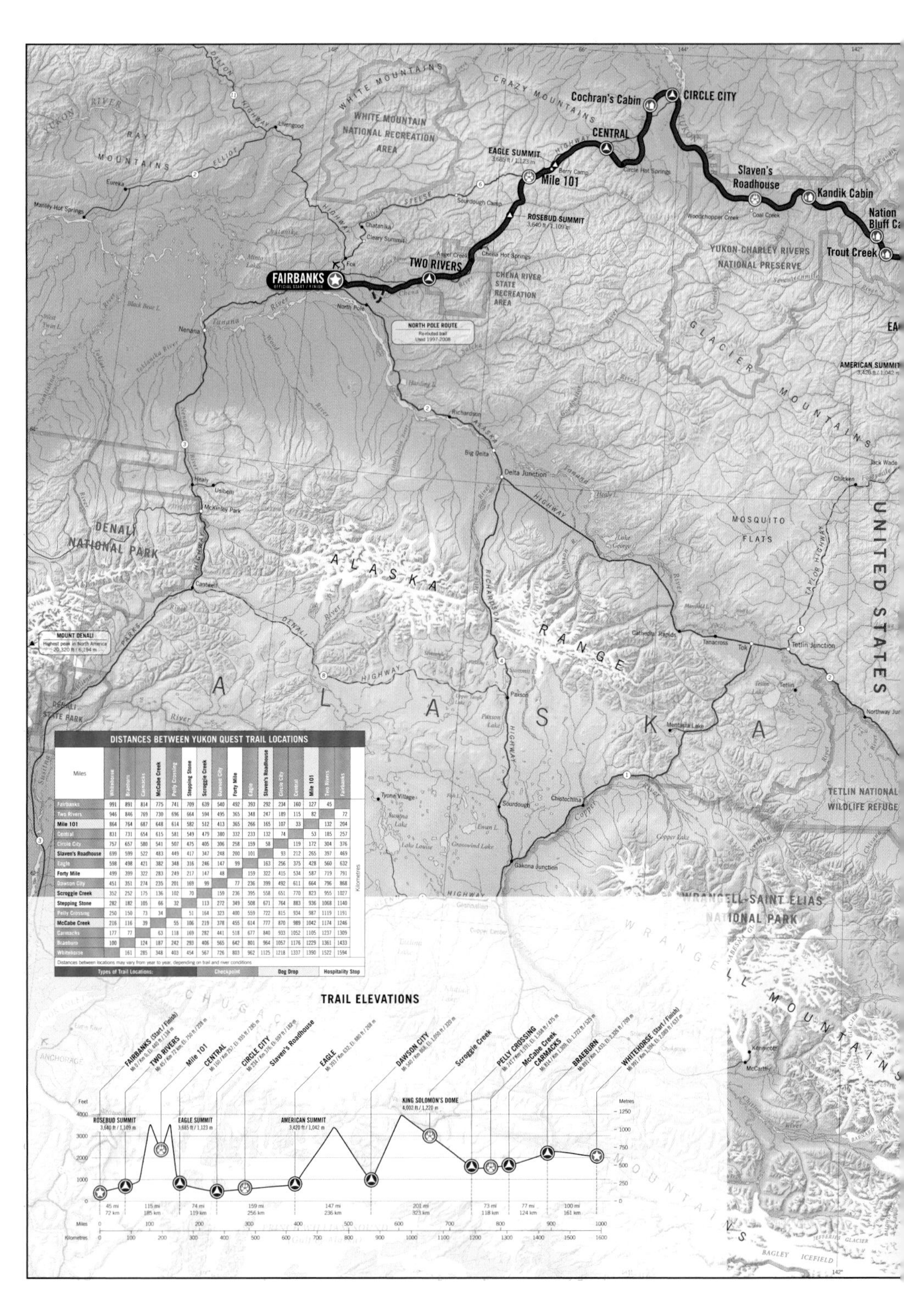

DISTANCES BETWEEN YUKON QUEST TRAIL LOCATIONS

Miles	Whitehorse	Braeburn	Carmacks	McCabe Creek	Pelly Crossing	Stepping Stone	Scroggie Creek	Dawson City	Forty Mile	Eagle	Slaven's Roadhouse	Circle City	Central	Mile 101	Two Rivers	Fairbanks
Fairbanks	991	891	814	775	741	709	639	540	492	393	292	234	160	127	45	
Two Rivers	946	846	769	730	696	664	594	495	365	348	247	189	115	82		72
Mile 101	864	764	687	648	614	582	512	413	365	266	165	107	33		132	204
Central	831	731	654	615	581	549	479	380	332	233	132	74		53	185	257
Circle City	757	657	580	541	507	475	405	306	258	159	58		119	172	304	376
Slaven's Roadhouse	699	599	522	483	449	417	347	248	200	101		93	212	265	397	469
Eagle	598	498	421	382	348	316	246	147	99		163	256	375	428	560	632
Forty Mile	499	399	322	283	249	217	147	48		159	322	415	534	587	719	791
Dawson City	451	351	274	235	201	169	99		77	236	399	492	611	664	796	868
Scroggie Creek	352	252	175	136	102	70		159	236	395	558	651	770	823	955	1027
Stepping Stone	282	182	105	66	32		113	272	349	508	671	764	883	936	1068	1140
Pelly Crossing	250	150	73	34		51	164	323	400	559	722	815	934	987	1119	1191
McCabe Creek	216	116	39		55	106	219	378	455	614	777	870	989	1042	1174	1246
Carmacks	177	77		63	118	169	282	441	518	677	840	933	1052	1105	1237	1309
Braeburn	100		124	187	242	293	406	565	642	801	964	1057	1176	1229	1361	1433
Whitehorse		161	285	348	403	454	567	726	803	962	1125	1218	1337	1390	1522	1594

Kilometres

Distances between locations may vary from year to year, depending on trail and river conditions.

Types of Trail Locations: Checkpoint | Dog Drop | Hospitality Stop

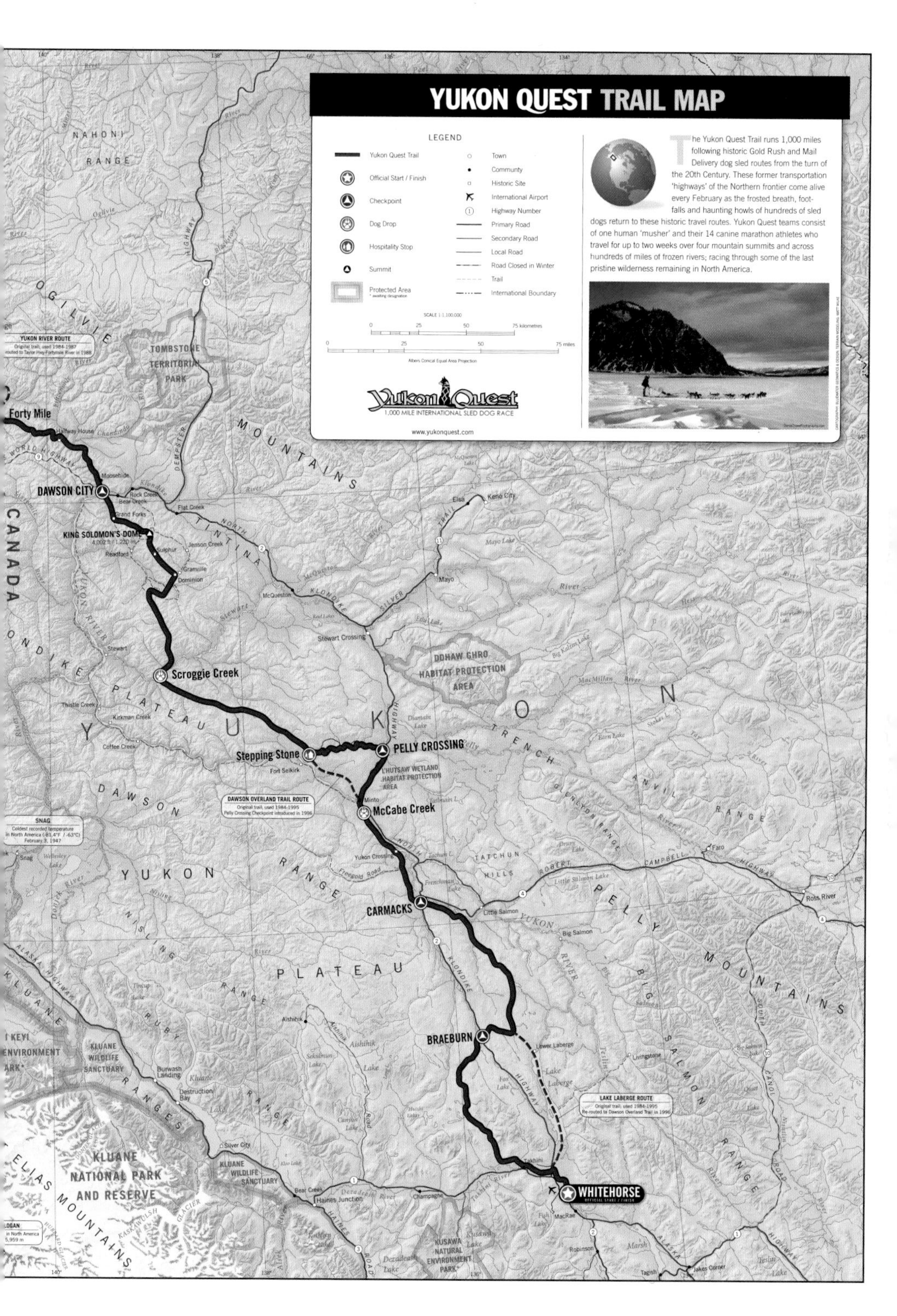
YUKON QUEST TRAIL MAP
LEGEND
Yukon Quest Trail
Official Start / Finish
Checkpoint
Dog Drop
Hospitality Stop
Summit
Protected Area
Town
Community
Historic Site
International Airport
Highway Number
Primary Road
Secondary Road
Local Road
Road Closed in Winter
Trail
International Boundary
SCALE 1:1,100,000
75 kilometres
75 miles
Albers Conical Equal Area Projection
Yukon Quest
1,000 MILE INTERNATIONAL SLED DOG RACE
www.yukonquest.com
The Yukon Quest Trail runs 1,000 miles following historic Gold Rush and Mail Delivery dog sled routes from the turn of the 20th Century. These former transportation 'highways' of the Northern frontier come alive every February as the frosted breath, footfalls and haunting howls of hundreds of sled dogs return to these historic travel routes. Yukon Quest teams consist of one human 'musher' and their 14 canine marathon athletes who travel for up to two weeks over four mountain summits and across hundreds of miles of frozen rivers; racing through some of the last pristine wilderness remaining in North America.
YUKON RIVER ROUTE
Forty Mile
DAWSON CITY
KING SOLOMON'S DOME
Scroggie Creek
Stepping Stone
PELLY CROSSING
McCabe Creek
DAWSON OVERLAND TRAIL ROUTE
Original trail, used 1984-1995
Pelly Crossing Checkpoint introduced in 1996
CARMACKS
BRAEBURN
LAKE LABERGE ROUTE
Original trail, used 1984-1995
Re-routed to Dawson Overland Trail in 1996
WHITEHORSE
TOMBSTONE TERRITORIAL PARK
OGILVIE MOUNTAINS
NAHONI RANGE
DOHAW GHRO HABITAT PROTECTION AREA
L'HUTSAW WETLAND HABITAT PROTECTION AREA
SNAG
Coldest recorded temperature in North America (-81.4°F / -63°C) February 3, 1947
CANADA
YUKON
KLONDIKE PLATEAU
DAWSON RANGE
YUKON PLATEAU
TINTINA TRENCH
PELLY MOUNTAINS
KLUANE NATIONAL PARK AND RESERVE
KLUANE WILDLIFE SANCTUARY
KUSAWA NATURAL ENVIRONMENT PARK
ST. ELIAS MOUNTAINS

to necessarily be a champion. Where mushers who rarely, if ever at all, won anything were considered equal and the accomplishment of completing the race earned the appropriate recognition. A race for purists.

"I said, 'There's got to be something besides this.' I mean, there's got to be more to long distance racing or there's got to be an alternative," remembered Leroy.

"Alternative. That word kept going through my mind. And I also thought of all those people in Fairbanks who invested all their time in the Iditarod. And they have to drive 500 miles just to start. And you finish in Nome. There's no highway back. You have to fly. It's expensive. And I thought, there's got to be something from Fairbanks....We wanted more of a bush experience. A race that would put a little woodmanship into it."

Roger had a more philosophical approach, "To me a dogsled race is still simply a dogsled race. It's the international and philosophical aspect of what we're doing. Sitting down with people from Alaska and the Yukon and everyone working for a common goal. That's what keeps me going. As far as the competition of the race...hell, that lasts two weeks out of the year. The rest of it. The complexities of running an international event. The logistics. The politics.

"The different philosophies of Canadians and Americans or the people who live in the villages versus the cities. Here in Fairbanks we think differently than, say, someone living in Maisy Mae or Biederman's Cabin or wherever. The only thing that brings all these people together and working for a common cause is the Yukon Quest."

The two men discovered on a fishing trip later that summer that they both felt the discussion in the Bull's Eye Saloon was more than just beer talking. However, when they finally suggested the idea to the people of Fairbanks, "They all stood up and laughed. They said, 'You can't do it. There's no possible way you can ever do it.' "

By February, 1984 they had cobbled together an organization in Alaska, recruited assistance from Canada, built a trail through the wilderness, found sponsorship to cover the costs, provided prize money and had 26 teams at the Start line. Even then they harbored doubts.

Leroy realized what they had accomplished early one morning in the Yukon River community of Eagle when race leader, Sonny Lindner drove his team into sight.

"It was in the morning and that sun was beating down there and you could see Eagle Bluff and he came around that corner through that beautiful white snow. And just as he popped around that corner, that church bell started ringing. And man! That just sent chills up my spine. I had tears in my eyes. I just said, 'Good grief.'

"And all those people were so excited because they had never seen a race before. They didn't even care who it was. They just said, 'Oh my God! Look at that! It's happening! It's him!' "

For Roger it was standing at the Finish line in Whitehorse when Lindner became the Quest's first champion.

"I could see these things in my mind where all these people said, 'You can't do it. Give up before you start.' When Sonny crossed that line – if nobody else ever made it across the Finish line, it could be done because one guy did it. It happened to be Sonny Lindner."

They didn't organize a race that needed to be completed as much as they created a monster to be conquered.

The rules are reminiscent of the Iditarod in its early years. More true to the independent frontier spirit of the North. Mushers have to be totally self-sufficient. They can receive no help from anyone other than another musher, an official or a veterinarian along the route – not even at the checkpoints, with the sole exception of Dawson City where their handlers can help with taking care of the dogs. Any assistance offered to a musher must be offered to every other musher on the trail. All mushers are to be treated equally whether they are front-runners or the tail end.

They use only one sled from start to finish. If the sled breaks, they repair or replace it while taking an eight-hour time penalty or "scratch" (withdraw) from the race.

The race starts from Fairbanks, Alaska, in even-numbered years. From Whitehorse, Yukon, in odd years. It follows historical stage roads, trappers' trails, abandoned freight trails, where dog teams once did the job of transport trucks, and traditional mail routes, where Canadian and American postal workers used their dogs to reach remote communities and homes along the Yukon River.

A particular emphasis is placed on dog care. The Iditarod allowed a musher to start with 20 dogs in a team and permitted them to finish with as few as six. While there were rules to protect the dogs from abuse, critics felt that the ability to "drop" so many injured or tired dogs at the checkpoints meant that the mushers could push their teams beyond their true capabilities. The Iditarod later reduced the number of dogs a team could start with to 16 and did address any legitimate concerns that had been

Quest Trail on Coughlin Lake.

raised. As far as the dogs are concerned, there has been no limit reached that a team hasn't been capable of achieving.

The Quest would have smaller teams (14) and limited the number of dogs that could be dropped along the way (6). The rule makers believed it would slow the race down but ensure better care of the dogs along the way. The lesser number of dogs would also make the race easier for smaller recreational kennels to participate. By 2009, the smaller team size for starting was still in place, but the number of dogs a team could drop had increased. Officials discovered that restricting the number of dropped dogs could potentially force mushers to continue running dogs that should be dropped.

The Iditarod, also known as "The Last Great Race," was always the richer, more competitive event for the larger racing kennels. However, over the two and a half decades the Quest has been in existence and universally acknowledged as the more demanding physical challenge, top mushers and recreational teams have made a habit of running both – often in the same year.

Four mushers have won both races (Jeff King, Joe Runyan, Rick Mackey, Lance Mackey) but only one, Alaska's Lance Mackey, has won both in the same year. He accomplished that feat twice, in 2007 and 2008. In 2009, he decided not to run the Quest. Hans Gatt, a three-time winner, was the only returning former champion. Four-time Iditarod champion and the man who ran the fastest Iditarod ever, Martin Buser, was running as a Quest rookie.

All mushers set up a schedule for their race. They determine, based upon how they've trained their dogs, how much run time and rest is required to balance speed and endurance. The most common basic schedule is "six-on, six-off," meaning a team will run for six hours, then stop and rest for six.

During the rest time the dogs will be fed a hot meal, get checked by their musher and catch a couple of hours of sleep. The musher might be lucky to catch an hour or less of cold and uncomfortable half-sleep, simply lying down on an insulated blanket on top of the snow or crawling into their sled bag.

Hans designed a schedule for Newton, not to win the race, but to complete it in just under 12 days. The reputation of the Quest is such that just finishing the race earns a lot of respect in a sport where respect doesn't come casually.

"People ask me if I think he can finish," said Hans. "That is not a question to me. That was the goal to begin with. I pretty much always reach my goals if I set them and we will reach that one as well."

Rest stop on the trail.

Two-dog nap.

Front runners have race plans that involve extra long runs at strategic times and cutting rest when necessary in order to gain the competitive edge. The early miles are spent trying to conceal from their competitors exactly how strong their team is while, at the same time, trying to size up their competition. Some teams will minimize their time in checkpoints and stop longer on the trail to conceal the amount of rest they are actually getting.

"People will leapfrog each other," Hans wasn't going to give anything away about his own schedule. "We won't know what's going on until somewhere between Pelly Crossing and Dawson City. I'm not one of these guys who is looking for weak competition. I always go to the races with the toughest competition because that is what racing is all about."

Buser, who was expected to be a challenger for the crown, agreed. "It's too early to be looking at standings. The length of the race. It's too far to worry about now."

All schedules look good on paper when they're drawn up but other factors will determine whether or not a team can keep to them. With a fast trail, the team could be better in some places. With a slow trail, everyone will be slower. The most important aspect of a race schedule is the rest time, when dog care is top priority, because it's the dogs who win or finish a race, not the individual driving them.

The first checkpoint was Braeburn Lodge, a lonely gas station, restaurant and cluster of outbuildings almost exactly 100 miles from Whitehorse.

The trail to Braeburn followed the Yukon River north from Whitehorse for approximately 15 miles, then turned onto a small tributary, the Takhini River for another 15. Eventually it left the ice and followed the old Dawson-Whitehorse Overland stage road, now part of the Trans Canada Trail system, to the lodge. Braeburn was one of the original roadhouses on the Overland Trail. There has been a lodge there since 1899. The highway from Braeburn to Carmacks was laid overtop of the Overland Trail for that distance.

It was a relatively easy start to the race – a good wide, firm path through a roller coaster series of hills.

What was important on the first day was to keep the team under control. The dogs were fresh and eager for the trail, full of power and speed. The musher needed to settle them down to a steady rhythm or they would burn out. It's harder to settle the team down on a fast trail and Buser called the run to Braeburn "probably the best 100 miles of racing, trail-wise, I've ever encountered." Nobody really wanted to stop in the extreme cold. "Not even for a fleeting moment. Not at these temperatures."

Newton's schedule called for him to run five hours from Whitehorse, rest for four and run another five hours into the checkpoint. But "the dogs didn't want to rest. They just wanted to keep on running." He passed a group of four teams stopped on the trail. Other teams including Hans passed him. Despite the fact that he didn't feel like stopping either, because the musher suffers from the same early energy surge as the dogs, he did finally manage to get them to rest on one of the pullouts built by the trail breakers.

Even with the break, Newton pulled out of the bush into Braeburn just before midnight, just a minute behind Hans and an hour ahead of schedule.

Rick Johnson was concerned Newton was going too fast. "I saw Hans' team arrive. There was another team close behind but we weren't expecting Newton this early. It was only when they started leading the team toward

Musher's view of the trail ahead.

the camping area that I saw the sled bag and realized it was Newton." He recalled Hans mentioning that he had a hard time keeping up to Newton on longer training runs.

Although Rick couldn't assist Newton in the camping area he did look at the team with a critical eye. The fast pace didn't seem to have taken any toll on them. Their tongues lolled out of their mouths and they all gave him a goofy grin as they passed by. They still didn't want to stop but a half dozen officials and volunteers didn't give them any option, hanging onto the tuglines and leading them off the trail.

The checkpoint was located in a clearing behind the lodge. As the teams approached, the headlamps worn by the mushers could be seen stabbing and dancing through the trees. Then the officials' headlamps would pick up fourteen sets of eyes as the dogs glided out of the cold mist in the trees. The steam rising from warm bodies, billowing from their panting into the cold air, illuminated from behind by the musher's headlamp gave them a ghostly appearance.

Overhead, in a perfectly clear sky that had provided brilliant sunshine all day, stars competed with headlamps for effect.

It's never really dark at night in the Subarctic. The snow on the ground reflects and magnifies the feeble light of the stars. The musher can see the trail but can't make out some of the subtleties of the terrain. It all looks flat so they rely on the dogs to pick the best path and use their headlamp to fill in the gaps. A moonlit night is bright enough that no lights at all are required to illuminate your way.

All teams had to stop at Braeburn for two hours for a mandatory veterinary check of the dogs. A small crowd of handlers, media, officials and the just curious turned up to watch teams come in, then floated back to the lodge to wait for the next one.

Inside the rustic restaurant there was chatter in four languages, and parkas, hats and boots draped over chairs. The tables were covered with giant sticky cinnamon buns, cups of coffee and oversized hamburgers. It's a small eating place, designed as a stop for trucks and tourists driving the highway. Not meant to host a small army such as the one the Quest brings to town, even if it is only for one night a year. The toilet had already plugged.

"Too many people using it," explained lodge owner Steve Watson. "They don't let the bowl fill properly then it gets plugged. Or someone puts something down it that they shouldn't." He didn't sleep that night, making sure everyone got fed and no one used the washroom. Later, the generator providing the place with electricity conked out for a short time as well.

There were sleeping facilities set aside for the mushers – three rooms with two beds in each one. As one musher left another would take his or her place but it still wasn't enough. Some just stretched out on the floor where people had to step over them to enter or leave the room.

For those who arrived later and couldn't get into a room, they slept where they could. Several leaned chairs back against the wall, pulled their hats down over their eyes and tried to ignore the din. Some actually dozed, as evidenced by their slightly open mouths and light snoring. Others pushed aside napkin holders, Styrofoam coffee cups and plates, folded their arms and buried their heads in their elbows. Hans looked for two chairs, then for a place where he might put them together so he could curl up in a fetal position on the seats.

The hardier ones went back outside and crawled into their sled bags. It was cold but quiet. When he finished feeding the dogs, settling them down on beds of straw and talking with the vets during the mandatory inspection of the dogs, Newton glanced at other mushers crawling into their sleds to sleep. “I’m not sleeping in the sled bag. It’s too cold in there. I can’t sleep when it’s too cold.”

He tried his luck in the restaurant where he was able to eat a giant hamburger smothered in ketchup – but got no sleep. Just after seven in the morning he was on the trail again, an hour later than his schedule called for. His dogs, well rested, still loped at a fast pace, chasing and passing every team they could see in front of them. An hour after leaving he went by Hans.

“You need to slow down,” cautioned Hans. “You’re still going too fast. You’ll burn out. Stick to the schedule.”

The schedule for the 77 miles to Carmacks was basically the same as the one that got him to Braeburn. A five-hour run, followed by a four-hour rest, then another five hours to the small village on the banks of the Yukon River. The trail itself got a lot harder and narrower than the first day. It weaved its way through tangled trees, the hills increased in elevation and steepness and it ran through a chain of small lakes connected by thin, twisting creeks before dropping onto the river for the last mile into the checkpoint.

There was one section, nicknamed “Ping-pong Alley” by the drivers, where the trail went down, to the side, up and all over the place as it braided through the trees. On a fast trail it would have been brutal on the dogs, sleds and mushers. The trail breakers had built it up so it would force the teams to run slower but even so, Brent Sass’s team went off course and one of his dogs, a brown and black husky named Thunder, collided with a tree. Sass massaged the injured shoulder but Thunder started limping and the shoulder “just blew up.” He carried the dog in his sled for the three and a half hours it took him to reach Carmacks.

When Newton caught up to Normand Casavant, instead of passing, he halted the team and fed them frozen fish. Both teams were running similar schedules, since both race plans had been designed by Hans, and they decided to run together for the next short while.

“We’re also the same in mind. We don’t pressure anyone,” Newton liked Normand. “We just like to go along easy and we laugh a lot. He’s a good friend.” They trained together for part of the winter. Normand lived in a cabin owned by Hans in Atlin, BC, where Newton and Hans did a number of their long training runs. When the Quebecer struggled in January with his preparations for the Quest, Hans called him.

“Normand, I’m going to help you. Come to my place.” The Quest was, according to Normand, the biggest race of his life and even though he had 22 years of experience under his belt, he was apprehensive about his ability to complete it. Hans drew up a schedule for him and gave him a good idea of what supplies to forward to each checkpoint. It convinced him that maybe he could do this after all.

Somewhere along the way one of Newton's gloves fell off the sled. Normand had an extra pair and loaned them to him. Normand hadn't packed enough snacks for his dogs so when they stopped for their four-hour rest in the early afternoon Newton shared some extras he was carrying.

When the dogs curled up for a short nap after their meal the air temperature was still -30°C. Newton was having problems keeping warm but felt he needed to get some sleep. He crawled on top of his sled bag. Lying on his back, he turned his head to the side and closed his eyes. The sun heated one side of his face while the other gradually froze in the shade. When he felt the sunny side had warmed up enough, he turned his head, thawing the frozen side in the sun's heat, while the warm side cooled off.

In the hour he spent on top of his sled bag he got maybe five minutes of actual sleep. He had so far been awake for approximately 40 consecutive hours.

His hands were so icy "they felt like they were burning." The extreme cold persisted with no indication it would get any warmer. The northern winter of 2008-2009 was one of the most consistently frigid in history for the Yukon and Alaska. The cold and snow had arrived in November and there would be no respite from it until the end of March. But, while uncomfortable, the below normal temperatures didn't concern Newton or Hans.

From the day he arrived in Whitehorse in November, 2007, Newton had shown a remarkable ability to adapt to extreme sub-zero temperatures. "We have been running dogs in 40 below this winter and for a Jamaican who had never seen snow in his life before last year," Hans said, "And being able to handle the cold as well as he does, that was quite an accomplishment."

It was the lack of sleep that concerned the veteran. Hans recognized that sleep deprivation was Newton's Achilles' heel during long runs with him the previous winter. If anything could stop Newton in the Quest, he felt, it would be his inability to get sufficient rest.

It's not what sleep deprivation does to the musher that matters, it is the impact it could have on the team that counts. If a musher can't take care of himself, he can't take care of the dogs.

The hands are most vulnerable and take the worst abuse. In order to check the dogs, unhook the lines or cook the food, the musher must remove his or her gloves. An overtired rookie might not notice when frostbite sets in. Cold hands are stiff and uncomfortable. Frostbitten fingers can be fatal. The fingertips turn black and become incredibly painful. Skin splits and bleeds. The entire hand swells grossly and the musher can no longer unzip booties, hold food bowls, undo small clamps or even hang onto the sled. The musher can't force the dogs to do something for him or her. They do it together or it doesn't work.

Veterinarians and race officials can involuntarily withdraw a team from the race if they feel there is unnecessary risk to the dogs. Race marshal Doug Grilliott had pulled one team out of the race in 2008 on the very first day for inadequate dog care.

Denying yourself rest while physically maintaining a high level of athletic performance is a place of emotional fragility. Your ability to function balances on a knife-edge, easily tipped to one side or the other. For rookies, who have never gone there before, small things out of the ordinary can seriously mess with their minds. The veterans long ago realized it is the brain that needs to be prepared to race a thousand-miler, but that knowledge doesn't come easy.

"You can train a person how to run dogs. Teach them everything about dog care. Survival in the winter and the wilderness," said Hans. "But your mind is the key to finishing. The only thing that can teach you how to race is the race itself. That you can't teach, but it must be learned to succeed."

Quest mushers live or die by endurance. Endurance is about conserving energy in an efficient manner so you can continue running on the edge without running out of gas. Experienced dog drivers avoid mistakes by conditioning their mind to a strict routine they follow on autopilot – including such simple things as placing their gloves in the same place every time or hanging them around their necks on "idiot strings" so they don't have to waste energy looking for them.

Every once in awhile the brain needs to shut down and take a break as well. Even the most experienced mushers need to sleep occasionally. When pushing to the Finish line some will deny themselves rest at the checkpoints or during their feed times on the trail. They tie themselves to the back of the sled and catch 20 minutes or a half hour of shut eye while the dogs are still running – that way, if they fall off, they won't lose the sled and the pain of being dragged in the snow will wake them up.

Every Quest and Iditarod veteran had been where Newton was going and they understood it would make or break him.

Newton wasn't aware of it, but just as there were people cheering for him there were others waiting for the Caribbean upstart to fail. For them long distance mushing was a northern sport – the realm of Alaskans. The mass arrival of Canadian, Europeans and Japanese into the sport three decades earlier had met with the same chilly reception. Even as recently as 2005, when Norwegian Robert Sorlie won his second Iditarod race, there was serious resentment from the mushing community.

It was that knowledge that had Danny, prowling the checkpoint in the Carmacks community centre, worrying that he was expecting too much of his protégé. That made Rick and Nettie anxious and prepared to do anything to help the young Jamaican they loved like a son. It inserted itself constantly into Hans' mind even as he tried to run his own race.

"I'll need two winters to train a musher," Hans told Danny when the plan for training a Jamaican musher for the Quest started to hatch in early 2007, "because the Quest is more than just a race. It's winter survival."

During the second winter of training, Hans, already a demanding taskmaster in their first year together, became even more exacting – pushing and challenging him constantly with ever-increasing standards of dog care and mental conditioning. He had done everything he could do to get Newton ready for the race but, in the end, it was entirely up to Newton to make it work.

Before Normand and Newton dropped out of the bush and onto the Yukon River where they could see the lights of the Carmacks checkpoint, Newton thought everything was going just fine. This might be where he could finally relax and get some desperately needed rest.

Then he noticed that one of the team dogs, McCoy, was limping.

Bags of food, equipment, clothes and dog booties are sent ahead to each checkpoint.

Devon, Smiley leading with Tallowa (L) & Chukka (R)

Devon

If yuh want good, yuh nose haffi run.

Jamaican patois: If you want to succeed, you have to work hard.

May, 2005

It started out as any ordinary day on the job for Chukka's operations manager. Vehicles breaking down. Horses deciding they didn't want to go to the stables. Gamboling instead through an open gate onto the lawn in front of Danny's villa. Cows finding a way to wander from a neighboring estate onto the Polo field. People not turning up where people were supposed to be.

Nothing that couldn't be dealt with.

Then the phone rang. It was Danny, calling from Edmonton.

"Doctor Anderson." "Doctor" is Danny's nickname for Devon because of his skill with horses. "I just saw something. What do you know about dogsledding?"

Devon was silent for a moment. "Dogsledding. That's, um, something you do in snow."

"No. It's on dryland too. Maybe it's something we can do here (at Chukka). I want you to learn about dogsledding. What do you think?"

Devon blinked. His first thought was, "How are we going to do that?" His initial impulse was to laugh. Then 25 years of working with Danny kicked in. "He comes up with the ideas and I do them. This one has something about dogs. It sounds interesting. Why not?"

"Yeh Mon," he shrugged, "Why not?" When he hung up the phone he went back to work. What will be, Devon knew, will be. Another off-the-wall conversation with Danny. Another ordinary day at the office.

Danny zeroed in on Devon as the candidate for musherhood not only because of his openness to new ideas but for the same reason Devon had been hired on at Chukka Caribbean back in 1984. He had a natural ability to work with animals.

"Devon is an incredible horseman. Devon understands horses," Danny knew immediately who he would go to for this project. "And, if you notice, everywhere he goes his yard dogs follow him also. I always know where Devon is working in the yard because I see the dogs first. He's good with all animals. He's kind to them. He's very unJamaican that way."

"Doctor" Anderson.

Born in the village of Dressike in Saint Mary Parish, east of Ocho Rios, on March 31, 1963, Devon grew up in the countryside. His mother was a basic schoolteacher so he acquired the education that many of his generation missed. His father, who worked as a supervisor for a banana company, owned a small farm. Devon worked with him when school was out for the holidays.

When the family went to visit his grandfather, a farmer in Trelawny, west of Runaway Bay, Devon would assist him with his horses and cattle. His grandfather, who loved working with horses all his life, noted how quickly he learned how to care for the animals and how easily he interacted with them.

"My love of animals I believe are in my genes – from my grandfather," said Devon.

His grandfather was also the operations manager for a large estate in Trelawny, Good Hope Stables, that had racehorses and cattle. When Devon reached his 17th birthday, his grandfather suggested he move from St. Mary's and take a job at Good Hope. He could stay on his grandfather's farm.

His first job was as a casual laborer cleaning stalls. When one of the regular employees decided to go to the United States as part of a farm work exchange program for Caribbean people, the American woman who owned Good Hope approached Devon's grandfather. Would there be any problem if she asked Devon to stay at the estate for a couple of months until they could find a replacement for the departing employee?

"No problem," his grandfather responded.

She asked Devon if he was interested and he jumped at the chance.

"Whatever needs to be done that's what I'm going to do," said Devon. "I never get too tired. I never quit. I'm always willing to make that extra effort to get things done."

The two-month job lasted five years.

The primary business at Good Hope was breeding thoroughbreds for racing. In addition, the stalls contained equestrian mounts and horses for trail rides. He learned the basics of grooming thoroughbreds and how to ride but his real desire was to learn how to train dressage horses. The opportunity was there. The owners gave him access to their horses, but offered little guidance. He learned by watching the owner's daughter, who did a lot of show jumping. When she was finished for the day, Devon would take a horse and imitate what she was doing.

"Most of my learning is not someone sitting down, trying to teach me and tell me what I'm supposed to do. It's observing other people doing things I think are constructive and will help you along the way. Then copying them."

Even as he was educating himself as an adequate trainer and rider he was starting to ponder his future and the possibility that he might not have one at Good Hope Stables. "I was getting frustrated. I had reached a line beyond which it appeared I wasn't going to be able to go.

"They were nice people but a lot of times they didn't provide the tools needed to make the job more professional. They were making money but they weren't putting anything back into the business so everything was starting to get run down. I felt there's no future here. It was time for me to consider a change."

One evening he was watching a horse jumping competition on television. One of the horses jumping was an Appaloosa and as it approached a barricade the television camera showed a massive wide field beyond the fence, bordering the jumping arena. Devon turned to a friend who was watching with him.

"That's where I want to work," he said. He had no idea where "it" was nor how he could possibly find it. All he knew was that he liked what he had seen on the television and wanted to work there.

Four months later the Disney Corporation came to town. They were filming *Return to Treasure Island* in various sites along the north coast of Jamaica. One of the locations was Good Hope Stables.

"They used a lot of horses and carriages for that film," Devon remembers. "A lot of the horses came from Chukka Cove."

Devon was provided by Good Hope Stables to assist with the horses. When he drove through the front gate at Chukka he recognized it immediately. Later, he learned it was Marc Melville riding the Appaloosa he had watched jumping on the television.

When shooting on the film at Good Hope wrapped up a week later, the horses from Chukka were being loaded into trailers to return home. Danny, working on the set as horse master, noticed that Devon had jumped on one of the trucks. "So where the hell are you going?" he demanded.

"I'm going with you, because I love what I see at Chukka," replied Devon.

Danny thought about it for moment, "You might as well ride up front then."

"When I got here (Chukka) it was just an equestrian centre, show jumping, dressage and riding lessons with a little bit of trail riding," Devon recalls. "I had five years experience with horses. Not great experience…but five years of it."

It was enough experience that Devon eventually moved into management, becoming one of the farm managers and ultimately operations manager. It was also enough to ensure he was kept on at Chukka when the business tottered on the verge of disaster in the 1990s. At one point the entire staff of Chukka Caribbean Adventures consisted of Marc Melville, Devon, one other manager and a bookkeeper.

"Devon is special," said Danny, "There's no doubt. From the beginning he's been like a big brother to my sons. They're very close. He has good instincts and can learn his way through a job. He learned early on that people can be inspired to do things they don't think they can if you give them the chance and the support to do it."

Substantial growth in business at Chukka started in the first few years of the new millennium. More staff were hired. Tours added and expanded. More managers were needed. More stables were built.

"All of a sudden there was a lot more for me to do," said Devon. His days start early. Just after dawn's first light he arrives from his home in the hills above St. Ann's Bay. Dressed in a black shirt and black shorts, the single father of six children runs three laps of the Polo field then changes into his office garb for the day – a baseball cap, a shirt partially tucked into his pants and joota boots, the rubber galoshes used on plantations.

Although there is a room with a desk for him that he might occasionally use, his workplace is the stables and workshops of Chukka Cove and the White River. Besides the yard dogs who trot along happily in his wake, his constant companion is his cell phone.

There is rarely a conversation or meeting that isn't interrupted by his phone. He answers all his calls immediately, not because it might be Danny calling but because he knows it's often the only way the employees know how to find him when he's needed.

Danny's second call, three days after his first, didn't interrupt anything.

"Devon, you're going to Scotland. Book yourself a ticket."

"Cool."

It was a few hours later, with his flight to Scotland booked that he, for the first time, started to think about what was happening.

"Dogsledding," Devon recalls thinking, "I really never even heard of that. Not even close. I had seen dogsleds on snow on television, but it never occurred to me....There had never been a single time when I even ever thought of training a dog other than just teaching him to be housebroken.

"It's something you just don't see in Jamaica. In a movie you might see it, but it didn't mean anything because nobody knew what it was."

He'd always sort of had dogs around. The yard dogs at Chukka, "they just seem to appear and just stay with me. They get on very well together. I adopted them. They adopted me." His youngest son, six years old, played constantly with the dogs.

Devon usually had a puppy as a pet while growing up. His first was a white mongrel named Sultan. Devon was five or six years old then himself and remembers there was no electricity or running water in his home the night Sultan died.

"I remember hearing this growling and fighting outside. My father woke up and said, 'Something is wrong.'"

They went out holding up bottles filled with coal oil with a cork and a wick stuck in the top. In the weak, flickering light they could see Sultan lying just in front of the steps to the porch. "I remember looking at him in the yard with his throat torn out," said Devon. Beyond they could see the eyes of the pack of feral dogs that killed him.

"As long as I remember, growing up, I always had dogs at home. And everywhere I went they would go with me. It's just something that seemed to come naturally to me. No one ever had to come and say 'this is what you need to do.'"

Devon was an experienced traveler. Danny had no hesitation sending him to other Caribbean islands to help set up new operations or rebuild after a hurricane had literally blown the entire business out to sea. He had seen most of Danny's ideas through either to their successful implementation or their demise.

But Scotland for dog mushing? Now for something completely different! Ten days passed between Danny walking into Badland Buggies and Devon standing in front of the immigration desk at Heathrow Airport in London, England.

"Where are you going?" the young man behind the desk looked him up and down, then focused on his eyes to watch the answers.

"Scotland."

"What is the purpose of your visit?"

"I'm going to learn about dogsled mushing."

The immigration official's piercing gaze faltered. This wasn't an answer he expected. He glanced at the passport. "Dog mushing? Coming from Jamaica?"

"Yeh Mon."

"Are you serious?"

"Yeh Mon. My boss sent me up here to learn about dogsledding."

The officer hesitated a moment, then stamped the passport. He shook his head as he handed it back, "Dogsledding."

"Yeh Mon."

"I want to know your boss and I want to know what he's smoking."

Alan Stewart and friend.

Alan

We run tings, tings nuh run we.

Jamaican patois: Control your own destiny.

June, 2005

When Alan Stewart went to Austria in 2007 to buy an Alaskan bred sleddog he didn't take a chequebook with him. Instead he took 67 bottles of Macallan Scotch whiskey and a 42-year old cask barrel. The deal for the dog, a five-year-old female named "Too Slow," had been previously negotiated by Alan and his long-time friend Dr. Gerhard Offer and sealed one night over bottle number 68.

"To be honest the dog was worth a lot more than the cost of the whiskey I gave to Gerhard, but money wasn't important. He was concerned about where she would end up and he knew 'Too Slow' will be well looked after and a much-loved addition to my kennel."

As unorthodox as the transaction was, it was in character for the wiry Scot. He had never really lived a "normal" life in the classic sense. The past year with the Jamaica Dogsled Team was proof of that.

The first contacts with Danny intrigued him but, like everyone else, he had his doubts. He couldn't have cared less about the business side of the project. His first concern had been about the dogs.

"My first instinct was, 'Wow. The heat. We were going to get dogs, all the equipment, but that's the easy part. Actually training them and working with them in the heat....It's just not on.'"

He wanted to get a feeling for a project that was, based on his conversations with Danny, in an ever-developing, ever-changing state of flux. "I needed to have somebody when we went over to Jamaica – that was the idea if we decided we were going forward – who knew what we were doing. I could help him big-time if someone from Jamaica could come over and I had him for awhile. If he was going to go back to Jamaica to select dogs I could give him an idea of what to look for.

"I do lots of courses here (Cairngorm Sleddog Adventure Centre) and a lot of people fail the course because they can't do anything with the dogs... they couldn't do anything. When we agreed that a chap called Devon Anderson would come over I went on Google and found a picture of Devon and Danny's sons and read a wee bit about him (Devon)."

The concept was so far-fetched he didn't want to make any mistakes. All his life he avoided them because he worked in a profession where any slight slip-up would cost him his life. Alan isn't a professional dog musher. Having a kennel and driving dogs is his way of relaxing when he returns home from his real job 170 meters below oil rigs in the North Sea.

Saturation diving is a technique that enables individuals to remain at great depths for long periods of time. It allows for greater economy of work and enhanced safety for the divers who, after their shifts, live in dry, pressurized chambers. It enables them to remain at extreme depths over the entire work period, which could be days or weeks at a time. The maximum stay at any one time is a month. The record for saturation divers was set in 1988 when a team in the Mediterranean Sea performed pipeline connections at a depth of 584 meters.

In such an environment there is no room for error and it takes a certain type of personality to do it.

"Some people call it being 'blinkered' or being a control freak," said Alan. "That's what I did in Red China, Angola, Congo. In the Mideast and for the past 19 years in the North Sea. You don't make mistakes under the North Sea or have accidents or you kill people. I spend most of my life working in horrible environments. You need to have total commitment to what you are doing.

"There are no words that can describe the feelings I have after a long time away deep diving and that first step into the dogyard. Taking dogs into remote snowbound mountain areas became my passion."

The sea has always been a part of Alan. He had been born in Glasgow in 1956 and raised in Ardrishaig, a small fishing village on Scotland's west coast. As a teenager he made a hobby of scuba diving. When he left school he decided to make it his profession. Moving to Australia, he took a job in the outback of New South Wales to pay for commercial diving courses at Sydney Harbor.

The work was so intense he decided he needed an activity or a sport during his off-time to unwind. He tried a few, but nothing really grabbed his attention until he came across dog mushing. It was as much a lifestyle as it was a sport. Not just for him but also for his wife, Fiona and eventually their son, John. Running dogs was a family affair.

He did his own version of "Dogsledding 101" and discovered that a Scot, Allan "Scotty" Allan, had, in his time, been the world's most famous dog musher.

Born in Dundee, Scotland in 1867, "Scotty" Allan traveled to the United States at age 19 to help break horses in South Dakota. When the Klondike Gold Rush started in 1897, Allan left his pregnant wife and two children in Oregon to head north to Dawson City to find his fortune. The gold fields had all been staked by the time he arrived so he found work as a teamster – moving supplies by horse and dog powered sleds. He moved further north to Fairbanks and west to Nome as more gold discoveries were made in Alaska.

His wife and three children rejoined him in 1910 after he established his reputation. He was one of the founders of history's first organized professional dogsled race, the 408-mile All Alaska Sweepstakes, starting and finishing in Nome, in 1908. With a purse of $25,000 it attracted the best the mushing world had to offer. Scotty more than held his own, finishing second in the first race, then winning the next three. His success did more than pad his bank account. It made him internationally famous.

He next trained dogs for the military during the First World War (Danny had also come across this record) before entering Alaskan politics and leaving the dog-mushing world behind. Alan Stewart identified with his fellow Highlander so strongly he set up a museum to him.

He and Fiona set up the Snowy River Sleddog Kennel, at the foot of the Cairngorms mountain range, in the eastern Highlands near Aviemore on the northwest corner of Cairngorms National Park. The large plateau surrounded by low, round glacial mountains, is home to five of the six highest peaks in Scotland. What made it perfect for driving dogs was the lack of road access and sparse population.

The major paths across the wilderness were trails created when drovers used to drive cattle through the mountains to market. The climate, temperatures drop as low as -27°C and winds gust up to 162 miles per hour, discourages people from living in the subalpine tundra and moorland that covers the area. It does get some snow in winter, which can hang around in the higher regions until late summer.

It is known for its abundance of wildlife and as a place of unique beauty. "It had a sublime and solemn effect, so wild, so solitary," wrote Queen Victoria after climbing Ben MacDui, Scotland's highest mountain and the United Kingdom's second highest, in the summer of 1859. "No one but ourselves and our little party there…I had a little whiskey and water, as the people declared pure water would be too chilling."

Alan also summited Ben MacDui during the winter in 1999 with his mentors in dog mushing, Rick Atkinson and Alister Taylor, and two dog teams that included every dog he owned at the time. It was the first time a sleddog team had crossed the Cairngorms.

Rick and Alister were both veterans of the British Antarctic Survey and drove dogs in Alaska for a number of years. Rick ran the Yukon Quest in 1985, 1987 and 1988, finishing as high as second (1985) and completing all three years in the top five. His place in mushing history came during a raging snowstorm on top of King Solomon's Dome, during the 1987 Yukon Quest, when he used mouth-to-muzzle artificial resuscitation to save Jeff King's dog Tommy. Alister did the Quest in 1996, finishing eighth.

"I've never done the Yukon Quests or the Iditarods," said Alan. "I've won two-week stage races in Ushuaia, Argentina and Chile. Shorter ones all over Europe and everything here in the UK. John won races in Ushuaia and here. Fiona won the women's Scottish 3-dog championship. But winning events here in my country had nothing on those few days on Ben MacDui."

The Macallan distillery provided him with empty whiskey barrels, which he cut in half and turned into doghouses. When he had enough for all the dogs, extra barrels became water reservoirs. When the dogs weren't running they sat in front of their houses and looked out at the view.

Eventually he and Fiona decided they wanted to start Scotland's first adventure sleddog centre. They had a couple of ATVs for dryland training and some racing rigs, a few snow sleds and dogs.

"I was looking to go further into the hills and mountains. But here in Scotland, just like all over the world, we have a problem with climate warming. My trails were cutting up all the time so we decided we would have to redesign a specialized buggy to cope with the heather and maybe get further up onto decent, steeper areas. I decided to speak with a couple of companies who actually work with extreme off-road buggies – one in Perth, Australia, and one in Edmonton, Canada.

"I felt that Canada was the best because it's got this huge sleddog market and Alaska was just up the road. Bruce, the guy from Badland, designed an extremely top class off-road cart. Everything was going great then Bruce, he phones me up and tells me he has some guy from Jamaica who's interested in talking to me."

He started to get convinced the project might work when he thought about using Jamaican dogs. All they had ever known was heat, so maybe the overheating concerns traditional mushers might have at zero degrees wouldn't be the same in a tropical climate. "For this venture, local dogs would have to be sourced. The more I found out about stray dogs in Jamaica it was not only the best way to go. It was the only way to go."

Still he felt there had to be someone there who could build the kind of relationship necessary and he knew from experience not everyone was capable of doing that.

Early on Devon's first morning in the mountains, the sky was clear and the winds so calm that both the Jamaican flag and St. Andrew's Cross hung limp on their flagpoles. Devon left the house to take a short walk and look at the Cairngorms.

"I looked out the window and there was Devon walking toward a herd of red deer. There were about 16 or 18 of them and he got close…real close. Something just clicked between them and him. That was incredible! If he could do that…I found out later that in Jamaica he is what could only be called a horse whisperer."

During breakfast Devon seemed pensive.

"You know, um, I love this area here," he finally said. "It's so quiet and so beautiful. It reminds me of home."

It would, Alan knew, take a couple of months to prepare a dog driver for taking tours but he had to start somewhere. He started him on his 10-day

Devon in the forests of Aviemore (L) and training in the Cairngorms (R).

Insight training course and did most of it at night. "We were in the middle of summer so the weather was playing an enormous part. It was cool at about three in the morning so that's when we actually started training the dogs. Devon was thrown into the deep end in pitch black." It would also be a test of the level of commitment he might expect to find.

The first day was a revelation for Devon. "I was excited about meeting the dogs. I'd seen Huskies on television and they were these big, fluffy things. I really wanted to see what these dogs actually looked like. I'd heard stories and I wondered, 'are these dogs aggressive?' but when we entered the kennel the dogs got as excited about me as I did about them. Within a few seconds I was relaxed, started to move around and pet them. Alan showed me around, telling me about the dogs and showing me who is who."

For two days Alan had him harnessing dogs, hooking up ganglines, feeding and watering, cleaning the kennels. In the evenings they talked about what Devon could expect to find when he finally rode in a sled and what he needed to know when he actually drove a team – especially in heat.

"I can read people quite quickly with dogs. He was very, very good. He had a background in horses so he took to the dogs very well."

On the third day Devon sat in the passenger's seat of the dryland touring rig behind a 12-dog team.

"I wasn't nervous getting into the sled. I don't get nervous the first time I do something. It's when I do it once, then have to do it again. That's when I get nervous because now I know what is expected."

"Hang on," advised Alan.

Fiona opened the gate from the yard and the dogs took off.

Devon hung on. "Oh my God!" he yelped, all the time thinking, "Is this for real?"

"The power of those dogs pulling was unbelievable. If someone had said to me, 'This is what you'll be feeling,' I would have said 'No Mon. It can't be

Alan, Devon and Newton.

true.' But I felt it and it was for real. When the dogs took off my heart came into my mouth. When I'm on top of a horse I'm in control. I have my hands to control the horse. But with the dogs we just have voice command."

When the team finally settled into a steady lope Alan brought them to a halt in the middle of the trail. "Are you going to try it?" he asked.

"No," Devon responded adamantly.

They sat silently in the middle of the trail for a minute. Alan waiting patiently. Devon considering the situation. "There are brakes. There's no engine. No steering – just by voice. The dogs know him but they don't know me – will they even listen to me? Will I be in control or will they?" He wasn't quite sure about this, Devon thought, but this was why he was here. It had to happen sooner or later.

"It's okay Devon," said Alan. "You can do it." Then he took a deep breath, "You know I've never done this to anyone. Nobody has ever driven my dogs except myself and my son."

"Alan. You trust me to do it?"

"Devon, you can do it."

"Okay," he finally conceded.

Alan sat in the passenger's seat and glanced back at Devon standing on the driving platform.

"Awk mon," he smiled, "You can do it."

Devon released the brake. "Hike," he said. The dogs started to run. Jamaica's first dog musher was driving a team for the first time.

Approaching McCabe Creek dog drop.

Newton's Schedule

Carmacks to Pelly Crossing

73 miles, 14 hours

The first thing Newton did after arriving in Carmacks was point out McCoy to the veterinarian who approached the team. "He's limping on his left rear leg. I think he has a bum knee. I'm going to drop him."

The vet looked at McCoy and agreed with Newton. As she walked down the line checking the other dogs she also looked carefully at Newton. The dogs seemed fine but he was obviously stressed as he followed along behind her removing booties and talking gently to the dogs.

As Rick unhooked McCoy and led him away to the dog truck where he would spend the rest of the race getting massages, going for short walks, eating and sleeping, the vet had a brief discussion with Newton about feeding the dogs.

"If they're getting skinny and don't eat, what do I do?" Newton asked. "They're not eating. I think they're stressed out."

Get some rest, she suggested, let the dogs get some rest then we'll see how they eat. A good sleep often made a significant difference in a dog's appetite. It also frequently made a difference in a musher's perception of how well the dogs are eating.

"That level of concern and care is a long way from the young man I first met two years ago," she noted as she left him spreading straw for the dogs to sleep on. Newton was still an hour or more away from being able to think about his own welfare.

Sleddogs are treated like Olympic athletes when they rest, both in checkpoints and on the trail. They are fed. Provided with a soft bed. Feet are checked and rubbed with ointments to help them recover. Wrists, elbows and shoulders are tested to see if there are any injuries that might flare up. Legs are massaged to increase blood flow and prevent cramping or stiffness. All of this must be completed before the musher can look after him or herself.

Carmacks is a small community of just under 450 residents, located approximately 100 miles north of Whitehorse via the Klondike Highway and 177 miles by the Yukon Quest trail. It had originally been a location for seasonal hunting and fishing camps for the Tage Cho Hudan (Big River People), the Northern Tutchone people who lived here before and since the arrival of K'uch'an ("Cloud People" or white men) in the 1800s.

Its central location earned it the nickname of "Hub of the Yukon" because from this community there is a highway to every major community in the territory. Before highways were built in the 1950s it was important as a riverboat stop and a roadhouse on the Overland Trail between Whitehorse and Dawson. It is named after George Carmacks, who built a trading post here in 1884 before eventually traveling further downriver where he became famous as one of the co-discoverers of the Klondike gold fields.

When the Quest rolls into town the population increases by about 25 percent. Most of the temporary additions can be found hanging around or in the community centre. The media dominates one room, lined with tables covered with computers. Handlers, hangers-on, media and mushers can get a meal in another room. There's a room with its floor covered with gymnasium mats for the mushers to sleep on.

Normand was sitting in the eating area when Newton finally came in. "Are you going to stay for five or six hours?" he asked.

"Six hours," Newton replied, "I'm going to stay for six."

"I'll head out with you if that's okay? "

"Yeh Mon. That's good, Mon."

When he finished eating Newton headed for the sleeping room but after a couple of hours he wandered back out.

"I can't sleep in there," he mumbled. "There's too much noise. There's people coming and going all the time." He went out to feed the dogs.

Rick stood by the team watching as Newton distributed bowls to the dogs, some of whom stayed asleep, others who displayed mild interest in the activity.

At some point during the feeding Newton decided he had to break from the schedule Hans had designed for him. So far he had stayed within an hour of his projected time, arriving in Carmacks only 50 minutes behind.

He hoped for sleep in Carmacks, but it hadn't come. Normand had already left, telling Newton he wasn't going to wait like they had agreed and he wasn't going to do the next run by the schedule either. He planned to run the entire 77 miles to Pelly without stopping for four hours, as planned, at McCabe.

"I'm taking a really long rest in Pelly," said a bleary-eyed Newton.

"Yeah," responded Rick. He had been getting increasingly concerned about Newton, "I think you should, man. If you need to take the time, take the time."

Newton changed his mind about staying for six hours. He started packing the sled and was ready to go after five. He noticed another dog limping as he hooked them up. Calling over a vet, they looked at the dog's leg. The vet couldn't determine without a more detailed examination if there was a problem or not but Newton decided to drop him anyway.

He stressed about dropping a second team member.

"Don't worry," advised Rick, "You can finish this race with 10 dogs, or eight. The dogs are strong enough to do it."

"You think so!?"

"I know so."

Later it was found the dog had a broken toe.

As Newton pulled up to the checkpoint to sign his departure form, the checker glanced at a note attached to his clipboard and advised, "On the north side of the road, out by the hill on the other side of McCabe, be aware of overflow."

The news visibly deflated Newton. Nobody likes overflow. Everything and everyone gets wet. On rivers it's bad enough, but in the bush it can be a nightmare. So far there hadn't been any, and the trail briefing before the start in Whitehorse had indicated there wasn't any on the trail all the way to

Rick Johnson and Newton at McCabe Creek.

Fairbanks. That had obviously changed. Newton drove off into the darkness of the early morning.

"He got out in good time," observed Dee Enright, a public relations consultant for the race organization. "But he's tired. He didn't get much sleep. He obviously didn't like the news about the overflow. He's down two dogs. He's second-guessing himself. I think he's pretty low right now."

The trail to Pelly is relatively flat and fast. It follows a road for the first while, hooks back onto the old stage road again before dropping down to cross a short stretch of jumble ice on the Yukon River near a hospitality stop named McCabe Creek. From there it travels a valley filled by a series of small lakes to the checkpoint. It is the last "easy" portion of the trail before the final stretch into Fairbanks, still almost 700 miles ahead.

Once past Pelly the terrain gradually becomes more brutal and demanding and the Yukon Quest truly begins.

Newton never did see much of the trail between Carmacks and McCabe. Instead of a frozen diorama of northern wilderness he found himself driving the team through Fern Gully, a former riverbed just south of Ocho Rios. The sides of the gully have a profusion of hundreds of varieties of ferns hanging from them, a towering rainforest standing tall on top of them. Hardwood trees and Lianas. Along the sides of the road that passes through the gulley are roadside stands built from bamboo that offer fruits, vegetables, carved-wood souvenirs and basket work. He spotted a bar on the side of the road with a Red Stripe beer on the counter.

He could hear the trees moaning in the breeze and a distant cataract tumbling out of the mountains. Birds flitted from branch to branch and sang as they can only sing in paradise.

"No," he muttered to himself, "That's not right. I'm really screwed up."

Sleep-deprived endurance athletes eventually find themselves occupying a sort of twilight zone where delusions, hallucinations and the illogical seem perfectly normal. In that stage, where their faces take on what is called "the thousand mile stare," it is almost impossible to determine whether people are awake or asleep even as they walk and talk. They will see and hear things they want to see and hear.

Naked women step from behind trees and ask for rides (this one is usually restricted to men). Men sit on brush bows blowing smoke rings. Their children suddenly appear on their sled bag and carry on a discussion like they were sitting at home. Imaginary wolves stalk the team. The trees march along the riverbanks with you. Entire orchestras play symphonies and relatives, who aren't within a thousand miles, conduct conversations with you.

Sometimes the illusions can be so strong that the musher will throw him or herself from the back of the sled to avoid the train that just came around the corner and is currently running through the team without the dogs even noticing.

His arrival at McCabe was almost a shock, seemingly coming so soon after leaving Carmacks, even though it had been five hours. There were half a dozen sleds in the yard as he pulled in, parked the team and fed them. When finished he wandered into the workshop where the Kruze family, owners of the farm, set out food and prepared a place for the mushers to sleep.

The time he spent with his hallucinations had improved his spirits. He seemed more relaxed. His sense of humor was back. He picked up a cinnamon bun, ate it, tentatively reached for a second.

"Can I have another one?" he asked.

"Take all you want," responded a woman. He reached over and took two handfuls.

"These are so good," he spoke with his mouth full, "You should send them to Jamaica."

He tried sleeping again, but gave it up after an hour. "That's okay," he shrugged off Nettie's concern, "I get plenty out on the runners."

Her face told him she didn't think he was, but she didn't say anything more.

He ate more cinnamon buns and fed the dogs a second time. Spoke with a vet about another dog he thought might be limping, but decided not to drop him so early in the race. Most of the time a dog will be able to run through a small limp. If he didn't get better, Newton could always load him in the sled for the short 34-mile run to Pelly. With daylight starting to fade he began hooking up the team.

Overflow usually happens during extremely cold weather. Creeks will freeze right to the bottom but the water, barely warmer than freezing, still needs a place to flow. So it finds its way to the top of the ice and pools there.

It can happen just about anywhere, on valley floors and hillsides, creek water flowing out over the top of river ice in a steaming, freezing sludge. Rarely does it appear as open water. Because it freezes so quickly after coming to the surface it is usually a spongy sort of ice covered by rivulets of trickling water. There is no way to know exactly how deep the water and slush is under the surface. It could be knee deep or barely enough to cover your toes.

All a team can do is go out on the pliable surface and hope they don't break through. It's easy to spot in daylight, either pea-green or a dirty yellow-brown in color. On a river it's easy to build a route or drive a team around the overflow. In the bush it's almost impossible to bypass. The trail markers may be missing but there are a series of trenches and open holes where previous teams have crossed and broken through.

Most lead dogs balk at crossing wet surfaces. Newton's leaders were no exception. He took the team through a narrow band of overflow, thinking "that wasn't so bad." On the far side he stopped and changed wet dog booties for dry. "If the Velcro freezes it can cut the back of their wrists."

He went through a second stretch, then turned a corner and found a wide patch of overflow 30 feet (10 meters) in length and about 18 inches (half a meter) deep. His leaders did a U-turn at the edge of the wet ice.

"Sometimes you have to go up to the front and take the line and lead them. Show them this is the right way to go. This is the path."

He got them started over the uneven surface. Without warning the sled tipped into a trench in the slush burrowed by an earlier team. Newton pulled the sled upright then, as the team jolted forward, slipped on the ice and dropped to his knees in the water-filled trench. His boots flooded. Realizing there was a problem behind them the dogs stopped and looked curiously back over their shoulders. He stood up, "hiked" up the dogs and they completed the crossing.

"It was uncomfortable and very cold. I don't think it was fun for nobody," Newton said. When he stopped to change booties again he realized he was dangerously low on them – having loaned Normand a bagful earlier in the race. If there was any more overflow he wouldn't have enough.

His own footgear he didn't change, opting instead to let his own body heat warm the water to a tolerable level.

There was no more overflow. When Newton rolled into Pelly Crossing that evening he was 250 miles into the race, three hours behind his schedule and hadn't slept more than a few minutes over the past two and a half days.

The dogs were covered in frost but their tongues lolled out of their mouths in happy grins. The limp he thought he detected in McCabe was gone. The vets went over the dogs with nods of approval as he spread the straw for them, stripped booties and applied ointment to paws.

In Carmacks a journalist had asked him if there was any time he would set aside his schedule and just run.

"I have the schedule and I will stick to it…unless something happens that means I can't stick to it," Newton had responded. "Then I will have to decide what to do."

He didn't know exactly how long he intended to stay in Pelly, but it was going to be longer than originally planned. The next checkpoint was Dawson City, 210 miles and a mountain range ahead. He needed sleep and, no matter how long it was going to take, he intended to get some.

Newton, Rick and Alan with dogs in harness.

Rick

Pudden cyaa bake widout fiah.

Jamaican patois: You need the right tools for the job.

July, 2005

Before he traveled to Jamaica to help set up a proper kennel Alan knew he needed two things. Dogs for one.

When Devon arrived back in Jamaica he suddenly realized he didn't know what kind of dogs he needed to find. He phoned Alan, "What kind of dogs are we going to look for?"

"Just find any kind of dog for now but don't get too many. We'll get a few more after I get there."

Professional help for two. He knew that two trainers working together were more effective than one working on his own. His son John was going to accompany him to Jamaica. He had the knowledge but not the experience. Alan thought of a sprint musher he'd met in the 1990s, at the Walt Disney

Iron Will race in Como Park, Minnesota. Rick Johnson had retired as a driver but was still a well-known gangline and equipment maker for dog mushers around the world.

Alan phoned Rick.

"He started talking about some guy in Jamaica who was starting a dog team," recalled Rick. "I thought, 'Yeah right man. Not gonna happen. Have another shot of Scotch.' I was waiting for some kind of punchline." The punchline never came. The conversation ended. There were a couple of emails and Rick realized that Alan was serious.

"Hang onto your shorts!" Alan finally typed in his last email in August. "He wants us to go down to Jamaica to help him."

His first morning in Montego Bay, Rick had breakfast with Danny's son, Daniel Jr., who had picked him up at the airport the night before.

"Have you met my dad yet?" enquired Daniel Jr.

"Nope."

"He's crazy."

"Oh really."

"Oh yes. He thinks up all these goofy tours and gets them going and we just run them." Then Daniel Jr. leaned forward and spoke in a confidential undertone. "Do not drink with my father," he warned.

Although it sounded somewhat like a challenge Rick heeded the advice during his stay in Jamaica. He wasn't used to turning down challenges. It all started with the kid behind him in high school.

During one of their classes a teacher asked for volunteers to ski jump. "This guy behind me – who was bigger than me – grabbed my hand and raised it." Even then he had to be convinced to go to the top of the slide where they informed him there was only one way down.

As Rick stepped out of the box and into the tracks on the jump he heard the only instructions he would ever receive about how to ski jump, "Don't forget to keep standing at the end."

He crashed. The challenge had been made and he was determined to meet it. Rick tackled the sport with a vengeance, until one of his crashes mangled his shoulder. Jumping was no longer an option so he took up downhill skiing and moved to Aspen, Colorado.

"Even then I liked being in the air…I really liked being in the air." He hooked up with a few friends and they started "really pushing the animal out there." They heliskied, went backcountry skiing in the mountains and charged headlong down double-groomed ski runs "designed to only do one thing – go really fast." Eventually he realized there was nothing left for him to challenge in skiing and the only future he had was seriously damaging himself.

One of his skiing friends was a hairdresser, Annette called "Nettie," originally from Minnesota who was as fearless as he was. When she decided in 1968 to return to Minnesota she left behind a pair of false eyelashes. Rick, looking for a reason to leave skiing behind, used the eyelashes as an excuse to follow Nettie "to return them."

They had a slight brush with dog mushing history close to Aspen, Colorado, when they went backcountry skiing in Castle Creek Valley – where the popular 1950s television series *Sgt. Preston of the Yukon* was filmed. However, it wasn't until 1972 in Minnesota that Rick and Nettie considered dog mushing themselves – not as sport but as a means of self-preservation.

At that time they had two dogs – one of whom had a bad habit of eating the living room furniture when he wasn't taken for his daily walk. They were leash-walking the dogs up a hill behind their house but the dogs were pulling so hard they ended up running up the hill every day.

"We can't keep this up," panted Rick one day, "it's gonna kill us." Then they heard about a fellow who built dogsleds and purchased one that they named "The Golden Goddess."

A couple of weeks later they heard there was a race being held. "We entered the 2-dog class. We didn't have a clue about how to drive dogs but we did meet a lot of people who knew what they were doing and we started learning that weekend."

After a year Rick wrote in his training journal: "We now have 17 dogs but will soon be down to a reasonable number."

"It went downhill from there, man, " he laughed. "Next thing you know, we bought a dog truck, then a kennel of dogs. All of a sudden we had 35 dogs in our backyard."

They needed a larger farm but weren't sure they could afford it. Nettie was employed but in the 1970s a woman's wage wasn't considered in the family cash flow when applying for a mortgage. Only Rick's income would be taken into account. They didn't have a lot of what they considered to be assets. To their surprise the bank approved the mortgage, accepting the dogs as collateral.

He did try a middle distance race but found that he still liked going fast so stuck to sprint racing for his 35-year mushing career. In the 1970s and 80s, Minnesota was the beginning of the professional sprint circuit. Teams

Rick and Nettie Johnson.

would start racing there in early winter, then work their way north, racing in Canada and finishing the season off in Alaska, in Fairbanks and at the Fur Rendezvous in Anchorage.

Rick and Nettie never made the trip to Alaska but shared their trails with the best the sprint world had – Alaska's George Attla, Gareth and Roxy Wright, the Streeper brothers from Fort Nelson, British Columbia.

By the late 1990s Rick started to notice a few changes. One was, his body couldn't take the abuse of racing any more. Another was that the other mushers weren't getting any younger. "There's a lot of gray hair. Not many kids." The cost of maintaining a team increased while the value of race purses and sponsorships dropped. More people were selling out than buying in. Even in Alaska the sport faltered. Anchorage's Fur Rendezvous race tottered on the edge of insolvency before being saved by a Canadian businessman from Winnipeg, Manitoba.

When they got Alan's phone call Rick and Nettie had already sold most of their dogs, retired from their regular jobs and were happily living on their farm making tuglines for other mushers. Their dog driving was limited to running their team purely for pleasure. If the lure of a two-week all-expense paid trip to the Caribbean wasn't enough, Rick was intrigued by the possibilities of what a Jamaican dogsled team might do for his sport.

At their first meeting, Danny turned to Rick, "Just tell me if this is feasible."

"Well," responded Rick, "the temperatures here scare the daylights out of me. Where I'm from we don't run dogs over 50 degrees (10°C). Anything over that, forget it. Even on days when it's freezing there are days I won't run dogs because the humidity is too high.

"In Jamaica?" Rick hesitated for a moment. "What can I tell you? I don't know."

While dogs had been trained in extreme dry heat in Australia there was no precedent for training dogs in a tropical climate where both temperatures and humidity were high.

"Overheating a dog is one of the most frightening things there is," Rick explained later. "I don't want dogs falling over and dying on me. I'm almost afraid to touch a dog far less make him move forward. If a dog overheats, they may survive but they'll never run again. They'll just overheat faster." Like Alan, he felt the unknown factor in their training might be the fact that the dogs were from Jamaica – they were acclimatized.

There were already three dogs in the kennel at Chukka Cove. Devon had gone to a private kennel, Animal House, in Lydford, close to St. Ann's Bay. A man approached him from the enclosure where a number of dogs were running free.

"What do you want dogs for?" asked the man. Devon tried to explain it to him. At first the man smiled. Then he laughed. Finally he gave him a price and showed him two dogs – Ronan, later renamed Smiley, and Salome, eventually changed to Jimmy, for the JDT's major sponsor. I have another one, he said, but it's my personal dog and aggressive.

"Okay. We'd like to see him." When the man reappeared he was being dragged by a powerful dog at the end of a chain.

"That's one we might be interested in," said Devon. Bruno became the third dog to join the Chukka dogsled team. Devon decided that was enough for now and he would wait for Alan to select any more dogs.

Alan and Rick started the dogs slow. Walking them on a leash with a stick or small weight dragging behind, worrying all the time – "How are they doing?" "Are they overheating?" They hooked a couple of dogs up to a three-wheeled cart but would only let them pull for a short distance. Then they realized the dogs were fine. It was the trainers who were overheating.

The biggest hurdle was that rather than training puppies to grow up into sleddogs, they were dealing with adult dogs who had already developed bad habits. The challenge was going to be convincing the dogs to overcome their life experience, learn to trust their handlers and work together as a team. Even something as simple as treating a dog to a cool treat was a problem.

"Jamaican mongrels don't know what an ice cube is," Danny watched the process with amusement. "They don't know how to eat one."

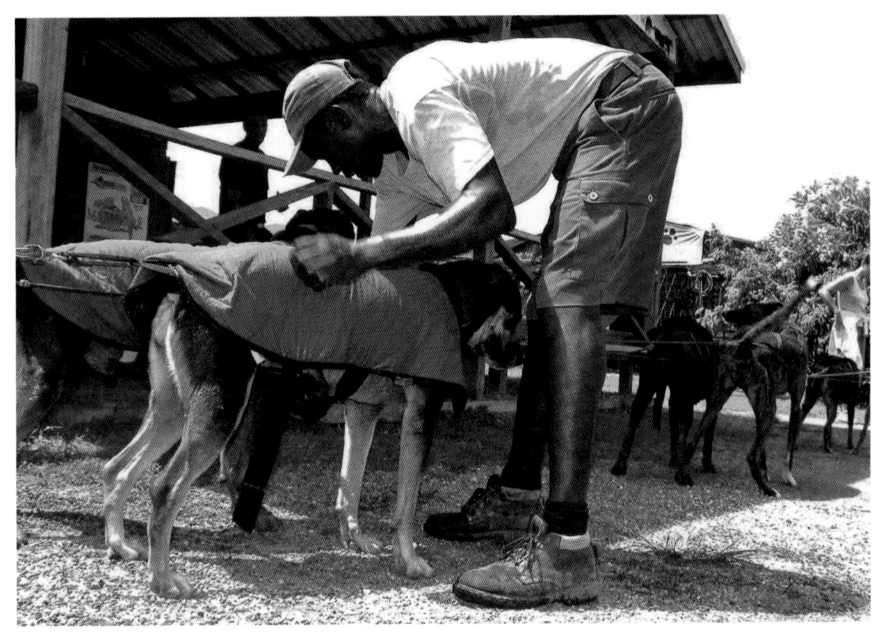

Blankets were soaked with water to keep the dogs cool.

"Those dogs that were rescued (from the JSPCA or Animal House), we have no idea what they went through," said Nettie when she came to Jamaica later that year. "Now it's another change in their life and they're wondering...what now?"

Alan, John and Rick traveled with Devon to the JSPCA compound in Kingston and Animal House in Lydford to educate Devon in what to look for in dogs and to continue building the team. They looked for the body characteristics that identified a potential candidate for the team – good body length, longer legs, the angle at which the legs ran out from the hind end, good posture, which indicates a positive attitude, and strong front shoulders.

Other dogs came from people who were moving from Jamaica and couldn't take their dogs with them. Chukka, Marbles, Tallowa and Isabella came to the kennel this way.

A site was identified behind the horse stables where a kennel could be built but doghouses didn't exist in Jamaica. The local tradesmen had to be shown how to construct even a simple one. Some modifications were required because of the climate. The structures were raised above the ground to allow air to circulate below the houses, keeping them cooler. A framework was built above the houses and covered with a sun-blocking material to shade the dogyard.

The paddock adjacent to the kennel was identified as the dog arena where teams could be trained. Alan and John walked the property and determined where an approximately one-mile loop trail for the dog tour could be located. They mowed grass and cut out underbrush. The trail took the tourists through a grassy meadow behind the kennel, through a grove of trees to the coast, to a landing where they could stand in the spray of the crashing waves and release sea urchins from the tidal pools that confine them.

Then to the location where the motion picture *Papillon* (Warner Brothers, 1973, starring Dustin Hoffman and Steve McQueen) was filmed. There they could rest on the same rock where Hoffman's character sat pondering his freedom and how he might be the first to escape from this dismal paradise (Devil's Island).

Finally, the tour went around the Polo field and back to the kennel.

It also soon became apparent that Devon, with his other responsibilities as operations manager, wasn't going to be able to do the whole project by himself. Alan suggested that he start looking for someone who might be able to help.

Devon never had any doubt about who he wanted. "There were lots of other people around, but there was just something about Newton that I knew he would be the best person to be a part of the dogsled team.

"He has a very gentle nature about him. He has spirit. I can't explain it but sometimes I just got this feeling that 'this is the person I want for this job.' I knew he would fit into this position. There was no doubt in my mind. Newton was the only person I thought of…nobody else."

He asked Natalia, one of the office staff at the stables, to call the horse riding operation at the White River, in the mountains above Ocho Rios. Newton was working there as a tour guide. He was saddling a horse when Miss Helen, the site manager, came out of the office.

"Newton," she ordered him, "Stop working."

"Why?"

"I got a phone call from Chukka Cove and they told me to tell you to stop working," Miss Helen stated.

Newton suddenly felt very frightened. He wondered if his job was on the line but couldn't think of why. "I didn't do anything wrong!" he pleaded.

"That's what they told me to tell you," she responded. "To stop working. You're supposed to wait in the office until someone calls."

"I didn't do anything wrong," he repeated.

"Newton, I need you to take care of some dogs," explained Natalia when she called back. "Can you take care of some dogs?"

Newton was prepared to agree with any suggestion at this point. "That's no problem," he replied. His first jobs were feeding the dogs, cleaning the dogyard and leash-walking the dogs around the dog arena. "They liked sneaking away through small holes in the fence."

Later, in a conversation with Alan he first heard mention of a dogsled tour.

"There was a rumor that Chukka was going to start a dog tour but I didn't have a clue what a dog tour was all about. I couldn't figure out how it was going to work. What are the dogs going to do?

"The only thing that came to my mind was leash-walking the dogs. I said to myself, 'I don't think that's going to work out.'

"I watched Alan and Rick train the dogs to pull sticks and weights and that just got me more confused." He saw them putting harnesses on the

The JDT Kennel.

dogs. 'They're going to have to drag the dogs,' he thought. 'This isn't going to be fun.' When the three-wheeled cart was put behind the dogs for short runs, with Alan and Rick hitching up only one dog at a time, 'the dogs are not going to pull that.' "

That's when Newton found out what his real job was going to be. He was put in front of the team and asked to run – to give the dogs something to chase. At first he was fast enough on his feet, then he had to start riding a bike and eventually an ATV.

Rick watched in amazement as Newton charged around the newly cut tour trail ahead of the dogcart. "I used to think that if Jamaica couldn't use him as a dog musher, by the time we were going to be finished they could use him in the Olympics."

Rick's two weeks were coming to an end. Alan and John would finish off the kennel and continue training Newton and Devon for another three weeks. Danny kept turning up almost every day, asking, "What do you think?"

Finally both Rick and Alan agreed. "We think it's feasible Danny. We think you can do it."

Instructing students

One rescued dog thanks Devon.

Shelter Dogs

Give them care. Give them kindness. Give them consistency.
Above all, give them time.

Zoya DeNure, Crazy Dog Kennel, Paxson, Alaska

One part of the animal welfare course the JSPCA puts on in their Outreach education program is teaching children that they shouldn't hit their puppies with machetes.

"You are not to kill them," said the JSPCA volunteer delivering the course to a roomful of elementary school children. "You are not to stone them. You are not to hurt them. You do not throw them in the garbage. Or in the sea. If there is a problem you take them and tie them. You call and we will come and we will remove them." Hanging on the wall behind her is a sign, *Education is key. It transforms lives.*

Walk any street in any Jamaican city, town, village or hamlet and you can find stray dogs. They're not really alive. They merely exist in perpetual black despair. Tick-infested, worm-plagued, flea-ridden, malnourished. Some dragging an injured limb or missing one altogether. Others covered with open sores or burns. Half-blind from untreated eye infections. Skeletons marked by knife wounds and infested with maggots. Females with their teats almost to the ground from bearing so many litters. Starving mongrels cowering in corners, waiting for death. Carcasses lying by the side of the road, victims of collisions with cars, taxis and trucks – some of them intentionally hit.

No one knows how many dogs there are on the island. Too many. In the eyes of many Jamaicans they are the lowest of the low. Undeserving of care and compassion. Some have never been touched by humans and are so terrified of people that any contact would cause them to urinate and vomit in fear.

They're called "Jamaica Boasties" because, despite their emaciated misery, when seen on the road they seem cocky, sure and arrogant. However, when they nose through garbage or rip into trash bags in search of morsels of rotting food there is, in their eyes, a tragic sense of loss. As if they understand this is their life but instinctively somehow know it could be different.

"I don't know that it (the abuse and neglect by the public) is always intentional," said JSPCA Executive Director Pam Lawson. She had been the Animal Welfare Manager at the Battersea Gardens Home, Britain's oldest charity before coming to Kingston and joining the JSPCA. "I fear that much of it is. The people in Jamaica are not a very natural animal loving country. Some of them care for them, but don't necessarily love them. They're not tolerant of their own (other Jamaicans), so how can I expect them to be tolerant of the animals."

Many dogs are feral and tend to roam in packs. Second or third generations of dogs who have never encountered any close human contact. Or, if they have, it's usually because someone is throwing a rock or shooting at them.

"To Jamaicans the dogs are just dogs," said Cyd Millar, a friend of Danny's who helped with dog care at the Chukka kennel. "They're dirt. You're not supposed to spend any money on them or train them. The dogs are supposed to know how to be friendly or be a guard dog by instinct only. If a dog doesn't behave the way they want, does something wrong or bites someone – they'll kill it themselves. Hang it from a tree. Poison it. Do some dreadful thing to kill it. Or they'll drive out to a highway in some remote place and just put it out on the road."

Cyd once stopped a man who was dragging a dog on a rope tied to the back of his car. She found two puppies "no bigger than my foot" tied in a sack and thrown into the rubbish.

Her sister stopped at a roadside restaurant on the road to Montego Bay, spotted two chains attached to the side of the building and walked around to see what they meant. She found one dog, still alive but "skin and bone." The other dog was dead.

"Jamaicans are very cold towards animals," Cyd added in a harsh condemnation of the attitude of her culture. "They're cold-hearted towards their own children much less their dogs." The people's indifference to the suffering of dogs was proof, to her, that her culture was broken. It is how a people treats its humblest members that ultimately determines who they will be.

Some Jamaicans see the island attitude towards dogs as retaliation for their mutual past.

Before and often after emancipation, dogs were used by slave owners to track down runaways and enforce discipline. Rather than being "man's best friend," dogs in Jamaica were feared as an implacable enemy. The British colonialists gave more humane treatment to dogs than they did to people.

Most Jamaicans, just three or four generations removed from slavery, still have a deathly terror of dogs and their natural reaction is to run or let fly with a "ground apple" (stone).

However, there was a time, in the two decades before Jamaica became an independent nation, when feelings toward the dog had mellowed.

"It was a gentler time back then," Danny said, "certainly in the rural areas anyway." He remembers spending time as a young man with farmers working on their hillside plots. The farmers were kind to their dogs, they often shared their modest lunches with them, but there was little warmth in the relationship. The dog had its place in their world, usually as home security, but not as a pet. Outside the cities, dogs are still used as home security.

What bothers Danny about modern Jamaica is the inner city "survival of the most cruel" mentality of much of the urban population, which shows little enough respect for human life, far less concern for "any damn dog." It is a downtrodden postcolonial culture where bullying and contempt are instincts used to bolster people's self-images because their life in poverty has little else of value to offer. The dog is an easy target for them.

The issue on which Danny and Cyd agree is that the attitude of Jamaicans towards dogs is representative of a need for education.

"It's ignorance. Not malice," said Cyd. "The illiteracy of it all. There needs to be education. To educate people about how to take care of their pets. What the JSPCA is and what it can do for animal welfare."

The JSPCA, founded in 1904 by Lady Lumb, believes that the way to reach adults is to teach their children. The Outreach program visits four to eight schools each month. In 2004, they educated 2,000 students ranging in age from five to 21 years. They also conducted a training course for the Jamaica Constabulary Force in an effort to bring the police on board with the program. There are no dogcatchers or dog wardens in Jamaica.

Teaching children to show love towards animals gives them a caring nature, said JSPCA volunteer Marcia Tomlinson. "If you learn to love animals you will love people as well." It seems to be working. People are becoming more aware and attitudes are changing slowly. "We're definitely getting a lot more abuse calls, abuse reports and people who are eager to help out."

On any given day their headquarters, kennel and veterinary clinic in Kingston will have 90 dogs on-site – a combination of dogs brought in by low-income owners for veterinary care and strays removed from the streets. They try to keep the animals as long as possible to give their adoption program an opportunity to find homes. In 2005, they adopted out approximately 50 animals per month, but some placements failed because the dogs were still semi-wild and didn't adapt to a home situation. Dog rescue is both joyful work and grim. They also had to euthanize 200 dogs every month.

"What do you do when someone brings two boxes full of puppies or kittens?" Pam sighed in resignation. "And there's always going to be more puppies and kittens than anything else. When we run at full capacity or are overcrowded – which we usually are – a case of Parvo (a usually fatal dog virus) could wipe us out. It's hard. We always want to say 'just keep them one more day,' but we run a huge risk of disease and we could end up losing everything."

Another part of the Outreach is teaching people the value of neutering and spaying their dogs.

Pam smiled deviously as she talked about the program. "Women have no problem bringing animals in to be spayed or neutered, but men are very resistant to the idea. I've had to tell men 'you put that dog on the table or I'll put you on the table.' I'm joking but they don't know that. I threaten them… my way of communicating."

Danny cringed when talking about it but agreed with her, "I don't think I would like to have my balls cut off and I don't think they would like it either. The difference is that a man's sexual drive can be governed by reason… sometimes. And birth control options are available to people. But dogs are driven by instinct alone and there are no controls available. Thus there's a greater chance for 'accidents.'"

From their headquarters in Kingston the JSPCA is also attempting to address what they believe to be the two other root causes of animal abuse.

The most recent two pieces of legislation concerning animal welfare in Jamaica are the 1965 Cruelty to Animals Act and the Pound Laws, leftovers from the British colonial era that have not been amended since. They protect animals owned by wealthy landowners, in particular horses and cattle, so the laws are harsher for hitting a horse than they are for being cruel or abusive to dogs, goats and pigs. This legislation grants minimal enforcement powers to the JSPCA.

Even with weak legislation the JSPCA is the only regulatory body in Jamaica for cruelty to animals. There are no animal hospitals in the country and no government department with a mandate to enforce the law.

"If you want to open a zoo or start a dog kennel in Jamaica," said Danny, "if you approached the government they would tell you – go to the JSPCA.

"We went to them because they believe in what we believe in, regarding the overpopulation of dogs. We need to get control of the situation."

Pets suffer from poverty the same way people do, and the people suffer along with them.

"I can walk into a community and just by looking at the children and the elderly I can tell what problems the animals have," said Pam. "In an economically challenged village, everything is in close proximity to everything else. If a dog has mange, the people have it. It's called 'scabies' in people.

"The children will have scabies. You can see the patches of hair missing off their head. Or scarring in the eyes. All connected to the stray animal population. So we can tell by looking at the children what is wrong with the animal population."

The Jamaica Dogsled Team is, for the JSPCA, a major new element in their education program, adoption program and fundraising. Danny's own contributions and influence in the national business community have increased donations, enabling them to advance their plans. The need for dogs to run the sleds has given the organization an opportunity to place dogs that may otherwise be euthanized.

The JDT is committed to assisting the JSPCA: (L to R) Pam Lawson, Executive Director, JSPCA; Dr. Paul Turner, Senior Vet, JSPCA; Newton Marshall; Paul Norman, CCA/JDT Resort Marketing Manager.

When Danny first approached the JSPCA "they were pretty cool about it. Of course we had to explain it to them and they inspected our facilities."

"Anytime I can save an animal, I will," added Pam. "If I see an animal I think they can use I give them a call."

Ultimately, Chukka gave them a spokesman who could speak to children and deliver a perspective on developing a relationship with dogs that no other Jamaican could. If you can improve one aspect of a culture, you improve the whole culture.

"A lot of animal welfare organizations put dogsledding on their cruelty list. We've had run-ins with one of the international groups over the matter," Pam looked exasperated. "But which is better? Leaving the animal to suffer on the streets in Kingston or anywhere in Jamaica. Euthanizing it. Or giving it proper care. Food. Love."

"That also gave the team a different story," Danny loved his multifaceted vision. "The rescue dog policy was as much about drawing attention to the way dogs are treated in Jamaica as it was about business. Of course, the dogs we took had to be able to pull too."

"They (the dogs) weren't on welfare (in the shelter) for nothing," said Alan. "Nobody wanted them. That was the bottom line. We had to get that respect and the connection back again.

Pinky.

Smiley.

"These were dogs from the street. Dogs that were horrendously looked after or not looked after at all. We had to get that out of them. We had to give them trust.

"We had to introduce harnesses. Then ATVs and carts. Then running fields and the track. We had to even actually introduce running."

As Devon, Alan and Rick discovered in their search for dogs, there are other kennels scattered around the country that also try to rescue strays from a life on the streets. Animal House in Lydford. The Montego Bay Animal Haven. Port Royal Dogs just outside of Kingston.

The independent kennels let their dogs run loose in their compounds, didn't clean the yards on a regular basis, had few if any veterinary services and, with the possible exception of Montego Bay, had no neutering or spaying program in place. They didn't agree with the principle of having dogs tied up on eight-foot chains and living in doghouses.

"If we did take a dog we would have to quarantine it," explained Rick. "All the JSPCA and Chukka Cove dogs have been wormed, had their shots, everything. I would not dare bring them (dogs from the independent kennels) into our population.

"Instead of looking at it like they are caring for a canine they are looking at it like it's their child. Well, it's not. It's a dog. It has different needs and requirements than a child and it needs to be cared for differently.

"They may say they're not happy that they (the dogs at Chukka) are tied up. But they're healthy and they're happy. They're well-fed and they get run well every day. Even when they get loose, they don't leave. They usually don't even leave the area… and there's no fences or doors to stop them from going.

"Most kennels where the dogs are kept in a run," Rick continued, "allowed to run loose, have no relationship with a human, if the dog gets out – they're gone! In 35 years Nettie and I had one dog take off on us and he came back the next week."

By 2009, the kennel at Chukka was home to 40 rescued dogs. Conditions at the independent kennels apparently improved.

Danny imagines a future where the quarantine laws are loosened and people from out of country can adopt dogs from the team. “Canadians and Americans often come to Jamaica, then try to adopt a dog to take home. But it takes forever and it costs a fortune. Our next step is to create an adopt-a-dog program for our sleddogs.

“Can you imagine strutting through Central Park in New York with your dog and people stopping and asking, ‘What is that?!’ ‘It’s a Jamaican sleddog.’ ‘You wanna run that one by me again!’

“Our first priority is to promote Jamaica. Promoting Jamaica is promoting Chukka. Our second priority is to increase the awareness of the plight of dogs in Jamaica.”

Official launch of the Jamaica Dogsled Tour at Chukka Cove on April 14, 2007: (L to R) Danny Melville, Carole Guntley-Brady (Director General, Ministry of Tourism), The Honourable Aloun Assamba (Minister of Tourism), Dr. Paul Turner (Senior Vet, JSPCA).

John Schandelmeier nodded his head in approval following the 2009 Quest when he learned about the shelter dog program at Chukka Cove. As a founding member of the Second Chance League in Fairbanks, Alaska, he understood the value of Danny's approach to building a dogsled team.

The Second Chance League was formed by a group of Fairbanks mushers in 2004 as an organization devoted to evaluating and training unwanted sleddogs from the Fairbanks Animal Shelter. They have a contract with the Fairbanks' North Star Borough, allowing them to select and remove sleddogs from the shelter. When a dog leaves the shelter it is given the rabies vaccine, spayed or neutered, microchipped (a small digitized chip inserted under the skin) and then either adopted outright or placed into a foster home.

The two shelter dog programs, at Chukka Cove and in Fairbanks, are very similar in appearance although they developed completely independently and without knowledge of the other's existence.

John and his wife, Zoya DeNure, own Crazy Dog Kennels in Paxson, Alaska. They have almost 40 rescued shelter dogs in their 50-dog Alaska Shelter Dog Race Team.

"My personal goal is to raise awareness, within the sport, of the ability of these cast-off dogs," said John. "It has always seemed to me there were a lot of dogs being overlooked. All dogs are capable of racing competitively."

It is Schandelmeier's role in rescuing shelter dogs that gives the concept credibility. A veteran of both the Iditarod and Yukon Quest, he won the Quest in 1992 and 1996, finishing out of the top 10 only twice in his 16 runnings. In the world of long distance racing he is considered to be one of the best dog men in the sport, known for his exemplary level of dog care under extreme race conditions.

He twice won the Veterinarian's Choice Award, in 1994 and 1996, for the most humane care for his dogs throughout the race. Race veterinarians learned to accept his psychic ability to notice even a slight change in a dog's gait and diagnose the problem correctly, despite not having any formal training. While most people think of him as being the strong, silent type, his dogs know him as the weak link on the team who talks to them all the time.

The Veterinarian's Choice is probably the most coveted prize a musher can receive. When 2008 Quest champion Lance Mackey also won the Veterinarian's Award that year, he broke down in tears at the podium. "This means more to me than winning," he declared.

While sitting in the Eagle checkpoint during the 1999 Yukon Quest, John proposed a unique idea to the other mushers in the room. Allow him to pick 14 dogs from the animal shelter in Fairbanks in September and he could have them ready to run and finish the Quest by next February. He didn't have total confidence in his plan and had only one rescued shelter dog when running the race in 2001.

One team he was running close to in 2001, driven by rookie Joran Freeman, was comprised of castaways, rejects and giveaways from other mushers. Freeman finished fourth and his performance got John's attention. Freeman hadn't gotten his dogs from the shelter but he had constructed his team in an unconventional manner, essentially ignoring the mainstream thinking of the time.

John decided the plan he concocted in Eagle was plausible after all. He also decided to have fun with the idea. By 2004, he had six shelter dogs in his team. He finished seventh. The next year he started with a team that included 10 shelter dogs and entertained the Start Banquet crowd with a wild tale about how he assembled his team.

One, he claimed, was a feral dog accidentally caught in one of his traps. Another a coyote he collected from the roadside while driving to Whitehorse because he was one dog short. "Named that one Lester," he joked. He had a "non-dog," named Snoopy, who "wouldn't hook up to a harness and he doesn't want to run."

Asked what he was trying to prove, John just shrugged, "I don't know if it proves anything. Realistically you'd have to be nuts to say I could win with them. I knew awhile ago I wanted to try this. We've been training for 10 months and we're continually working forward. People need to take a closer look at it. Maybe some mushers should think twice before they decide to have another eight-dog litter and just keep three of them. It's been interesting. But they're starting to look good. They're starting to look like a real dog team."

He reached the finish of the 2005 Quest in 10th position.

Most competitive mushers were skeptical of the idea. It's been a long held belief that bloodlines are more important than training in determining the quality of a team. The problem with shelter dogs was there was no way to determine their bloodlines properly. Even some veterinarians had doubts.

"John (Schandelmeier) had done great things with kennel dogs," long-time Quest vet, John Overell from Dawson City is one skeptic. "But breeding is still the bottom line to a good sleddog team. Most of these dogs were from sleddog lines. What I think he did was emphasize just how important training is."

The highest finish Schandelmeier has had with a shelter dog team was third in the Copper Basin 300. "That's respectable, but it's not good enough," said John.

His wife, Zoya drove the team in the 2008 Gin-Gin 200, finishing just two minutes behind winner Lance Mackey.

There is even discord inside the shelter dog rescue groups. John tried selling some of the rehabilitated animals on his Internet website "just like you would do with a bred dog. You put a price on them."

He got calls from other rescue dog organizations and the Second Chance League.

"You wouldn't believe the flack I got. Those guys told me that shelter dog were valuable, but when I put a value on them they didn't want to hear about it."

"You can't do that," he was told, "they're rescued dogs." He kept the website but did drop the prices.

However, the idea has been garnering begrudging support from other kennels. Yukon Quest musher, Iris Sutton, used a shelter dog named Twiggy as one of her leaders – one of five rescued dogs in her 2009 team. "I fostered her and ended up adopting her. She's turned into a wonderful, wonderful dog. I really believe that it's the relationship you have with your dogs rather than bloodlines."

In the 2009 Quest Sebastien Schnuelle ran a shelter dog, Frankie, whom he had rescued eight years earlier. It was Frankie's seventh long distance race. Another driver, Wayne Hall, had one of Schandelmeier's rescued dogs in his team in the 2006 Quest.

"We're retraining these 'discarded' dogs and running them in the main team or placing them with the appropriate musher," Zoya revels in her role as a dog rescuer. "We're excited to say we're making a difference, one dog at a time."

In Jamaica, Rick and Devon made one of their periodic trips to Kingston to check out the dogs at the JSPCA. As they walked into the holding area filled with grey metallic cages, Rick noted the dogs looking downtrodden, their ears and tails down, their eyes mournful and afraid. He knew it wasn't just from being mistreated. They were afraid of containment after a life of living in the open.

One of the dogs, a brindle hound, caught his eye almost immediately. "What about him?" Rick pointed.

"Would you take him?" the JSPCA volunteer seemed incredulous.

"Take him?" responded Rick. "You betcha."

Benji was a month past his euthanasia day. Just days away from finally having to be put down. Rick couldn't believe that no one wanted him but was informed that in Jamaica the color "brindle" – a coat coloring in animals where streaks of color are darker than the base coat color – is considered to be an evil color. It's the reason the dog was in the shelter in the first place.

"Brindle to me is one of the strongest, most beautiful colors one can find in a dog," said Rick. Later, he noticed a coffee cup he was using had a design of a stray dog strolling along a Jamaican road. Idly he wondered if a design of the Jamaica Dogsled Team would end up on a beer mug.

That night Benji, sentenced to death in his first life, started his journey to a second chance.

Benji – a second chance.

Jimmy Buffett at the JDT launch in December, 2005.

The Godfather

If we couldn't laugh, we would all go insane.

Jimmy Buffett

December, 2005

"Everybody kind of thinks back to the Jamaica bobsled team and how ridiculous that must have sounded to people in the beginning," JDT "godfather" Jimmy Buffett sat comfortably in his loose shirt, baggy shorts and flip-flops – the perfect image of what his legion of Parrothead fans believe him to be. "Then the results were pretty gratifying to everybody from it just being a sense of something that brings a smile or a laugh to your face. A sense of completion. I kind of compared that same feeling when I first heard Danny mention the Jamaica Dogsled Team.

"What is it about this island's infatuation with the cold? I missed out on the bobsled years. I don't intend to miss out on this one. I take harebrained schemes and make them happen. So it's nothing new to me. I didn't know anything about racing dogsleds but it sure sounded like fun. I just thought, 'wouldn't it be cool if this could happen?'

"I just love the whole idea of it. I love the absurdity that when we first did this, people laughed and thought it was a joke…and guess what?! It isn't!"

Danny had finally told his sons what he planned to do. Their reaction was as he expected.

"Most people thought we were crazy anyway. Even my sons and business partners probably thought I was a little bit nuts."

They resisted. At best the tour would probably be able to support itself. Framing the worst-case scenario they insisted the JDT was a waste of money.

Danny persisted, "It's a tour. Every time we go away (to compete out of the country), we're promoting Jamaica, by extension our tour, and by further extension all of our other tours."

The media and press would be good for Jamaica, they agreed, but publicity for Jamaica didn't specifically show up in the bottom line for the business itself. Chukka Caribbean would invest in the project, they finally relented, but there was a limit and Danny had to live within it.

They enthusiastically agreed when Danny wanted to keep it confidential within the Chukka management – although probably not for the same reasons. Jamaican businesses are notorious for stealing ideas and copying them if the proper protections aren't in place. Danny wanted to be sure all the logos and names were trademarked before the tour became public knowledge. The others likely hoped it would stay a secret and eventually disappear.

His plans had also continued to grow. Some were a little "out there." "We're going to have the Jamaica Dogsled Team restaurant and you know what we're going to serve…hot dogs! 365 different types of hot dogs!"

But one was starting to establish itself as a centerpiece of his concept. "My first thought was a tour because I'm always looking for tours in our business. But the next thought was the racing. If we're going to do this we need to race. That's the spectacle! That's the thing that will build credibility, give us experience and put us right out front of the public."

Racing out of country wasn't going to be cheap. Even if they built a good team in Jamaica, they couldn't take it abroad because of quarantine rules. If he was going to race, he would have to lease teams from other kennels and that would take more than Chukka Caribbean was prepared to provide. To succeed, the JDT would need financial input from other corporations and individuals.

"I knew that if I wanted to be serious about it," said Danny, "it would take a lot of money. It needed sponsorship. It would be a very low volume tour. You can't make much money with a low volume tour. Especially this tour in this climate because it isn't cold and dog mushing is seen as a cold climate activity.

"So I started thinking about potential sponsors."

In June he received an invitation to go on a helicopter ride from Montego Bay to Appleton – where Appleton Rum is distilled. The Margaritaville Restaurant franchise owners in Jamaica had the idea they could run a railway tour for tourists between the two communities. It would expose visitors to the interior mountains and sugar cane fields while indulging them with good food and rum. There was once a railroad operating between the two cities but it had been shut down since the 1990s.

Danny was invited because Chukka Caribbean Adventures was the largest supplier of tours on the north coast and had the marketing expertise and operations people who might be able to run it. The owner of the franchise, entertainer Jimmy Buffett, would be on the trip.

"I didn't know Jimmy Buffett. I didn't know much about Jimmy Buffett. Carole was more into Bocelli than she was Buffett, but she at least knew who he was." As he was leaving the villa to drive to Montego Bay with his sons, Carole handed him a camera.

"Please get a picture with him," she instructed, "because I don't know what he looks like."

The first part of the tour was flying from Montego Bay to Appleton over the proposed route in a helicopter while it was explained to them that Jimmy, who already had his own beer label, also wanted to market his own brand of rum. And he wanted to use Jamaican rum to do it.

As they were boarding the helicopter Brian Jardim, one of Jimmy's Jamaica business partners, turned to the musician. "Jimmy," he said, "Danny's wife doesn't know what you look like so we need to get a photo of you with him to show his wife."

Danny was embarrassed.

Jimmy laughed, removed his baseball cap, revealing his receding hairline and threw his arm around Danny.

Jimmy Buffett, Newton, Chris Blackwell and Danny Melville.

This is one of those guys who would understand, Danny realized. They flew to Appleton, following the abandoned train tracks and spent an hour or two sampling rum blends for the proposed Margaritaville brand. Then they flew to YS Falls, a spectacular waterfall on the south coast of the island. There they were served a plantation-style lunch on a veranda framed by jungle growth and topping limestone cliffs, where waterfalls dropped 120 feet into massive pools ideal for swimming.

The dozen businessmen sat back, socializing, sipping on a couple of drinks. The atmosphere was relaxed but Danny found himself anxious, biting his lip. "This is the kind of guy that will just get the idea," he was thinking. "He's sort of off-the-wall. I may never get this opportunity again."

He blurted it out, "Jimmy. I'm starting a Jamaican dogsled team."

His sons started laughing because the announcement had been completely unexpected. It was, so far as they were aware, still supposed to be a secret. Jimmy's business partners started laughing, two of them so hard they could hardly stay in their chairs and had tears running down their cheeks. Jimmy laughed too, but just for a minute. Then he sat quietly for another minute. He turned to Danny.

"I like the idea. I want to be part of it." The laughter stopped and, to Danny's amazement, everyone sat in shocked silence. Jimmy pulled out his cell phone and punched in a number. "Can you put me on the air?" he asked the disc jockey at Margaritaville Radio, then announced to the Parrothead world, "We're going to have a dogsled team in Jamaica."

A week later Danny was in New Orleans pitching his new tour to the cruise ship industry. During his spiel his cell phone rang. It was Jimmy's business manager.

"How's the presentation going?" he asked.

"Fine," a surprised Danny managed to stammer.

There were two other things about the dogsled team that appealed to the American-born entertainer.

First it was coming from Jamaica. Despite the fact that Jamaican police had shot at his plane in 1996, believing it to be a craft used to smuggle marijuana, he still loved the country. In all of his concerts he wore a red, green and gold sweatband (Rastafarian colors and the colors of the Ethiopian flag) and he referred to himself as a "second-home Jamaican."

Starting with his "Let's go to Jamaica! Go to Negril! Get down! Red Stripe man!" days when he was in his early 20s in the early 1960s, he traveled frequently to the island. He had a 20-year association with Jamaica-based record producer Chris Blackwell, who had produced Bob Marley to international stardom.

Chris was another who decided he wanted to be a part of it. He never came in as a sponsor but his film company, Palm Pictures, produced the first documentary about the JDT, *Sun Dogs*, in 2007.

"I span a wide spectrum of Jamaican experiences and I think what I take from it is the fact that they (Jamaicans) are a wonderful, wonderful people," said Jimmy. "There's this love of life and spirit of fun that has always been there. Jamaica to me was Bob Marley and Reggae music. That still is my music. I don't listen to me on the beach. I listen to Bob Marley."

The JDT's policy of using shelter dogs appealed to Jimmy's social conscience.

"He's one hell of a humanitarian," said Danny. "I've learned a lot about him in the past couple of months."

Jimmy co-founded the "Save the Manatee Club" to become a leader in the preservation of Florida's endangered Manatee population in 1981, funded the "Singing for Change Foundation," which provides funding for disenfranchised groups, environmental groups and ventures dedicated to children and the family, in 1995 and raised funds to assist hurricane victims in Florida, Alabama and the Caribbean islands in 2004.

At the time of the JDT launch party at Chukka Cove in December, 2005, Jimmy was also raising funds for relief from the damage caused by Hurricane Katrina on the gulf coast of the United States.

He liked the idea of using shelter dogs and he liked what the project could potentially do for young Jamaicans.

"It's not only the look of happiness on the dogs' faces, it's the look on the faces of Devon…and Newton in particular," explained Jimmy, "A kid whose simple love of animals, with a very complicated and harsh background of life as he has had to live it, (the JDT) simply has changed his life for the better. It started maybe as a tourist attraction and now it's something the whole country could take a little pride in."

The entertainer also had experience with ownership of sports teams, being part owner of two minor league baseball teams: the Fort Myers Miracle and the Madison Black Wolf. He understood that being involved in sports at a high level often brought out the crazy side of otherwise rational people. That an owner who is willing to spend more than his competitors can carve out an advantage in sport's financial landscape. Teams are better served with entrepreneurial owners who are passionate about their sport but he was also aware that owners often run their teams with more passion than brains. They take the risk because, to them, the vision and accomplishing it is the payoff.

Jimmy was a folk-rock busker in Nashville in 1970 when country and western performer Jerry Jeff Walker took him down to Key West, Florida, where he discovered a lifestyle waiting for its music. For a budding artist who had been born in Mississippi in 1946 and raised in Mobile, Alabama, the introduction to "Island escapism" was an inspiration that changed his life.

He combined a little bit of every genre of music – country, folk, rock, soca and reggae – and created his own sound, sometimes called "gulf and western." He cultivated the image of an easy-going beach bum who happened to play a little music and discovered there was an audience of beach bum wannabes all over the world – who formed themselves into an international and fanatical fan club consisting of self-described "Parrotheads."

"I'm not that good a singer. I'm no virtuoso on any instrument. I would give myself a B as a writer. But as a shameless performer I'd give myself an A. You play your strongest suit. You may not be the best player but you try to find the best image that fits into what you're trying to project.

"*Margaritaville* was a song, then it became a lifestyle. People had been living it for so long but my version of it seemed to catch on. I think simply because it comes from the heart and it's pure escapism. Everyone needs a little bit of it and particularly in these days and times.

"I need it too, so it's kind of fun to go out to Chukka Cove on a quiet afternoon and watch the dogs. Somewhere in the dogsled team I find a place where I could be Jimmy Buffett without having to be on stage."

Margaritaville became more than a lifestyle. It also became a restaurant chain throughout the Caribbean and the United States. It was through that brand that Jimmy provided his sponsorship to the JDT.

"The first thing I want to say is that I'd only had one Appleton and Ting (a Jamaican soft drink) when I made my decision to endorse Danny's crazy idea," said Jimmy as he stood at the podium in his *Mush Mon* T-shirt at the official launch party.

"I think a lot of people make a living out of having fun. When someone brings you ideas that have any ounce of fun and immediately brings a smile to your face…I learned a long time ago you've got to pursue those. And you never know where it's going to end up."

The day before he had met his dog namesake, Jimmy. After briefly posing with the human Jimmy, the canine Jimmy looked around at the crowd of media and entourage, and then bolted into his doghouse.

When Jimmy Buffett saw the team run for the first time, he clapped his hands above his head, and then sprinted onto the track after the dogs went past.

Chris Blackwell, standing next to him, laughed as he watched the collection of motley mutts lope around the trail. He said to Jimmy, "They look exactly like a Jamaican dogsled team should look like."

When the launch party was held the JDT had two mushers, Newton and Devon, and nine streetwise dogs. Once underway, they could run four-dog teams relatively well. The dogs still all wanted to pull in different directions when they

Danny pitches his idea to Chris Blackwell and Jimmy Buffett.

Jimmy the man meets Jimmy the dog.

started each run but eventually they figured it out.

The project had been sanctioned by the International Federation of Sleddog Sports (IFSS) when a committee, including the JSPCA and a representative of the national veterinary organization, set up the Jamaica Sleddog Federation (JSF). On the recommendation of Alan Stewart, IFSS president Tim White went to the island in September to talk to the committee and sign them up as a member.

In April, 2008 Jimmy broke with one of his own personal guidelines when he traveled to Mont Tremblant, Quebec, for a dogsled ride.

Jimmy.

"I tend not to go to cold climates very much in my lifestyle," he once claimed. "I spent a lot of time in them earlier. I choose not to now."

He stood on the runners while his tour guide, Yves Kirouac, rode in the sled basket. The power and speed surprised him. So did falling off the sled at one point, but he followed the number one rule of dog mushing – never let go of the sled. He also had trouble sitting down comfortably for a week after hitting the snow.

"Now I know what it's all about," he mused. "Everybody should do this once in their life. Now I can swap mushing stories with Newton and Robb."

Jamaica's first musher on the trails at Aviemore, Scotland.

Aviemore

If you can fill the unforgiving minute
With sixty seconds' worth of distance run
Yours is the earth and everything that's in it
And – which is more – you'll be a man, my son!

Rudyard Kipling

January, 2006

Devon wasn't only physically exhausted – he was emotionally distressed and frightened. Not for himself, but for Macallan.

It was the end of his first day of racing at the Aviemore Sled Dog Rally. For the second half of the day's distance he and three other dogs, Aladdin, Buffy and Angie, had carried Macallan in the basket. The Siberian husky wasn't small or light. The final hills had taken their toll on the team.

"That must have been a hard four miles," observed one bystander.

"It's something I was always scared of," Devon had tears running down his face at the Finish line, "not wanting to hurt them. I was very concerned. Almost wanted to stop. I didn't know if I wanted to continue with the rest of the race. I was still worried about them for the second day."

The time had arrived for the Jamaica Dogsled Team to make its appearance on the world stage. Danny and Alan had decided that Devon was ready to take part in his first major race. They selected the United Kingdom's oldest and largest race, run by the Siberian Husky Club of Great Britain.

The Aviemore Sled Dog Rally was started as a dog mushing event on snow in 1984, with only a dozen teams braving a stiff wind and cold temperatures. The race trails on Cairngorm Mountain had been identified as a potential race site when they were used to train the winner of the British Broadcasting Corporation's Dream-of-a-lifetime competition – who had decided his dream was to race the Iditarod. The original races were held lower on the mountain but a lack of snow forced organizers to shift the site up to what are called the Forest Enterprise trails higher on the slope.

Two things had vanished since the early days of the race. The first to go was "Water Butt Turn," a sharp turn in the trail which was popular with spectators because mushers, one after the other, would fall off their sled into the snow, landing on their butts. Although it still had the same name it had been rebuilt into a gentler curve.

The other thing to go was the snow. One of the main attractions for Aviemore when the race was founded was the snow. However, it had been several years since the weather had been cold enough for any significant amount to fall on the mountain – even in the dead of winter. There had been some light dustings for a couple of days before the 2006 race, but it melted by the time the teams hit the trail. What started in 1984 as a true snow rally had turned into a dryland dog race in 1996.

The snowfall that night was Devon's first experience with snow, "I can say I've experienced snow. If I never get another chance in my life, I've experienced it. To see it and feel it. I didn't know with snow that you get wet, just like rain."

The change in weather didn't hurt the growth of the event; it probably helped it. All the other British races are dryland and Aviemore was where most mushers gained their winter experience. The trails, narrow in some places, not much wider than the racing carts, were very accessible from Alan Stewart's kennel.

There were over 200 teams running in excess of 800 dogs in 2006. It was a very polite race. When asked to give way to a faster team coming up from behind, slower teams did pull over. As the quicker sled went by the overtaking musher said, "Thank you."

Before making the trip to Scotland Devon and Danny spent three weeks at Rick and Nettie's home in Mahtowa, Minnesota, in October getting a short refresher training course. It was a cold autumn in Minnesota with frigid air and wind chill combining for a temperature of -29°C.

"I was afraid he (Devon) was going to freeze to death," Rick laughed. "Instead he was outside back in the woods with me laying out the trail and loving the cool weather."

Devon took part in the North Star Sled Dog Club's annual fun run and finished second in a local race, the Pro 4 Dog Rig Class at the Byllesby Dryland Classic in Cannon, Minnesota, on October 14 and 15.

He also raced in the East Meets West Dryland Competition at the Brainerd International Raceway on November 18 and 19, where he finished sixth overall in a field of 86 teams.

For the organized events he drove a team owned by Ken and Donna Davis of Elfstone Kennels from Twig, Minnesota.

"We want to race in the States," Danny had informed Rick. "I need a good team and a good trainer."

When they arrived in Minnesota, Rick drove them over to Twig and introduced Ken.

"Here's the guy that can do the job for you," Rick said.

Danny and Ken sat down and negotiated a deal to provide Devon with race training, a team, one dryland race in each of October and November, 2006, and a race on snow in February, 2007. The local media coverage during and after the dryland races suggested to Danny that he was on the right track.

"After that," said Danny, "we want an entire season, so we have to sit down and make this work."

When Devon and Danny arrived at Alan's kennel in Scotland a week before the race, the training continued as they tried to establish exactly which dogs Devon would be racing on the weekend. The day before the race Alan and Devon drove carts around the trail to reacquaint him with them. Devon had driven the trails when he was first in Scotland in July but now he had to understand them as a competitor.

Indicating one slope Alan instructed Devon, "The secret is not to blow yourself up out here. Let the dogs pull. Our dogs are quite powerful." He reminded Devon that this race was for experience. He would discover things about the dogs and himself that he didn't yet know.

"It takes years to run and work a sleddog team. It's not just driving a car. It's easy to change tires and have mechanics all around. But with the dogs there are so many things. They're not machines. You're working with live animals in front of you. You have to read the dogs," said Alan.

The race itself didn't intimidate Devon. "I've been in competition before with horses. It's different but as long as I have something to do with animals, there's no fear. Once you get moving, everything just becomes normal. You're just going and trying to get them to go further."

It was the international media attention he found unnerving. Newspapers from Scotland, Jamaica, Australia and India were interviewing him constantly.

"It really does feel like I'm representing Jamaica with all the publicity we're getting."

"Don't kid yourself," added Alan, "This guy is under a lot of pressure. He's got all of Jamaica and most of Scotland riding on the sled with him."

The 4-dog team started strongly and Devon helped on the hills by running behind the sled. Everything seemed to be working well until Macallan stopped pulling. The other dogs, sensing a problem, slowed down. Devon applied the brake, bringing the sled to a dead stop. Three dogs remained standing but Macallan lay down. For a moment Devon hesitated, uncertain of the next step. He had never had a dog or horse stop working before. It devastated him.

A spectator stepped in from the side of the trail and held the brake for him. Devon went forward, unhitched Macallan and carried him back to the sled, stuffing him into a bag, included on the sled for precisely this reason. Then he continued, the extra weight and reduced pulling power making the hills more demanding. He pushed, the dogs pulled and Macallan watched it all from his new vantage point.

As they started climbing what he knew was the final hill, he could feel himself starting to falter. Running around the Polo field hadn't pushed him as hard as this final climb to the Finish line. His legs felt like they had anchors tied to them. His arms burned. His chest hurt. He started calling to the team, "Going home! Going home!" They picked up the pace, finished the ascent and loped across the Finish line.

When the sled stopped he leaned over the mud-spattered handlebars, utterly spent, wiping dirt, tears and perspiration from his face. A veterinarian lifted Macallan from the bag and took him to be checked.

"Macallan's fine," Alan said later. "Dogs just give too much and he was the hardest, toughest dog in that team. You have to keep your eye on the dogs all the time because they're going to be giving 180 percent. You must be as a complete team and Devon did exceptionally well."

After a night's sleep Devon was able to put the incident into perspective, "He overheated. It happens to people and animals too. But it was my first time experiencing it at this level so it was a shock to me. Macallan is pretty much back to his normal self, so I'm very happy about that. I'm better prepared today.

"I've been encouraged (by other mushers) that it happens every day even to the best of dog mushers. It's something that happens because they're animals and they push themselves to a limit where, normally as an athlete, you would stop. But dogs and horses don't stop. They'll just run themselves into the ground. It's pretty clear that everyone here is an animal lover. You watch the way they care for their animals."

The second day's run was completed without any problems. The dogs pulled Devon to a top 10 finish for the day. Overall, in the JDT's first major international race, he finished 27th of 40 teams in his category. Devon also laid claim to the award for being the musher who traveled the furthest to compete.

"What happened in Scotland was nothing short of unbelievable." Danny was thrilled with the media attention they had attracted. "The fact that one newspaper was able to say that we were putting them and their dog race back on the map. My Scottish friends may laugh at me but the fact is, we really pumped up the volume there."

"I've gained that experience," concluded Devon over a post-race beer. "It's something that will live with me forever."

Devon tries out the local fare.

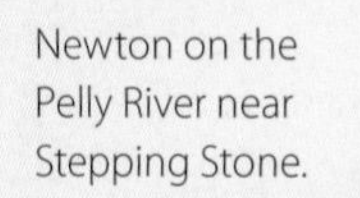

Newton on the Pelly River near Stepping Stone.

Newton's Schedule

Pelly Crossing to Dawson City

210 miles, 45 hours

The front running teams spent 15 minutes in Pelly. They signed in, dumped the leftovers they didn't use on the way from Carmacks, grabbed bags of food and extra gear that would get them through the next two days to Dawson City, signed out and were gone. The veterinarians had time to quickly go over the dogs. They didn't ask many questions of the musher. They understood that the teams at the front of the race were highly experienced. If the mushers had any dog problems they usually told the veterinarian which dog to look at and what to look for.

Some of them would shut down at Stepping Stone, a hospitality stop just four hours down the Pelly River, or camp out on the trail. However, most of the teams took time to stop. Pelly was a favorite among the mushers. It became a checkpoint, not because it lies along the Overland Trail, but because it didn't and it seriously wanted to be a part of the race.

The Overland-Yukon Quest Trail had crossed the top of a large hill called Minto Mountain, about 30 miles south of the community, until the 1996 race. In 1995, Teddy Charlie, a resident of Pelly, contacted the Yukon Quest and asked if they could become a checkpoint on the race.

"There's no trail to Pelly," he was told.

"Yes, there is," he replied. "We just finished building it.'

That same desire to be involved still permeated the enthusiastic atmosphere in the community center that served as the checkpoint. It sometimes seemed that all 300 residents of the village were working at one job or another while the teams were in town.

Pelly was originally established as a construction camp and ferry crossing during the building of the Klondike Highway between Whitehorse and Dawson City in 1950. When the road was completed riverboat traffic on the Yukon River ended and the entire population of Fort Selkirk, a community 40 miles downriver from Pelly, moved to the highway town site. When a bridge was built across the Pelly River in 1958, the main source of employment, the ferry across the river, was shut down but the village persisted. Many of the people are subsistence trappers, hunters, fishers and wilderness guides.

For the people of Pelly the Yukon Quest is not just the main event of their winter. It marks the beginning of the end of it. It happens late enough in February that the daylight following the race gets a little longer each day, spring creeping ever closer with each sunrise.

"If it makes the mushers, vets and officials happy," said checkpoint manager, Dave Bennett, "then it makes us happy. It's the volunteers and the people who give up their time to come and help out."

"They seem to want to accommodate people better," said race vet Jan Weaver. "And provide a nice, big place for people to sleep. This is my favorite checkpoint."

It was the sleeping area that Newton went looking for after he took care of the dogs, had a big bowl of moose stew and chatted a bit with the media. He sank to the gym mats on the floor. He closed his eyes, thought of the comforts of home and the pleasure of good, warm, thick Caribbean air and finally fell asleep – almost 72 hours after waking up the morning of the race start.

While he slept, the overflow just past McCabe forced one of the mushers out of the race. Jean-Denis Britten had been ahead of Newton when his dogs found a wet, soft spot in the ice.

"The ice broke and they were completely underwater. My three best dogs. Three to four hours earlier there was no water." Jean-Denis pulled them safely out and continued to negotiate a section of trail littered with timber but noticed the three dogs didn't want to pull.

After resting in Pelly for a couple of hours and consulting with the vets he realized he had to drop all three dogs, plus two more who were nursing sore wrists. Rather than continuing with just eight dogs he withdrew from the race, loaded his dogs into his truck and drove home.

"I've run those dogs for six winters and never saw them like this. I'm not going with just eight (dogs). I had to think about the sponsors and all those who helped us start. But this is really all about dogs, so it is better to stop here," he said.

Repacking the sled properly at Pelly Crossing was important. By the time the teams left, the sleds, which usually weigh about 35 pounds empty and 150 pounds when fully loaded between checkpoints, would be up over 200 pounds. It may seem like a lot for the dogs to pull but the sleds, constructed with aluminum and composite materials, glide on plastic runners, minimizing friction between the snow and the sled. Sled designers have made them one of the most energy efficient means of transportation, although their narrowness has made them fundamentally unstable. When the dogs are pulling well, riding on the back of the sled can be akin to a magic carpet ride, but a magic carpet that could tip over at any moment without warning.

The distance the teams had to travel without resupplying meant carrying spare sled parts, extra bags of booties, dog food and snacks – usually chopped-up frozen pieces of fish, beaver, chicken or lamb.

"I overpack," said Whitehorse musher, Michelle Phillips, "I'm always worried that I'm going to run out of dog food."

Normand Casavant, who stayed at Pelly for seven hours, also loaded up on extras. "If I get stuck I absolutely need to have extra food for them."

So far teams had been able to travel at an average speed of about 10 miles per hour, including rest stops on the trail and at hospitality stops. The estimated speed through the hills to Dawson City would be just over four miles an hour.

For the first 32 miles to the hospitality stop at Stepping Stone, the trail follows the Pelly River. This year it had frozen fairly level and the trail passed easily through a series of wooded islands and over short outcrops of riverbank. As they approached Stepping Stone they could see the trail to Dawson City on the other side of the river.

In 1995, when the trail was changed to include Pelly Crossing, the mushers didn't want the organization to eliminate Stepping Stone, another roadhouse on the Overland Trail used as a hospitality stop. When the original Quest trail dropped down from Minto Mountain it came right through the yard of the former homestead.

For the last few miles into Stepping Stone the trail from Pelly runs on the south side of the river. When the teams depart Stepping Stone they have to travel a few miles back toward Pelly on the opposite side until they reach the cut-off that takes them north. After leaving the Pelly River the trail runs through rolling hills for 70 miles to a dog drop and hospitality stop at Scroggie Creek, a gold mining area since 1898, where the teams turn for a short stretch on the Stewart River. Once leaving the river, they start a long climb through the Black Hills – a grueling creep up switchbacks for over 30 miles, inching slowly toward the top of Eureka Dome, the highest point on the Quest Trail at 4,325 feet (1,440 meters) above sea level. The series of ridges and creeks that dominated the landscape had been named for their resemblance to the Black Hills of North Dakota by gold seekers in the 1880s. Gold was discovered in small amounts in 1898 and the hills were still sporadically worked by miners.

Dropping down from Eureka, the teams cross the Indian River Valley, a well worked mining region and part of the Klondike gold fields, and then start a long, gradual ascent to the summit of King Solomon's Dome, the trail's second highest summit at 4,045 feet (1,341 meters). Once over King Solomon's Dome, the trail runs downhill all the way to Dawson. This one section of the race was longer than the island of Jamaica.

Rick, Nettie and Moira Sauer, a friend of Susie's who was accompanying her on the race, took turns guarding Newton's sleeping space from the media who were wandering around trying to find interviews. When Newton eventually woke up and headed out to feed the dogs and start organizing his sled, Rick informed him that recent reports had more overflow on the trail before Scroggie Creek.

He was concerned because he knew Newton had almost run short of booties in the overflow before Pelly.

"Are you sure you should have given them (his extra booties) to him (Normand Casavant)?"

"Yeh Mon. He's a friend and I still have plenty of booties."

"But it's a race Newton," Rick was frustrated. "Part of being in a race is the preparation. He should have had more booties. What happens if you run short?"

"But he's a friend ...."

Newton had been four hours behind his schedule when he arrived in Pelly. When he pulled the snow hook (the dogsled's parking brake) to leave Pelly after a nine-hour layover, he was seven hours behind. His team dropped quickly down from the dogyard in front of the recreation center and turned toward the bridge across the river. His headlamp caught the

Newton's team in the Pelly burn.

reflective tape on the first trail marker. As he lifted his head the light illuminated a reflective string of markers down the ice into the darkness.

These markers are simply wooden stakes, topped with a piece of reflective tape and set in the snow along the right side of the trail so the mushers know where to go. There is also a form of code in the markers. A series of two markers set side by side on one side of the trail means there is a turn coming to that side of the trail. Two markers, one on each side of the trail marks the beginning of the correct trail. If there are other trails intersecting the race route, as frequently happens, the musher knows which one to take.

Two stakes set up in an "X" formation indicates there is a dangerous or tricky portion of the trail ahead and the musher should take whatever precautions are necessary.

This year there was a problem with the stakes on the trail to Dawson. A large pack of wolves ranged from the river through the hills to Eureka Dome. Biologists later identified 24 animals in the pack. They didn't bother any of the teams although a couple of mushers did spot them and the trail was littered with wolf scat. They took a liking to the trail markers, knocking them

Yuka Honda.

over, stealing them and chewing others into piles of splinters alongside the trail.

"I saw a lot of them (trail markers) lying down," Newton noticed that something had happened to the markers, but didn't know what it was. "And there were places where there weren't very many markers on the trail at all."

The well-rested team made a fast run down the river, arriving at Stepping Stone just over three hours after leaving Pelly Crossing. Signs nailed to trees every few hundred yards for the last mile or so into the homestead advertised what the musher could expect to find when he or she arrived. *"Nachos"* one read. *"Burritos"* and beyond that, *"Chocolate chip cookies."*

Alongside the trail approaching the squat, dark buildings huddled in the trees were candles burning in translucent bags. A haze of smoke lingered over the clearing where the dog teams were parked. After parking and snacking the team, Newton stopped to read the "Mushers' Menu" – an old schoolroom blackboard hanging on the side of the steps leading into the cabin:

Hot Coffee
Muffins
Chocolate chip cookies
Tea
Soup of the Day
Burritos
Lasagna

Another sign indicated a barrel where he found warm water to make meals for his dogs. On the trail dogs won't usually drink water, but they need to be hydrated. Putting heated water with the kibble and chopped meat makes the water more interesting to the dogs and they will usually drink the fluid in which they find their food. A dog that isn't eating will not only get hungry, it will also dehydrate.

Inside was a clothesline to hang clothes for drying. A kitchen table around which the mushers sat to share food and conversation. There were beds where Newton could sleep if needed or he could sleep on the floor in the storeroom, beneath the shelves lined with bulk foods in large boxes and giant tin cans.

Some more isolated hospitality stops were also used as dog drops – where a musher had access to veterinary assistance and could leave an injured or sick dog behind without penalty. Stepping Stone was too close to Pelly to be used as a dog drop. Like many of the cabins along the trail, it's just a place where mushers know they are welcome and can take a little time out from the race.

Newton stayed for seven hours, enjoying the food, socializing and feeding the dogs. What lay ahead of him would make most people hesitate to leave. He waited for Japanese musher, Yuka Honda, who had arrived a couple of hours behind him, to depart. It would be easier to travel with company than alone. When he did pull the hook he was eight and a half hours behind schedule.

A few minutes behind him, Quest rookie Jerry Joinson of Fort St. James, BC, also departed. As Jerry dropped over the steep embankment back onto the Pelly River one dog jammed her shoulder and another hurt its back leg. Neither could run any further, but to load them into his sled meant he would have to unload most of his food.

The best option was to take the injured dogs back to Pelly, then come back, pick up his food and continue. Instead of crossing the river on the trail to Dawson City, he started back down the same trail he had arrived on. Then Jerry realized that by the time he got back, ravens and foxes would have had hours to raid his food supplies. He decided to scratch when he reached Pelly.

"I was down to nine dogs. The Quest has been a dream for years. I really wanted to finish. I was hoping for the Red Lantern (the trophy presented to the last person to finish the race). I couldn't have kept on going. I couldn't get to the Scroggie Dog Drop," Jerry said.

"It's very disappointing. But I'm more concerned about the dogs than my feelings. This is such an expensive race that I don't think I'll be able to do it again."

When they reached the overflow Rick had mentioned to him in Pelly, Newton's team stopped. He walked to the front of the team and taking the leader's neckline, he led them through. There were several areas of overflow, separated by challenging runs on narrow trails over steep hills and through tangled brush. Newton had listened to Rick and made sure he brought all his extra dog booties with him. On the last one, the water flowed over the top of his own boots and filled them.

"Water was so cold I had goosebumps on my teeth," Newton shivered with the memory of it.

Team arriving at Stepping Stone at night.

Yuka's team balked at the edge of the last overflow. They refused to move when she tried to lead them.

This wasn't her first attempt at the Quest. She had tried the race twice before and had yet to finish. In 2006 she was one of six teams airlifted by helicopter off Eagle Summit when snowstorms trapped them on the exposed Alaskan summit. The next year she scratched in Dawson City after one of her dogs died.

Her third attempt at the race and her leaders had already caused her concern. Her main leader, Olive Oil, quit on her just after leaving Carmacks. She tried several other dogs before coming across Talcum, a young dog with lots of enthusiasm but no leadership experience. She had been forced to switch the leaders constantly, using Olive Oil when experience was required and Talcum when the team needed a lift. At the overflow neither one wanted to go.

Leaving his team with Yuka, Newton went back through the overflow and convinced her team to follow him across.

Together their teams trotted slowly toward Scroggie Creek. It was slow going as they slipped along the trail, mostly silent, through the washed-out backdrop of countryside. What had taken other teams between eight and 10 hours, took Newton and Yuka almost 15. The "Welcome to Scroggie" sign came as a welcome relief although the sight of the "Stewart River Hilton" itself didn't give people much reassurance.

This single small cabin with thin walls and a flimsy door offered no protection from the elements. The cracks between the boards were large enough for a dog to walk through, according to the Canadian Rangers (Canada's northern paramilitary force) who operated the dog drop. There was a vet on-site to check the teams – this far from a checkpoint the mushers and the race organizers didn't want to take any chances with the dogs. Any dogs dropped at remote dog drops were usually evacuated by aircraft that would land on skis on the river ice.

A chimney jutting out of the cabin roof had smoke pouring out of it into the frigid -30°C air, proof that there was at least a fire inside to warm up beside. A gas generator produced electricity for a few lightbulbs, a microwave oven and a battery charger for the ham radio. There were a couple of small, dilapidated homemade tables and overturned buckets served as chairs.

Newton was soaking wet from the overflow and freezing cold. He hung his clothes over the fire to dry but it had been built with green and frozen

At Scroggie Creek dog drop: (L to R) Quest veterinarian, Wayne Hall, Colleen Robertia, Yuka Honda.

wood and didn't give off much heat. One of the Rangers stuck his boot liners into the microwave oven and tried to dry them on "high."

Colleen Robertia, who started the race just ahead of Newton, was still there giving her team a good rest before heading into the Black Hills. Wayne Hall, from Eagle, Alaska, was traveling close to her.

"Dawson City," Wayne muttered to himself while sitting around the fire, "thirty-six" (referring to the mandatory stop for the teams in Dawson).

Colleen, sitting next to him, had been half asleep, but jolted awake. "Dawson City. Dirty Sex?" She wasn't sure she heard him correctly. She cast a wary eye toward Wayne.

"What vitamins does this guy take?!" she wondered.

There was only room for two people to stretch out on the dirt floor to sleep by the fire. A tent next door was being used as a sleeping room but Newton found it too cold. He bedded down beside the fire and nodded off. Finally, he had learned how to grab a short nap during a rest stop. In the time he spend dozing, he crept closer to the fire to keep warm – too close. Even with low heat the fire burned a hole in the sleeping bag.

Nineteen hours ahead of Newton the race was beginning to develop.

Six teams juggled the lead for almost 500 miles, each one taking its time up front, as the mushers evaluated each other. Although the first team into Dawson City receives four ounces of Klondike gold, that isn't the ultimate goal. The run into Dawson is a place for a team to make a statement or to continue hiding in the snowdrifts.

Jon Little was the first team to top the barren windswept Midnight Sun Dome, the last climb before a 25-mile downhill run into Dawson. He glanced back over his shoulder but could see no headlamps coming up the road along Sulphur Creek. He relaxed a little. He wasn't in Dawson yet, but if there was no one close behind he would be the first to arrive.

It might be time to get rid of his nickname, "Fourth-place Jon" – because he was always a contender but had never won a race.

"He doesn't push his dogs," his handler Mike Barnett was waiting in Dawson. "He's laid back and in tune with his dogs. It shows in how his dogs perform."

Being out in front of the race at this point was testimony to Jon's ability to work with his dogs. He had been cutting his rest time "because I think it's all the dogs need." It was also a very emotional race for him. He was fortunate to be here at all.

In January he and Mike had been training two teams in front of ATVs. At one road crossing, the brakes on Mike's ATV failed and the team burst out onto the road. A speeding truck flew over the hill, went right through the team and kept on going. Four dogs died instantly and a fifth was seriously injured but did survive. Little had a small kennel by Alaskan standards, just 24 dogs, and the loss hit him hard.

"I've been thinking about them a lot. It's definitely dedicated to them, this whole race is," Jon said.

Then he made a mistake on the summit and headed down the wrong trail for about 20 minutes. Realizing his error he turned the dogs around and got them started on the correct route. Once again reaching the top, he still couldn't see any lights on the hill behind him.

His team trundled down the mountain for a couple of hours and onto the Bonanza Creek Road that would take him to the Klondike River and Dawson City.

"When I'm a mile outside of town I'm thinking, 'Oh, I can get my wife some gold. That's really cool.'" Then his team stopped running. "One of my leaders, Adidas, was wanting to dip snow (scoop snow with her mouth) and she stopped the team. And (William) Kleedehn went blowing by me. I knew he was potentially right there, but I never really looked behind me."

He trailed William into Dawson by two minutes.

Earlier William had trailed by a couple of hours but made a long 100-mile run from Scroggie, stopping only once to snack his dogs near Indian River Bridge, approximately halfway.

"I paced my dogs different. I was running to win the race, not be the first into Dawson. I passed him on the Klondike River." William's headlamp batteries were dying so he had run without lights for most of the last 30 miles into Dawson. "I couldn't even see anything and all of a sudden I saw a dog team right in front of me. I figured they were a recreational musher or something and it turns out it's Jon. So my dog team just went straight by."

He had been a force in the Quest, finishing in the top five for most of the past nine years including two second-place finishes. Despite his success at the Finish line, this was the first time he had been the first team to arrive in Dawson.

Raised on a farm near Hanover, Germany, William immigrated to Canada in 1978 using the insurance money he received for losing his leg in a motorcycle accident. While living in western Ontario for a number of years, he got into middle distance racing using a group of older "retired" sleddogs and a beat-up junker of a dogsled given to him by a family from The Pas, Manitoba. He finished second in his first race, in Minnesota, won the next and never finished out of the top two for several years.

"I got mostly dogs with mental problems, but those are the best dogs with which to learn. Problem dogs."

His first Yukon Quest in 1990, which he finished in 17th position, convinced him to move to the Yukon. The 2009 Quest, he had already decided, would be his last.

Hugh Neff, who splits his time between Whitehorse and Tok, Alaska, was just an hour behind.

Born in Tennessee and raised in a suburb of Chicago, Illinois, Hugh made a virtue out of poverty. "I don't really respect money. Twelve years in Catholic school teaches you there's more to life than money. Life should be about helping your fellow people."

His love of the North came from reading novelist Jack London, poet Robert Service and tome writer James Michener. Working in a dog kennel owned by Ramy Brooks, the Yukon Quest champion in 1999, he declined to accept a traditional wage. Instead of money, he took his salary in dogs. For his first Yukon Quest in 2000 he had 14 dogs and a sled but no means of transporting them. He, the dogs and a loaded sled hitchhiked from Fairbanks to Whitehorse for the start. Over the next few years, he received training and support from 1995 Quest champion Frank Turner, William Kleedehn, Hans Gatt, and Thomas Tetz, a former musher who was a race judge for the 2009 race.

"I'm here because I'm a dog man. I keep racing because I know I have a lot to learn still," said Hugh.

He matched William step for step from Scroggie until one of his dogs, Zirl, came up lame and he had to stop and load the dog into the sled bag. The extra weight slowed the team down for the long haul up King Solomon's Dome.

Hans Gatt was the fourth team in followed by another Whitehorse musher, Sebastien Schnuelle – a garrulous musher whose hair looks perpetually like he has just stuck his finger into an electrical outlet.

Sebastien had actually withdrawn from the Quest before the race started. He had been depressed about his team's performance in the Copper Basin 300 in early January.

It had been his pattern since starting racing long distance in 2005 to run both the Quest and Iditarod in the same year every year. He wondered if he should skip the Quest, give his dogs more training and just run the Iditarod, which started in the first week in March.

At the last minute he asked the race organizers if he could withdraw his withdrawal, and they agreed.

The former automobile mechanic from Wuppertal, Germany, found his way into the North by canoeing one of the world's great rivers, the MacKenzie to the Arctic Ocean in 1996. He moved to Whitehorse following the canoe trip and decided he wanted to learn about dog mushing. His Blue Kennels team was a successful dogsled tour business. He also trained mushers to run the Yukon Quest.

Sebastien felt lucky just to reach Dawson. On the trail to Pelly he had a crash with the sled. While tipping the sled upright, freeing it from the brush and untangling the team one of his dogs slipped her harness and ran down the trail.

"There goes my race," thought Sebastien. When a team loses a dog, they can't continue until the dog is found and returned. If the dog isn't returned, they have to scratch. A few miles down the trail he came across his dog and put her back in harness.

Sebastien never seemed to be racing his team. He displayed patience and discipline with his dogs and was known for his dog care, earning the Veterinarian's Award in the 2007 Quest. He spent as little time in checkpoints as possible. "I've been camping alone. I run by schedule. I don't care where I'm at, even if it's one hour out of a checkpoint."

Brent Sass was just minutes behind. In his sled bag was one of his leaders, Madonna, who he had carried for over 60 miles. "I didn't stop kicking or poling from the second I put her in the sled until the second I got here,"

Brent said. "The dogs definitely sensed my urgency. I'm probably going to have to drop her, which is a real bummer. That's probably the biggest blow we're going to take throughout the entire race."

The Minnesota-born musher had arrived in Alaska in 1998 to study at and cross-country ski for the University of Alaska in Fairbanks. He watched a neighbor run his dogs one day and decided that was something he wanted to try. Brent's first totally out-of-control experience driving and crashing a sled, careening wildly through the bush with cross-country skis as runners and no brake, simply served to convince him he loved it.

Trained by Susan Butcher and 1988 Yukon Quest champion Dave Monson, he consistently finished in the top 10 of the middle and long distance races he entered. His only win so far was the Yukon Quest 300 in 2006. His goal was to win the Quest and Iditarod in the same year. He was happy being just a few hours out of the lead.

"The best thing I did in this entire race was start slow from Whitehorse. If I had tried to keep up with those fast guys, I would have blown the team up," said Brent.

One of the pre-race favorites, four-time Iditarod champion Martin Buser made a rookie mistake. He ran short of food on the run from Pelly to Dawson. Slowing the team down, he kept them going on snacks and a reduced diet of warm meals for the last 100 miles, rolling into Dawson almost eight hours behind the leaders.

"I felt bad that I couldn't provide them as much food as I should have... and that's a typical rookie mistake. I could see the handwriting on the wall so in Scroggie I didn't feed them as much as they wanted to eat," said Martin.

"I must admit if I had not had a reasonably clean run I would have underpacked. This is my first long race that I've come in with a totally empty sled...and I don't like that."

Running short of food wasn't something Newton had to worry about. If anything, he always carried too much. If he had leftover bags of snacks from a previous run, rather than dumping them, he would hoard them and add them to his snacks, packed for the next stage. His sled gained weight with each checkpoint. It was a leftover, he said, of not having enough to eat when he was growing up and often going to bed hungry.

Food wasn't on his mind though as he drove his team into the misty rolling ridges past Scroggie. It was the cold. He hadn't been able to completely dry out his gear and the temperatures down on the Stewart River had stayed near -30°C.

It didn't take long before he started seeing snow-encrusted machinery alongside the trail, remnants of long abandoned gold mines or current mining operations waiting for the summer to get back to work. This part of the route is called "The Gold Trail" because it travels through the Klondike gold fields. In the early years of the Quest, dog teams and cat trains used to encounter each other on the trail and they learned to live together.

Cat trains were convoys of trailers, pulled by caterpillars, and loaded with equipment destined for the Black Hills gold camps, traveling on winter roads punched through the snowbound wilderness. The massive diesel-powered iron earthmovers scraped the snow away, exposing frozen shale and bedrock. Often when a cat encountered a Quest team, they would move aside, leaving a narrow gap through which the team would pass. It was an unnerving experience for both since one minor error by the cat skinner (driver) could kill dogs and musher in an instant.

The switchbacks started. Newton would climb for awhile, push the sled around a steep corner, continue pumping his foot or running behind the sled while still climbing. If he looked down the hill he could see just a short distance directly below him the trail he had just covered. They seemed endless and went on for hours. The ridges appeared one after another. Eventually, he emerged from the treeline and the massive hump of Eureka Dome blotted out the horizon in front of him.

In one section, where the trail leveled off, he rode the runners, letting the dogs set their own pace and giving his own legs a short break. He took the time to look around and spotted something that seemed strangely familiar, but totally out of place up here near the summit.

He looked again and it still looked like a machete handle sticking out of the snow. He reached out and pulled it out as the team loped past. It was a short machete. Where it came from and why it was there he never found out. But there it was.

Before leaving Whitehorse he had joked, "I would rather carry a machete. I know how to use a machete. We use them to mow the grass back home and cut firewood. I don't know how to use an axe."

Now he had what he had wished for. He tucked it into the sled bag. He would probably have a use for it later on the trail. For the moment it just made him feel a little warmer.

The descent was uneventful. His iPod batteries had died. He rode the runners, controlling the sled just enough that it didn't pressure the dogs. Occasionally, he rode in silence, listening to the steady patter of feet, the

Jason Mackey passes an abandoned dredge just outside Dawson City.

jingling of dog tags and the panting of the dogs. Every once in a while he broke into song. The dogs, he believed, ran better when they listened to Reggae.

His scheduled stop was at Indian River Bridge, just 50 miles from Dawson, in a wide valley of snow covered "tailing" piles, a rhythmic series of small ridges created by mining dredges, and mining roads that seemed to lead everywhere and nowhere.

"It was miserable cold and there was nothing there. I used the machete to cut some firewood and built a small fire to keep myself warm while the dog food was cooking. When I had everyone fed up and a little rested, I pulled out and ran all the way to Dawson."

The climb up King Solomon's Dome was long but gradual, following an unplowed road up a narrow valley. It parallels Sulphur Creek, one of many creeks that feed the Indian River and, like the valley he had just crossed, it also had been torn up by the dredges. A skeleton of one of the massive three-story tall dredges could be seen about half way up the ascent. Piles of scrap metal and rotting cabins lined the hillsides.

It was the gold mining history along the trail that lured rookie Warren Palfry from Yellowknife, Northwest Territories, to the Quest. As a child he had heard stories about his grandfather going to Dawson City in the Klondike Gold Rush in 1898 and running mail by dogsled along the creeks of the gold fields.

Author Jack London wrote of two men who raced their dog teams 50 miles from a gold claim they had both staked simultaneously by the Indian River, to see who could get to Dawson City first to register their find. They arrived neck-and–neck at the recorder's office and a Mountie suggested they split it equally – which they did. It turned out to be worthless.

"It was really neat to hear those stories and realize I was running...quite possibly on the same trails as him between those cabins that date back over a hundred years or so." The race, Warren believed, was as close to history as one could get because of the distance between the checkpoints and the camaraderie of the mushers.

"It's the code of the North," recited Warren, "Do unto others as you would have them do unto you."

When he reached the communications towers crowning the mountain, Newton could look back and see, vaguely lit by the stars that peeked out between broken clouds, the valley through which he had just passed. Ahead he was looking at the roof of the world, mountaintops as far as his eye could see.

King Solomon's Dome has been the source of many Quest tales of the supernatural. From the old man who appeared to musher Don Glassburn in 1987, during one of the coldest Quests ever run, and told him to take a rest because he was too far from Dawson to make it in one shot. (Don made the run anyway and discovered the ghost had been right.) To an imaginary mineshaft into which Frank Turner believed he drove his team. There is a large open pit mine through which the trail passes, but there are no underground mine shafts near the mountain.

Newton was no exception. The sky was mostly overcast. There was no moon and the psychedelic Northern Lights didn't appear (the winter of 2008-2009 was the worst year ever for Northern Lights).

"I know it sounds strange when I talk about it, but I saw a bright light in the sky near me. It came closer towards me, then went away. Then it flew close to the treetops and disappeared. I don't think I was hallucinating. I think I saw the light, but it was no flying saucer or anything like that."

Newton and his dogs looked at each other. They appeared to have seen it as well. The trial of miles fosters an unsentimental kind of intimacy between team members. As it does with anyone – hostages, shipwreck survivors – who survive in dire circumstances under duress. At such times they seemed to be able to read each other's minds.

However, as they started the final descent to Dawson, they couldn't read the minds of those who awaited them. They had no idea of what was about to happen.

The power had to be felt to be understood.

Ultimate Athletes

The best long distance runners eat raw meat, run naked and sleep in the snow.

Alaska Airlines advertisement

The marriage of man and dogs is as close to long distance perfection as the animal world can produce.

It is strongly believed that only three species in the world are biomechanically built for long distance running – the horse, man and the dog.

Over a short distance, almost every animal is faster than man, including the dog and horse. Even the world's fastest man, Jamaica's Usain Bolt, must take a back seat to the sprinters of the wild kingdom. Over a long distance, because we are capable of traveling extreme distance at a consistent pace, man can outlast and is faster than everything – except the dog. Men have won the vast majority of 50-mile man versus horse races over the past two decades.

It was that theory that prompted Alaska's Joe Runyan to wear running shoes instead of bunny boots (heavy, waterproof winter boots) and run behind his sled for almost 1,000 miles to win the 1985 Yukon Quest, then repeat the strategy to claim the Iditarod title in 1989. He believed he could not only aid his team by reducing the amount of weight they had to pull, but that he could run with them for the entire distance. So that's what he did.

Twenty-five years later his strategy might not work. Not because man has gotten slower. In fact, human sprinters and long distance runners have improved marginally every decade or so. It's because the dog has proven to be faster and stronger than ever before believed possible.

When mushers started running both the Quest and the Iditarod in the same year, they often had two teams – one for each race. Then they started running a few dogs in both races, usually dropping them at some point during the Iditarod when the musher decided the dog was tired. When Lance Mackey started winning both races in the same year, he was running almost the same team for both races. The majority of dogs who ran both, finished both. Not just completing them but running almost 1,900 miles

Foot care for the dogs is vital.

in two stages, separated by only a two-week recovery period, and winning. With times that were over two days faster in each race than the best teams in the 1980s were capable of running.

Being a sleddog is a natural instinct.

"It's a reverse reflex," said psychologist Stanley Cohen of the University of British Columbia in Vancouver, BC. "If you have an uncontrollable dog on a leash, some people suggest using a harness to control the dog. Big mistake.

"You put pressure against a dog's chest, instead of holding them back, the canine reaction is to pull against it. Put a harness on a dog, you can turn a terrier into a malamute. A sleddog is not necessarily pulling a sled as they are reacting to pressure."

Humans have recognized this trait in dogs for over 2,000 years and not just in dryland dog driving regions of the earth. Arab literature of the 10th century describes dogsledding in the Siberian Subarctic. Explorer Marco Polo (13th century) talks about dogsledding on snow in his writings on central Asia. There is archeological evidence of Alaskan natives using dogsleds for over 1,000 years. An illustration by Arctic adventurer Martin Frobisher in 1675 shows Inuit hunters using a dog to pull a pulka or canoe-type sled on snow.

Dogs had been around for about 47 million years before humans turned up. No one is exactly sure how contact between the two species occurred or how they not only learned to live together, but to bond on an emotional level. It is believed that contact was made over 130,000 years ago, long before humans started living in settlements or practiced agriculture.

While it is likely the first reason for joining forces was to enhance hunting capabilities, at some point humans started breeding dogs to serve other specific functions. Newfoundlands and St. Bernards are draft animals. Borzois and Wolfhounds are hunters. St. Hubert Hounds are scent dogs as are Bloodhounds and Bassett Hounds. Heelers and Collies are herders.

There are at least 150 different breeds of dogs in existence, many of them in danger of becoming extinct. One consequence of creating purebreds is that many disease-causing genes have become concentrated in those breeds. In particular, according to veterinarian Charlie Berger of East Thetford, Vermont, who has worked on five Iditarods and two Yukon Quests, the type of breeding used for beautification of show dogs has destroyed many of those breeds. Burmese Mountain Dogs, for one, have had their life expectancy drop to an average of four or five years.

Northern breeds are usually identified by the region they're from rather than by their purebred lines. Siberian Huskies are from northern Russia. Mackenzie River Huskies from the region bordering the river after which they were named. Alaskan Malamutes were used along the northern coast of North America. Yukon River village dogs come from hamlets along the Yukon River in Alaska and the Yukon. There were few if any breeding programs for them. There was no need. Working dogs could be as homely as they wanted to be. Crossbreeding was common.

Developing bloodlines for dogs for racing never really occurred to anyone until after the All Alaska Sweepstakes in Nome, Alaska, in 1908.

The initial idea was to try and combine the best features of different types of dogs into one dog – making him or her faster, stronger, smarter and more durable than any other dog on the planet. Different mushers had different opinions on how this could be accomplished.

Thus when a musher says he has an "Attla dog," he has a dog whose bloodline was determined by the program employed by sprint racer George Attla, and it would be vastly different from a "Gatt dog" since Hans was breeding for a totally different reason. No combination of breeds was too strange or different to try in the search for the perfect sleddog.

Dogs run on their toes. Their heels don't contact the ground and the pads on their feet absorb all the impact of running. Having tough feet and a tough skin on the pad keeps the feet healthy. Siberians have good feet.

Large sleddogs were once popular among racers until they discovered that smaller, lighter dogs were faster and just as strong. The Malamute, in comparison, is a smaller, faster dog. Mushers want dogs who can build a superior bond with their driver and respond quickly to direction. Belgian sheep dogs have those attributes.

A dog with longer legs will cover more ground with each step than a dog with shorter legs if they are both racing at the same pace. It's a minute difference with each stride but it adds up significantly over 12 days. Greyhounds were introduced into the mix.

Foot speed was also important. Border collies provided that along with advanced intuition and reasoning capabilities.

Long distance running is an aerobic activity. The greater the lung capacity of the dog, the stronger and more durable it would be. The British Bull Dog, not famous for much more than powerful jaws and being truly ugly, also has exceptional lung capacity.

For almost 90 years it was mostly hit and miss. There was some basic science applied – urine testing to determine lactic acid build-up or blood tests to see if someone could identify the mysterious metabolic switch that sleddogs are able to turn on during a race – their metabolism changes. They are able to keep their metabolic rate at the same baseline that is found in resting subjects – even as they run up to 200 miles per day. It makes them fatigue-proof, and consequently, less susceptible to illness or injury, but no one has been able to figure out what it is or how it works.

Some bloodlines worked. Others that should have, didn't. Dogs that came from successful breeding programs – Jeff King, Martin Buser, Hans Gatt, Frank Turner, Susan Butcher and several others – became mainstays of successful racing teams. Eventually the dogs from the programs crossbred and often started a whole new bloodline. It was odd, but sometimes the mating of two successful bloodlines produced a dud. It was a veiled warning that, like show dogs, along with the interbreeding of racing lines came the possibility of achieving the goal at the cost of the dog itself.

In the past decade advances in medical and veterinary science have improved the odds of developing successful breeding programs and heading

off potential disaster. Hans Gatt was one of the first professional mushers to start tracking the genetic records of his dogs.

"He's always been cutting edge when it came to genetics," said John Overell, a veterinarian widely experienced with middle and long distance races. "Now we're encouraging all mushers to keep genetic records, then we can identify whether what we're looking at is a medical problem or a genetic issue. We can look through the breeding lines, see the issue is genetic and tell the musher, 'Okay. You shouldn't be breeding this line anymore.'"

One example of genetic influence was a group of dogs who were born with their eyelids turned in backwards, so the eyelashes were scratching the cornea of the eye. The short-term solution was minor corrective surgery. The long-term solution was even simpler. By looking at the breeding record, John was able to identify the problem as being genetic in origin. The musher stopped breeding that particular line and the problem vanished.

"Mushers are breeding for strength and intelligence," said John. The ideal sleddog runs forever happily, eats nothing, can pull large loads and never gets injured. And, if it's racing, does all this more quickly than the competition."

The sport has come under attack by various animal rights organizations. Their protests, while occasionally justified, are primarily focused upon the political need to stand with the appropriate emotional conviction in front of financial backers and convince them they are doing something. They have accomplished limited success and made the sport slightly more humane. Not every person who owns sleddogs should own them and the rights groups have been effective in rooting out those the mushers didn't find on their own. But, their arguments are based mostly upon flawed science and not wanting to understand the dog.

"You know," adds John, "you listen to the heart rate of one of these (sled) dogs, then you go and listen to the heart rate of the average house pet....You wonder how any blood gets out of the (house pet's) heart."

2009 Quest veterinarian Bernadine Cruz agrees with John. "These animals are in better condition than 99 percent of the animals we see in our regular practices. They are well cared for, more used to people, are used to being examined and cared for by veterinarians."

Mushers are true dog lovers. Not just one who sees them as pets, but instead views them as colleagues in life. They see them differently from other people. They respect their dignity. They recognize their exceptional physical gifts and mental acuity. A lead dog has the remarkable ability to almost perfectly recall a thousand-mile trail that it races only once a year. There is an intelligence and a fundamental ability to reason that can take a person's breath away.

The musher doesn't just see a dog. He sees the ultimate athlete whose individual personality has all the same complexities as a human – with none of the human faults – and who wants to deliver the best possible performance. Even with many years of driving dogs under their belts, seasoned veterans often still marvel that the dogs are willing to pull them through the woods and take them places they would otherwise never go. What human, they wonder, could ever ask for more?

"Dogs are not stupid," said former Quest musher David Sawatzky. "They do what they're doing because they like to do it. You might be able to force them to do something for a short period of time, but you can't force them to do it for a thousand miles. They're going to lie down and they're going to quit....When the going gets tough and a dog is afraid of you, it's going to get worse. If the dog loves you, it's going to pull through for you."

"All you have to do," said two-time Quest champion John Schandelmeier, "is convince a dog that's been running all night and is tired that it's the greatest thing in life to be out here with me."

There is something surreal about spotting a musher standing in front of his team, arguing with his lead dog about which trail is the right one. Both of them respecting the other's opinion and neither of them prepared to concede the point. The odd thing is that the dog wins as often as the musher does, usually because they're right.

A study written by Dr. Michael Davis for the American Psychology Society in 2007 identified the three areas where sleddogs are superior in physiology to all other dogs and addressed the question of why they have made humans the weak link in the team.

The aerobic capacity of the sleddog is second to none. They can take in and absorb phenomenal amounts of oxygen, enabling them to maintain high energy levels and mental alertness for extended periods of time. During the dog mushing off-season, their heart is normal size. When they're racing, the size of the heart can increase by up to 25 percent, increasing blood flow and muscle development.

Second, they convert food into fuel very efficiently. Veterinarian John Overell provided an explanation, "The sleddog metabolism is different from the human process. In humans, fat is converted to fatty acids, then to glucose that can be used. In humans that can cause lactose buildup, which hampers your muscles' ability to function efficiently. That doesn't happen in dogs. The fat is converted directly to glucose. No fatty acids. No lactose."

The third area was something that scientists and mushers discovered at the same time. The scientists found it by poring over mileage charts and results for the top teams. The mushers saw it by watching their dogs.

Sleddogs adapt well to exercise and the more exercise they get, the better they get. One hundred years after they started racing dogs, mushers are just now discovering they haven't tapped into the full potential of their dogs. Rather than burning a dog out by running it too much, mushers now realize that the dog simply adjusts to its new exercise schedule and performs at levels never before believed possible. If there is a point where the dog peaks out and performance starts to lag, it hasn't been reached yet.

Robert Sorlie was the first to utilize that knowledge when he won the Iditarod in 2003 and 2005, while pioneering the idea of long runs and short rests. Lance Mackey took it to a higher level when he ran basically the same teams in the Quest and the Iditarod in 2007 and 2008, winning both races in both years. Sebastien Schnuelle almost did the same thing in 2009 and Hans Gatt came close in 2010.

Dr. Davis was conducting blood tests on dogs during the 2009 Quest, trying to determine if there was a measurable limit to the canine capability. Based upon his observations, "once they find that extra gear, they can keep going for at least a week or two more."

Some teams never seem to have any problems on the trail. The dogs never get stressed or sick. Dogs that are dropped are usually the result of an injury.

Others appear beset with issues – lack of leaders, sick dogs and females in heat. Ninety percent of the time it is the result of going too fast, not getting enough rest or not eating properly.

Problem solving is a mindset, not science. It's the musher having unlimited patience, trying out all sorts of different ideas and not losing heart until a solution is found. If dogs start suffering from diarrhea the best solution might be to add powdered rice to the food. Or it could be to continue running them without feeding them for a long while. Either one can settle a stomach down. If a dog isn't eating, the musher tries different types and flavors of food and meat until the dog finds something that interests him.

The difference is in paying attention to details. Experienced mushers are aware of how much their dogs need to eat – exactly how many calories are in a single piece of kibble or a four ounce piece of pork fat. During the race the average sleddog will need to consume 10,000-12,000 calories per day. Dogs won't usually drink water on the trail. They will scoop snow with their mouth but the majority of their liquid intake comes from the water their food is cooked in.

Every time the team stops, whether it's along the trail or in a checkpoint, the driver knows to check the dogs' feet. As goes the feet, so goes the team. They look for worn booties or wet ones (even booties damp from the sweat of a dog's foot cause irritations). If they find feet that look chafed or cut or slightly swelled, they will apply foot ointment. The ointments aid in improving circulation to the feet and drying them.

Massaging legs during snacking time, meal times on the trail or while resting in the checkpoint helps to reduce stiffness in the muscles, prevent shoulder lameness and reduce the possibility of joint injuries. If they are aware of any swelling, the musher will wrap the leg immediately in a tension or neoprene bandage, keep it warm and reduce the swelling. Massaging the legs helps the dog sleep better because they're more relaxed. It also helps them run better because they don't have to run off any stiffness.

The mushers try to do all of this effectively and efficiently in as short a time as possible. The less a dog is disturbed, the more it will rest.

The veterinarians who greet the teams at every checkpoint understand this as well and they have developed a system of giving a team a complete physical exam while the musher is still signing in with the race officials.

It starts with the way they lope into the checkpoint. The vet watches for the dogs' demeanor – signs that indicate how the dogs feel. Are their tails wagging? Do they lie down as soon as the team stops? Do they try and clean the snow off their feet? Are they curious and looking around? Are they bright and alert?

The vet will walk down the team. To the casual onlooker they look like they're just petting the dogs, but in fact they're checking for hydration – pinching the skin on top of the head or along the spine. If the skin doesn't deflate back to its natural state, the dog could be dehydrated. The top of the head is more reliable because some styles of harnesses can push the skin on the dog's back into positions where it could give a false reading.

While pinching the top of the head, the vets also pull back on the eyelids so they can see the eyeball. If it's clear, no problem. If it's red – eye infections are often indicators of other injuries that might not be obvious.

They also put their thumb into the dog's mouth, running it over the bottom of the teeth. Testing again for hydration by feeling how dry or slick or tacky they are. There is a small pink spot on the dog's gum the vet will look at. If it's not pink, it should be. If it is pink, the vet presses on it. It should blanche, then return to its natural color. This is a test for hydration and blood circulation.

The finger in the mouth also tests the dog's body temperature. A dog's body temperature is slightly higher than that of a human. If the mouth feels too hot, they will use a rectal thermometer to determine if the dog is overheating.

Passing their hand under the dog's jaw, they check the lymph nodes. They shouldn't be swollen but if they are it could be an indicator of an infection. They also check other lymph nodes under the armpits and between the rear legs.

"Each part is like part of a puzzle that ultimately leads you towards a reasonable diagnosis," explained John Overell.

Occasionally the vet will bend down and reach between the hind legs of the dog. They're checking the femoral artery – taking the dog's heart rate. They check it twice, once on the way up the team and again on the way back down. The speed at which the pulse decreases indicates the speed of recovery and the overall condition of the dog.

Now, for the first time, the vet will actually look like they're doing a medical exam. The vet uses a stethoscope to listen to the heart and lungs. By this time, the musher has finished showing the officials his mandatory items and signed in.

They check the feet, picking up the paw and inserting a finger between the toes looking for infections or "wet cracks," small cracks in the foot caused by snow melting between the toes. They can be treated by foot ointments. "They're not serious but they could get serious if not treated," said John.

Pushing their finger against the back of the dog's wrist they watch for the dog wincing or try to feel any springy resistance in the tendon or muscle. Wrist problems can usually be resolved with a few hours of rest. Swelling will go down and the tendon or muscle loosens up. "While they're running the swelling usually doesn't cause the dog any discomfort, but when they stop the swelling can reoccur quickly."

The leg is then bent at the elbow to see if it distresses the dog and lastly, the vet will place a finger at the front of the shoulder joint, and then pull the leg gently forward and pull it back to check range of motion.

They'll ask the musher if they have any concerns or want the vet to look at any of the dogs in particular. "After all, we only see the dogs at the checkpoints. They are the only ones who see the dogs out on the trail," John continued. Communication between the mushers and vets on the trail is usually excellent.

"It's easier to explain something to a musher because they've taken the time to learn. They not only take the time to know what antibiotics or foot creams to use, but they understand why one works better than the other for certain things and why sometimes they shouldn't be used at all."

2009 Quest head vet Kathleen McGill echoed John's feelings, "Mushers take great pains to inform themselves and become very knowledgeable. What they may not have in medical training they certainly make up for by knowing their dogs very well."

One part of the mandatory gear the musher must carry during the race is a book where vets can write details about each dog's health at each checkpoint. Each dog has its own page. When they reach the next checkpoint, the musher provides the book to the attending vet so he or she will know if there's anything specific to be aware of.

The time to do a complete check of a 14-dog team is approximately 28 minutes. Mandatory vet checks must be done at Whitehorse, Braeburn, Dawson City, Twin Bears and Fairbanks. At all the other checkpoints or dog drops, the vet check is optional. If a team plans to only stop for 15 minutes to change food bags and reorganize the sled, then the veterinarian will usually just rely on their first observations as the team comes in and ask the musher if there are any dogs he or she wants looked at. In John Overell's experience, not one musher has ever declined the invitation.

A typical dogsled team has four components to it. The dogs in front are leaders. They are generally more intelligent than the other dogs, better at learning and remembering commands and superior in being able to stay focused on the job they need to do.

Right behind them are the swing dogs. These are either leaders-in-training or experienced leaders who perform at a higher level under certain conditions, like being able to locate a trail in storm or whiteout conditions where there is no visibility, or climbing a hill that no other dog in its right mind would consider tackling.

The two dogs closest to the sled are wheel dogs. They are generally the strongest because they are the ones who physically turn the sled when it

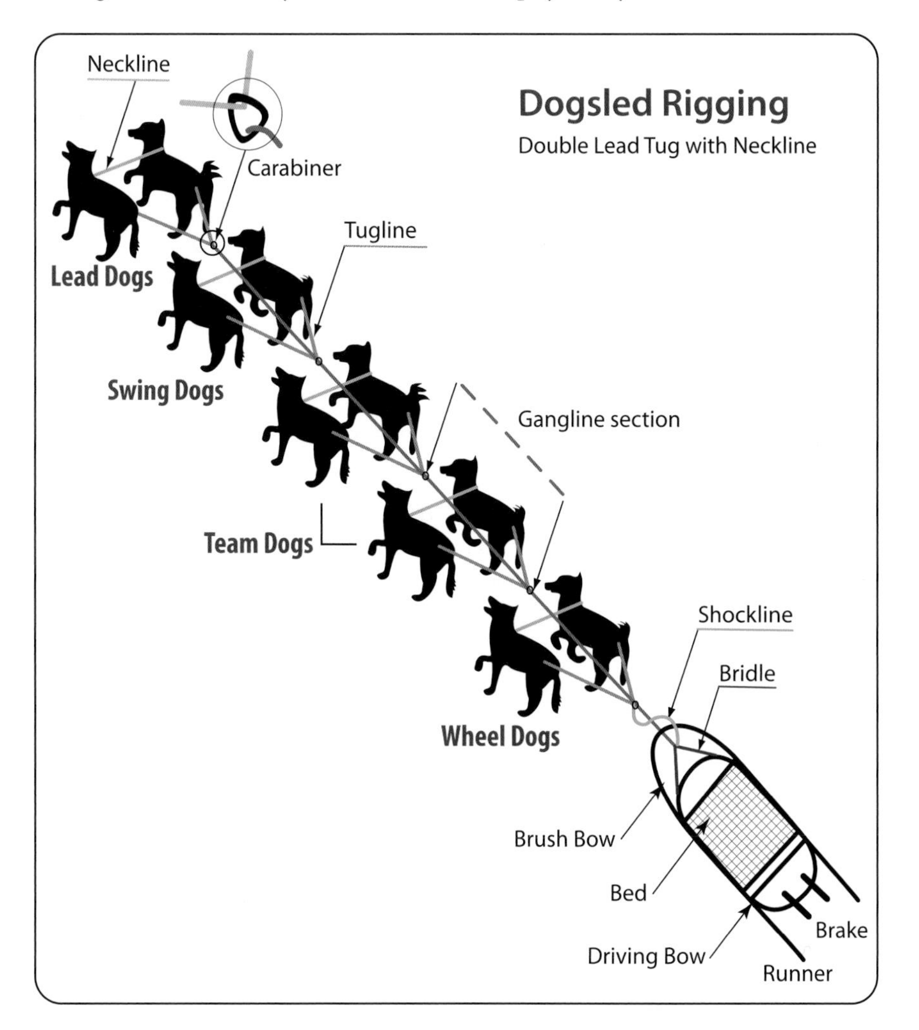

goes around a corner. Between the wheel dogs and the swing dogs are the team dogs. Good pullers who maybe couldn't learn the commands as well so they simply follow the dogs in front. They know their place in the team hierarchy. Or possibly a place for a musher to hide specialized lead dogs that he or she doesn't want the other mushers to know about. They'll pull as team dogs until placed in lead for whatever purpose they are needed for – which could be a strategic purpose such as speed or passing other teams rather than one dictated by terrain, a leader for trails obscured by blowing snow or steep hills.

There have been technological improvements to equipment and food over the years that have contributed to improved performance by the teams.

The sleds, once big, bulky, weighty and built with wood are now sleek, lightweight and constructed with composites and aluminum, turning the team into one of the world's most efficient users of energy.

New harness designs have improved the way the dog pulls and new materials make them more comfortable to wear. Even the dog booties have changed so that they are easier on the feet, lightweight, quick dry and faster to put on or remove; a doggie shoehorn has been invented that eliminates the hassle of tugging at the material to get it over the paw.

Some mushers use ski poles to help the team power down the trail. A sit-down sled was invented by former Quest champion, Jeff King so the mushers themselves could be more rested.

High performance dry dog food has mostly replaced meat. In the early years of the Quest, just the amount of food required to complete the run between Dawson City and Pelly Crossing weighed almost 300 pounds (136 kilograms). Combined with all the other gear a sled could weigh 500 pounds (227 kilograms). Now the sled, food and equipment combined weigh just over 200 pounds.

In the early years of both the Iditarod and the Quest, mushers used to build fires to cook dog food. Today, alcohol stoves can do the job much faster and with less chance of the food getting burned. The mushers now carry their own food frozen in sealed plastic bags. They can drop the bag into the water being heated for the dogs. By the time the dogs have been fed, the musher also has a hot meal waiting to be eaten right out of the bag.

While the dogs eat over 10,000 calories per day, the musher also needs about 6,000. Many of them use junk food, potato chips, nuts and chocolate bars to provide quick energy. Sebastien Schnuelle eats gummy bears, "nobody ever got food poisoning from gummy bears." Kelley Griffin eats fruitcake because, if she puts enough alcohol in the recipe, it doesn't freeze even at minus 40. Others like to use the small energy gel packets favored by long distance runners.

Sugars and carbohydrates give quick energy boosts. It is fatty foods that provide endurance once the quick boost is over. Dan Kaduce loves pre-cooked bacon.

Thermoses of juice, either hot, cold or slushy, and electrolyte drinks like Gatorade and Powerade are the beverages of choice. Just as the dogs need to stay hydrated, it is equally important for the musher.

However, all the drivers realize that it's not who's driving the sled that will determine the team's performance, it's the dogs. Everyone has access to the modern equipment and foods, but not everyone can be a dog driver. If it was easy, everyone would be doing it. However, it is theoretically possible that every dog can be a sleddog.

One Alaskan musher, John Suter, ran a team of Standard Poodles in the Iditarod from 1989 to 1991. Not ideally suited to the northern climate they required a substantially higher level of maintenance to complete the race. They weren't competitive but he never expected they would be nor did he ask them to be. Their job was simply to prove it could be done.

"What I see that still gives me chills every time," former Quest head veterinarian Kathleen McGill said, "are dogs that have the strength, endurance and intelligence to run 1,000 miles and still cross the Finish line with their tails wagging, ready to lick their musher's face."

Ready to run.

Minnesota

Too much callaloo mek peppa-pot bitta.

Jamaican patois: Too much of a good thing can spoil everything.

April, 2006

One of the first things Rick realized when he and Nettie arrived in Jamaica to provide further training was that the program seemed to have stalled. Devon had his regular work responsibilities and had been away racing in Scotland and the United States for three of the past six months. Newton ran and took care of the dogs, but lacked the knowledge to provide any real guidance in the training program and still didn't understand what it was all about.

He didn't even know the proper commands for the team, so he just used the language he knew. Instead of "hike" to get the team started, he would say "G'wan." He didn't know the word "mush" even existed until he saw it on a T-shirt.

"It was difficult because we would get the dogs to a certain level, then we'd leave," said Rick, "but they wouldn't continue with it. For them it was a job and, to them, not a very good one at that. They didn't get (that) they had to keep working the dogs."

Newton was a natural-born dog man.

Diamond.

He also noticed the mocking Newton was receiving from the other employees at Chukka Caribbean. In their eyes, looking after dogs was a demeaning job. In Newton's eyes it was a demeaning job, but it was his job so he did it.

At one point during the winter, Devon asked Newton if he wanted to continue working with the dogs.

Newton recalled the fun he had when he drove the dogs for the first time. "I just keep on laughing. I can't believe it. The dogs are really pulling me." He saw tourists were taking pictures of the team and asking the guides what the dogs were for. He enjoyed being greeted each morning with unbounded affection. "Horses don't jump up on you to give you a kiss."

In particular he remembered a dream he had. Newton put a lot of stock in his dreams because, for him, they suggested possible futures. That night he dreamed the dogs were running really well. The next morning he hitched up three dogs and they started running on command and went where they were supposed to without anyone to run in front of them. "It was a dream come true."

Tallowa – a strong leader.

"Yeh Mon. I want to keep working with the dogs," he replied to Devon, so he stayed with the kennel and the other employees continued to tease.

When he walked past someone they would growl at him, bark or make dog noises in his direction. Newton never complained but Rick could see the teasing bothered him. He understood that Newton needed to view the dogs differently, as something more than just a job. One afternoon he stopped him in the kennel and pointed at the dogs.

"Newton, these dogs are going to take you places you've never imagined. These guys," indicating a couple of Chukka employees hanging around the back of the stables, "they're still going to be here sweeping stables. So ignore them. Give them a smile. Go take care of the dogs and you'll be fine.

Chillin' in the dogyard.

Chukka

Visitors to the JDT can go for a dog-powered scooter ride.

"I guarantee you, these little dogs down here will get you places you've never even dreamed of going. And you'll have somebody paying you to do it.

"So just keep looking ahead man. Do what we're doing now. Learn it. Follow it. Do it. You can do this. And the rest of these guys will be sitting here doing exactly what they're doing now…nothing. And going nowhere."

"You think so?"

"I know so."

The original plan had been to have Rick and Nettie at Chukka in Fall, 2005, but Hurricane Katrina postponed those plans when it trashed the U.S. Gulf Coast. The five-month delay meant that to get the program back on track they had to go back to basics with the dogs. Newton had to learn how to train the dogs because, when Rick and Nettie left and Devon was away, Chukka wouldn't have anyone else who could do it. Failure to accomplish this meant failure of the entire program.

"This is the experiment we've got to work with," said Rick. "We're going to have to do this because when we leave, they've got to have people in place that are trained and can continue on."

While Newton had his dream day with the perfect run, for the most part, the dogs themselves still had questions: "Why am I in this harness?" "Why am I tied to this line?" "Why is this dog beside me?" "What are they doing behind me?"

Shy and Doc in harness.

They pulled enthusiastically, but not all in the same direction. One of them, Diamond, was proving to be a challenge to educate. While the other dogs leaped in the air, barked and wagged their tails in anticipation of going for a run, Diamond would sit with an unhappy expression on his face. The only reason he eventually stood up was because the other dogs would relentlessly drag him forward – but even then he would dig in his feet and end up in an undignified pose, resembling a dog trying to take a bowel movement.

"It takes time," explained Nettie, "until they figure out they can do what you set them up to do. He (Diamond) is afraid he can't do it and he doesn't understand why he has to do it.

"It's not like a car. You can't just turn on the key and it goes. You've got to kiss it. You've got to hug it. You've got to love it. If you don't love them (the dogs) and you ask them to do things for you…they're not going to do them."

In the end Diamond never did make the cut. He started hanging around the stables, the riding area and near the gift shop where the tourists gathered to start their tours. He rolled over on his back to have his stomach scratched or dug a hole in the dirt and lay down to sleep. That's what Diamond did best – sleep.

Bruno, one of the original three, didn't ever lose his aggressive nature. He kept tangling with the other dogs, constantly striving to establish himself at the top of the canine food chain. Rick and Nettie started leaving him in the kennel and watched him.

"He didn't like it. He didn't like it one bit. I thought if I left him there it would either bend his nose out of shape or he would quit. He wanted to go. When he realized his behavior dictated whether he ran or not, he stopped fighting."

In the end it was Newton who brought him back to the team. He simply ignored Bruno's aggressive nature, walked him out of the kennel and hitched him up.

Nettie couldn't believe her eyes when she saw them together. "Here he was, with his dog that just scared the bejezuz out of everyone else, walking him on a leash like he was just another dog."

Bruno started watching Newton, like a sleddog watching his or her musher, and responding to his commands. One morning when Newton was running Bruno as a single dog in front of the scooter, the scooter tire snagged on a tree root and tipped him into the mud. Bruno ran for a minute with the scooter banging along behind him, and then realized he wasn't pulling any weight. He turned around, came back to Newton and used his head to nudge him back to the scooter.

"He pulled me straight up. It was very nice. When Bruno was ready to go, he was going." He turned into the team's strongest leader until he died in 2007 in an accident in Kingston, breaking his back when he fell from the back of a moving truck, while being transported to a tourism show in the capital city.

"Newton has a natural ability with the dogs that very few people have," Rick just shook his head in amazement.

As the older dogs gained experience, Rick and Nettie started adding new recruits from the JSPCA. They found Benji, the brindle hound, who looked the part of a classic sleddog. When they put him in the middle of a team of experienced dogs, he twisted sideways and then tried to run across the gangline. The other dogs just watched him with disgusted looks. Eventually they got him straightened out.

They found another small, but tough leader in Tallowa – a dog with "roots (hardworking, genuine, principled)."

While at the JSPCA Rick spotted two puppies he liked. "Look at these," he said to Devon. "It'll be a benefit to bring some young dogs up. They'll play and whole idea is to have fun." Doc and Chance became the Junior Dogsled Team.

It wasn't just dogs they added. Early on they realized another person was needed at the kennel. That's when the teasing from the other employees stopped.

The JDT comes together: (L to R) Damion Robb, Devon and Newton.

"Once the program got started, other guys wanted to join. You could tell just by talking to them that they looked at it as a ticket to ride," said Rick. One girl told them she couldn't shovel dog poop or ride the scooter because she had a bad back.

"Then why are you here?" asked Rick.

She shrugged.

One of the bartenders, Doc, approached Rick, "Are you going to bring anyone into the dog thing?"

"Actually we're looking for someone because Newton is coming up to Minnesota to do some training and a race or two. We need somebody else to look after the kennel."

"I have someone, my nephew, that will do it."

"If we bring this kid in," Rick looked hard at Doc to ensure he understood, "he's got to toe the mark. There is no fooling around. If we see he's not going to do it he's out of here. But if he's interested…you talk to him. You tell him. Then bring him around to talk to Devon and we'll see how it's going to work."

A couple of days later Damion Robb turned up and joined the Jamaica Dogsled Team.

"I could see right away that Robb could turn his charm on and off," Rick said. "He turned it on for the tourists and for the cameras. And he does a good job of it…which is his job."

Time was running short before Rick, Nettie and Newton would be heading to Minnesota, so Robb was introduced quickly into the training regime. When he found out the training took place early in the morning, he told Newton he would be around later in the day and run his dogs then.

"It doesn't work like that," Newton responded. "We train the dogs when it's cool."

His first day on the job, a couple of the dogs started fighting after they had been hitched up to the gangline for a run. Newton held the sled while Robb went to break up the melee. One of the dogs turned and nipped Robb in the groin. He jumped back, straight into a barbed wire fence, and the barbs drove him forward again, right back into the middle of the fight – frightening the dogs so badly that they stopped fighting.

Robb didn't stop there. He stood up quickly and headed down the trail toward the stables, looking for a ride to the hospital. It wasn't a bad bite and he was back with the dogs an hour later.

Newton wasn't of much help to his new workmate. He was laughing too hard.

The dogsled team came as a bit of a surprise for Chukka's neighbors. One afternoon, a man walking down the road on the east side of the Polo field was suddenly confronted by what he believed to be a pack of dogs charging down the road in front of him. When most Jamaicans see a pack of dogs coming toward them, they usually try to get out of the way.

He jumped off the road, over the fence and started running across the Polo field. Reaching an almond tree, he climbed rapidly into the branches and bumped his head directly into a wasp nest. The wasps acted predictably, attacking viciously. He dropped back to the ground as Robb and Newton, on the sled, swept past him staring in astonishment.

When Newton saw him later, with his head swollen from the wasp stings, he asked him why he climbed into the tree.

"A whole heap dogs coming at me! What do you expect?"

When the dogsled tour opened in April, 2007, Robb learned on the very first paid trip not to include new dogs in the team without more training. Pulling Lisa and Fred Garder from Charlottesville, Virginia, in the large sled behind a six-dog team, the team did well for the first part of the loop. When they hit the final stretch up the west side of the Polo field there was a goat tethered by the horse stables.

Cove, who was the last dog to be adopted from the JSPCA before the tours officially started, was running near the middle of the team. She saw the goat and decided to go after it, pulling the rest of the team to the left.

"She was so strong," Robb noticed he was losing control, "the rest of the team realized they couldn't pull her back, so they seemed to agree, 'Okay Cove, whatever you say….' They stopped running, looked at the goat and the whole team started chasing the goat."

When they reached the goat, the team hesitated, not sure what to do now that they had caught their prey. Fred and Lisa jumped out of the sled and helped Robb hold the dogs back. Daniel Melville Jr. also turned up and waded in to help.

"The guests were holding dogs," chuckled Robb. "We were holding dogs trying to get everything untangled. Mr. Melville was holding Cove and all I could hear was Mr. Melville saying, 'Okay. Someone's got to take this one from me. I can't manage this one.' Cove was still trying to get to the goat.

"I'm so glad the guests were so relaxed. It was like an adventure – not just for them but for me also. They sent me a T-shirt later with a picture on it of them in the sled and me behind them with 'Can Charlie come out to play?' written on it."

Charlie was the name of the goat.

When Robb and Daniel Melville Jr. apologized for the detour, Lisa and Fred laughed. "Don't worry about it. This was the best adventure we've had on our vacation."

The decision to send Newton to Minnesota wasn't part of the original plan. It was something that Rick thought of during a talk with Danny. Other than the dogs at Chukka, and a few films on mushing so he would know what a dogsled team should look like, Newton had never seen a dog team in action.

"I have Newton training dogs," Rick said, "but we think he needs to learn what a working team can actually do. He's never seen a racing team. Until he can see that, he really has nothing to draw on. He needs to know the possibilities of what he can do with the team."

Danny, having seen how Devon benefited from his experience in Scotland and Minnesota, agreed.

"Devon was still the musher," said Danny, "but we needed him at Chukka. Newton went to Minnesota mostly for the film (*Sun Dogs*). He would learn dog mushing from Rick and Annette and the film crew would take advantage of that."

"We're going to bring you up to the snow and show you how to run them (dogs) as a team on snow," Rick explained to Newton when he told him he was going to Minnesota. "Think that'll be okay?"

"That'll be okay," grinned Newton, and then he hesitated. "Snow. I don't know about snow. I'll just wait for that to come."

A couple of weeks later he encountered bureaucratic incredulity. When applying for his passport the government official referred to him as a tour guide. "I'm a dogsled musher," Newton corrected him.

"A dogsled musher?!" the official laughed, "Oh that's very good. So you are the one who will represent Jamaica on the next dogsled mush?"

"Yeh Mon."

"That's good. We'll see you internationally then."

When he left Chukka he went to say good-bye to Devon.

"All the best," said Devon, giving him a big hug. "Enjoy and try to make the best of it. And may you cool down and freeze your balls off."

Newton's previous experience with flying was riding in a small plane from a glider school he had once worked at. He had been flown from the field to Runaway Bay and back. He also had a couple of short rides in the glider itself and one helicopter trip from the field to St. Ann's Bay.

"Being up in the air and being able to see so far. Everything was so different." Newton was awed, " The first time the plane took off, it was going through the clouds. It was shaking and I couldn't see anything. I thought the plane was catching afire because the clouds looked like smoke.

"Coming out of the airport in the parking lot (in Minnesota), it was cold like hell. I was trying to get on more clothes. And they're giving me coats and hats. Oh God, it was cold! It was a burning cold. It was piercing. The cold kept poking me and poking me."

When he saw snow for the first time he just stared at it. "This is snow," he thought, white stuff falling from God. "You see it on TV."

"I tried to pack it together. I was happy. I was smiling all the time. It was really good." His first day in Minnesota, he made snow angels, threw snowballs and ran the dogs. The documentary crew filmed everything. They had to. It was springtime. The snow was melting rapidly. The next day, it was gone.

Rick showed him a dogsled built to run on snow.

"I've never seen a sled for snow before," said Newton as he balanced on the runners and rocked back and forth.

"We'll give you a three-dog team first," explained Rick. "If you survive that we'll have you on a four-dog team and see how you do."

His first sled ride on snow stunned him. "They (the dogs) were jumping for it. I couldn't believe it. I couldn't believe the dogs were just ready to pull...right now!"

"When you go across some of those bare spots you're going to feel the sled pull a little," said Rick. "Don't panic. It's got plastic runners on so it's meant to slide across stuff. It's just not going to slide on the dirt as it does on the snow."

"Okay," Newton nodded, "you're scaring me now."

Then the team started to run. "Oh my God! It was crazy. They just wanted to go. They just wanted to run!" Before he returned to Jamaica, he had progressed enough to drive an ATV behind a 12-dog team. "I thought I was going to fly. So amazing to see dogs move that fast!"

Rick taught him how to build a gangline. Nettie introduced him to a diet of American gourmet food and Fig Newton cookies. When he wasn't training they took him to see some of the sights. The size of everything, even the local hardware store, overwhelmed him. He rode on a rollercoaster in the Mall of America – one of the world's largest shopping malls.

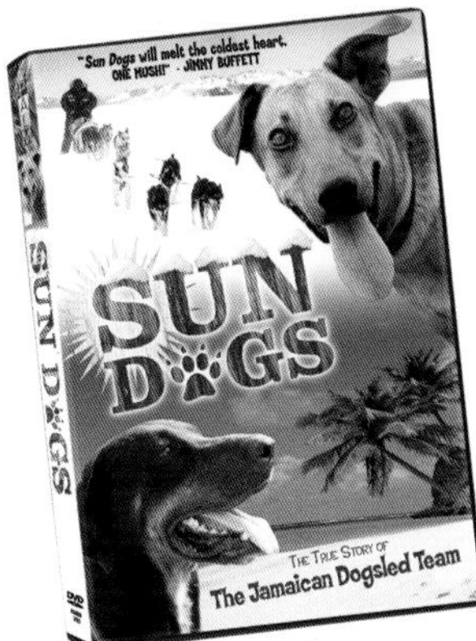

Through everything he was the focus of attention for the film crew. It opened a world of experience for him, but presented a dilemma for those around him. Newton had no idea how to deal with all the attention and potential fame from being a central figure in the film.

"When they started making the movie, you could see some changes in Newton," Devon is still disappointed he didn't see it coming. "Not with the way he worked with the dogs. But with his personality. He started to act like he should be the center of attention. He started to treat people differently. He started to act like he was owed something.

"There were some positive changes. He started to have more light – 'I'm part of the world now!'

"But he started to lose respect for people. In Jamaica, people always address people as Mr. Oswald, Mr. Anderson, Mr. Melville, or Mrs. Melville. But he stopped doing that and would address people by their first name. No respect."

Newton in the dog's tent set up in Dawson City for their 36-hour layover.

Newton's Schedule

Dawson City, Yukon to Eagle, Alaska

165 miles, 43.5 hours

When Europeans arrived in the interior of Yukon and Alaska in the mid-1800s, they were looking for the same thing Europeans were looking for when they first arrived on the shores of Jamaica.

Gold.

The earliest Caribbean conquerors from Europe, the Spanish, never found the gold they sought in Jamaica because they didn't understand that gold wasn't just a valuable metal. Jamaica's gold was the capacity of the land to grow just about anything that could be grown, especially sugar cane, a large part of the British economy in the 18th and 19th centuries.

In the far northwestern corner of the North American continent, however, where not much at all could be grown because of the severe winters and barren soil, Europeans of English, Scottish or Russian origins did find what they were looking for.

The first major coarse gold discovery in the Yukon River watershed was on the Fortymile River in 1886, near what eventually became the border of the United States and Canada. Coarse gold was the prospectors' goal and the find established the area as a major mining district.

According to the *Dawson City News,* evidence was discovered in 1907 suggesting that Russians mined for gold in the Klondike Valley as early as the 1830s. According to the *City News* just as the British used slaves to finance their empire with Jamaican sugar, "the bones of a couple of men were found past a cave-in which had evidently imprisoned them beyond all rescue…on their legs there still clung the heavy manacles with which Russia in the old days hobbled their political prisoners."

However, what brought one of the world's most isolated regions to world attention was the discovery of gold on Rabbit Creek, later renamed Bonanza Creek, on August 17, 1896. The mountain from which Newton was descending with his dog team was named after the mythical lost gold mines of King Solomon in Africa, because from it radiated six of the richest gold-bearing creeks ever found on earth. It wasn't the world's biggest gold field or its wealthiest, but the find in the Klondike River Valley was possibly the best-timed discovery in world history.

In 1896 the United States, along with most of the industrial world, was in the throes of a four-year depression that showed no signs of easing. Unemployment ran rampant. People wandered aimlessly in search of anything that might suggest the possibility of a future. Almost a third of the population lived in shantytowns – temporary way camps for homeless vagabonds. Governments fell because they had no answers and major corporations, once the dominant force in their particular industries, vanished without so much as a whimper.

Then came the siren call: "Gold. There's gold in the Klondike." Rumor had it that the gold was just lying on the ground for the picking! The stampede was worldwide. It is estimated that over a million people started the journey to the gold fields. The very fact that it gave people hope and created opportunity woke up stagnant economies, which began a quick recovery. By 1900 the depression was over and the United States, one of the first nations to benefit from the renewed activity, was on the verge of becoming the dominant economic power in the world.

One hundred thousand made the trip to the Klondike. Some got as close as the Alaska panhandle but only 40,000 actually arrived in Dawson City – the instant city that grew up in a swamp at the junction of the Klondike and Yukon Rivers.

Rich men. Poor men. Hungry men. Brave men. The disillusioned and lost. They saw new riches, a new challenge, a new meaning to life hidden in the icy gulches. In its own way, Dawson City was a destiny for Newton, not just a destination.

At its peak Dawson City, the "Paris of the North," was the largest city in North America north of San Francisco, California, and west of Winnipeg, Manitoba. By 1902, gold finds further west in Fairbanks and Nome had lured the gold seekers to Alaska. What remains today is a monument to its former glory. The government of Canada realized the importance of preserving history and started restoring buildings in the 1960s. Gold mining still forms the backbone of the community as the Klondike, worked over several times since Discovery, continues to produce the noble metal.

As Newton's team climbed up the short incline that brought him to the top of the dyke protecting the town from the River's floodwaters in the spring, he thought he was doing just fine.

The dogs were healthy and he was almost halfway to Fairbanks. There was an early morning ruddy glow strengthening in the southeast sky. Danny had always insisted the goal was to finish and Newton had not lost sight of the goal. Reaching the Finish line, he felt, was something he would be able to do, "No problem Mon."

Being behind schedule didn't bother him too much. After Braeburn, he was told by Hans to slow down so he wouldn't burn out the team. When he told Rick he wanted to take a long stop at Pelly, Rick encouraged him to do so.

He was feeling pretty good when he sank the snowhook at the Dawson checkpoint. Busy talking with the checkers and race officials, he heard the spectators clap and cheer and didn't notice the unusual silence from his own crew. Danny and Carole, relieved to see him emerge from the darkness, gave him big hugs. So did Rick and Nettie.

Susie rode the runners with him to the dogyard. Only Newton and Susie know what was said on the way across the river, but his mood had dampened significantly by the time they reached the dogyard.

The conversation continued as they unhooked the dogs and led them to their straw beds under a blue tarp where they would spend most of the next 36 hours. "You have a top-ten team. You're 13 hours behind your schedule. You spent nine hours in Pelly and seven in Stepping Stone. You shouldn't be in 20th place," lectured Susie.

"Rick said I should get some rest in Pelly," he responded.

"Rick said that?"

"Yeh Mon."

Earlier Hans had ripped into an accredited journalist following the race, accusing him of preventing Newton from getting sleep in the checkpoints. "I was told that you were talking to him while he was trying to get some sleep. I don't want you to talk to him at all for the rest of the race!"

He later apologized when the allegation turned out not to be true.

The outburst shed light on how intensely he believed that if Newton failed, he failed. Failure was not in Hans' vocabulary. "When I start something, I usually finish it." It also illustrated how much Newton's race was interfering with his own. A veteran champion with a reputation for being totally focused couldn't keep his mind off a team of dogs almost a day behind him and it was frustrating him. "At this rate he won't even make Fairbanks before the banquet," Hans said.

The afternoon before, while Newton was starting to cross the Indian River Valley, Susie told Hans not to talk to Newton about his frustration. It would, she said, turn into an argument from which no winners would emerge. She would deliver the message to Newton. She chose to talk to him in confidence, while they were alone on the sled crossing the river.

With the dogs unhitched, bedded down and his handlers now looking after them, Newton walked away from the tent.

"I thought the whole purpose of this was to just finish," he said. "I didn't think it was important to be so competitive," his shoulders sagged noticeably as he looked dejectedly at the Yukon River. "They keep changing things on me."

Later, in his hotel room, he repeated the words, his voice cracking.

"Have something to eat. Get some sleep," he was advised. "You can work this out with Danny tonight." However, when the door closed and he lay alone in the dark, sleep didn't come easy.

"I ask myself, 'What am I doing here?' I don't really want to finish this. I don't even want to be here. I just wanted to quit and go home. I felt like telling Susie, 'I don't need to take this stuff from you. I'm running this race for Mr. Melville....Not you!' "

However, as Newton finally dozed off, even Danny had gotten caught up in the competitive drive and probably wouldn't have been sympathetic to his feelings.

"He could be doing better," Danny insisted. Carole kept her counsel to herself. Yet when someone mentioned that the goal had been changed for Newton without him knowing it, she nodded in silent agreement.

While Newton slept greater changes happened in his support team. Susie, citing her knowledge of the dogs and being in better health than Rick and Nettie, fired them as Newton's handlers. She and Moira, to Moira's surprise, were replacing them.

The firing was apparently done in a confrontational manner and, according to Rick, part of the reason was the advice he gave Newton about taking a long rest in Pelly. While unhappy with the manner in which it was carried out, he and Nettie also conceded that the change was probably good for Newton.

"We never intended to be his handlers, man!" said Rick. "We were actually surprised to be asked. We have no experience with a race like this. We're not young and we can't do some of the heavy lifting any more. And when it came to setting the camp up here in Dawson we weren't sure exactly how to do it. We were constantly second-guessing ourselves. So I guess this is good for Newton but I feel it was handled very poorly by Susie, Hans and Danny."

Nettie was not quite so understanding. She was just flat out angry. "We may not have been the best people for this job, and we knew we weren't. But we did the best we could. Nobody should be spoken to and treated like that."

They did follow the rest of the race, going to Fairbanks to watch Newton finish. But when it ended so did any relationship between them and most people involved in the JDT. The only person they would stay in touch with in the future was Newton himself.

Handlers have a unique role in the Yukon Quest. For most of it, they are simply cheerleaders, standing on the outside, required by rules to be hands-off and not permitted to assist the musher in any way. Only when their team finally leaves the checkpoint does the handler go into action, cleaning up the straw and dog poop left behind.

The exception is Dawson City. Here, for 36 hours, they become the primary caregivers for the dogs while the musher takes the opportunity to catch up on sleep, consume extra calories for the cold days still ahead, study the trail maps and work with the vets to ensure the dogs are being taken care of. Handlers are not necessarily retired dog mushers like Rick and Nettie. Some are spouses, relatives, children, college professors, electricians, writers, plumbers, schoolteachers, military personnel, merchant marines or young world travelers just looking for an experience. Without exception, they all have a love for dogs and every one of them would do the thankless job again.

Like all checkpoints, Dawson City is all about time management – looking after the dogs and reorganizing. The handlers construct the dog hotel, a large blue tent, protected from the wind and snow with dog beds made of straw. A chain runs up the center and the dogs are tethered to it so they don't wander off by themselves.

Even with the chains and the watchful eyes of the handler the dogs can sometimes find their way out of the tent. While Newton rested, his lead dog managed to slip his collar and started meandering down the road toward the ice bridge across the river to downtown Dawson. One of Yuka Honda's handlers noticed him, caught him and escorted him back to the tent where he clipped him back into place.

Every few hours, the dogs are fed. Then walked, medicated and massaged. Like Olympic athletes, dogs are randomly tested for illegal performance-enhancing substances or drugs that mask pain. When not looking after dogs, the handlers are repairing damaged sleds, doing laundry, sewing, and repacking bags for the musher.

Susie, now the official handler, looked over the dogs. "They look great," she concluded. "Their feet are good with one exception and he's always had sensitive feet. Everything is good. A 36-hour break should resolve any small issues."

Former Quest champion Frank Turner, seeing the team as it arrived in Dawson, was impressed with the dog care. "That team looks in great shape. He'll make up some good ground in the second half."

A few hours later Hans unexpectedly withdrew from the Yukon Quest. His dogs were fine. "I probably have the best-looking dog team here in Dawson I've ever had." Poised to potentially win his fourth title, the musher himself was off his game. He might be able to shake his competitors, but he couldn't shake Newton.

The reason he stated for scratching was that his team was healthy and strong now and he wanted to prepare them for the Iditarod, but that logic escaped most of the officials and other mushers. Race Marshall Doug Grilliot was surprised by the withdrawal, stating he had never heard of anyone scratching because their team looked too good to carry on.

Brent Sass was confused, "I understand he has priorities but I would never do it."

Newton's race was obviously an unspoken factor in Hans' decision to scratch and the second half of Hans' press conference dealt with Newton. "Everybody is very smooth trotting. He has 12 good-looking dogs. It's what you'd expect. They have more rest than they ever had in a race before. He's been talking to people in checkpoints and just getting a lot of distractions and not following his plan. He's over-resting big time," Hans added.

That night Danny and Carole hosted a dinner for everyone in a house they were renting. Newton was already there when Hans arrived. After they both had a bite to eat, Hans took Newton out to the front porch, away from the crowd. There was no confrontation. His decision about scratching having been made, Hans simply moved to the next issue on his agenda – getting Newton to the Finish line.

"They had the trail briefing today," Hans set up a hand-drawn map of the trail between Dawson and Eagle, "so I'm going to fill you in on what you can expect."

The trail to Forty Mile Newton had already run the previous year in another race, the Percy DeWolfe. It follows the Yukon River for 50 miles. There were few surprises along the way, a little overflow about 10 miles out of Dawson but the trail breakers had simply opened a route around it. Since he would be reaching it at night, Hans advised, he should keep a close eye on the trail markers because, if he missed them, he would get very wet.

The Fortymile River, which Newton had never traveled before, is a narrow, winding stream with high steep rock walls on both sides. It would be dark in the canyon. Even on a clear day the sun can't penetrate the dark recesses of the trail. Then there's a short steep climb, which takes teams to the Taylor Highway, a summer-only road that crosses American Summit.

There he would find a tent with wood for a fire. Once on the highway, he was to follow it up to the summit, traverse for about five miles across the exposed slope, then descend to Eagle. American Summit is possibly the most underrated mountain on the Quest. On a nice day, the beauty of the area can take your breath away. On a bad day, the winds could suck the life right out of you.

If a storm hits while a team is crossing, there is nowhere to take shelter. A team caught in a blizzard, screaming out of the north and blasting a swirling murk of grey snow and ice crystals into their faces, must somehow keep moving forward – or die trying. In previous races, teams had to group up and help each other across because a team on its own wouldn't have made it.

There are rolling hills on the summit, described Hans, and a tremendous amount of "side hilling," where the trail traverses across hard-packed slopes formed by drifting snow or glaciation. It takes strength and finesse to stand on the uphill sled runner and hold the sled level so it doesn't skid down

"It was the first time I knew he cared." Hans Gatt and Newton.

the slope sideways, pulling the dogs with it. At times, a musher can reach left and touch the snow without bending down, while the right side is a sheer drop to the bottom. Looking down a musher would see a broad trench between the mountains and a slope that could carry musher, sled and dogs potentially hundreds of feet to the bottom of it.

Newton sat quietly, absorbing the information, but his heart wasn't in it. He still intended to talk to Danny. It was a couple of hours after the trail briefing, when the evening was drawing to a close, that Hans pulled Newton aside once again.

Newton was shocked to see tears running down the Austrian's cheeks.

"Newton, you have to finish this race," he said. "Scratching is not an option."

"The way he said it," Newton recalled, "I felt like I wanted to do this. I never really knew Hans cared until Dawson when he started to cry. Up until then he was very hard. He had a point. Sometimes he made it too much. Wasn't too calm. But I guess he needed to be hard to make me a dog musher.

"For me right now, it's past and gone. I'm really glad I get the opportunity. Now I understand why he was hard. He wanted me to do good. But I never knew he cared that much until Dawson."

At that point Newton understood he didn't need to straighten anything out with Danny. Whatever issues he may have had with Susie and Hans could be dealt with later. He knew what he had to do and, although he wasn't privy to each individual's motivation, realized for the first time how emotionally involved everyone was with his Quest.

He may have been the one standing on the sled runners but the various dreams, aspirations and reputations of others rode on his shoulders. Everything depended upon him reaching the Finish line and doing so in a manner that would turn heads.

All around Dawson other mushers were getting ready to get started again. Sebastien Schnuelle had gotten a bad taste in his mouth when he arrived in Dawson. His handler had instructions to have something ready for him to drink and tossed him a bottle of Gatorade when he pulled into the checkpoint.

"I was all happy I got something. I looked at it and it looked okay so I opened it and took a big gulp....I keep fish oil for my dogs in Gatorade bottles ...," Sebastien was doing the math. "I really wasn't racing until I got to Dawson. When I realized how fast we were going I began to realize I had a chance to win."

Jon Little was more worried than he wanted to show. His strategy hadn't worked the way he had hoped. "I tried to do a few things to set myself apart from the crowd. But I didn't lose the crowd and when I left Dawson I was pretty worried."

He also had a few dogs suffering from diarrhea. "I'm going to have to take it easy. If someone wants to run a hard race I'm going to have to let them go," said John.

Hugh Neff wasn't thinking about the trail ahead of him at all. "I love Dawson. It's part of my heart and soul. I was here a hundred years ago." He and William Kleedehn spent part of their rest time having a couple of beer in the "Snake Pit," the bar at the Westminster Hotel.

Mark Sleightholme was concerned about the jumble ice he had been warned was all the way down the Yukon River. "Okay," he thought, "I've had the good trail and the good weather. Now I've got bad ice to look forward to."

A few hours before his departure time, Newton rediscovered the machete he found on Eureka Dome. "I like the cutlass for chopping fire wood," he laughed while demonstrating his skills on firewood in the campground and a willow bush on the side of the road. He left the machete behind when finally leaving. There was an international boundary ahead of him and he didn't think it would get through U.S. Customs.

Working with Susie and Hans to hook up the dogs, he suddenly realized that something was different. "Where are Rick and Nettie?" he asked.

"They're not handling anymore," responded Susie, "I am."

Newton stood silently surprised for a moment then continued with his preparations. He wasn't sure he liked the change but there was nothing he could do about it.

When it was time to go the team slipped silently down the snow-covered road then through a small gap in the brush onto the Yukon River. He heard

The "General Store" at Forty Mile.

a last faint cheer behind him as he headed up the empty frozen river and then human voices gave way to the eerie silence and flat monotony of bluish snow that is the northern night.

The run to Forty Mile was relatively easy. He found the trail around the overflow, then another around a second overflow that had occurred since the trail briefing. There was no glare ice and the rough ice he had been warned about was buried under a fresh layer of snow.

When he pulled up in front of the lone occupied cabin at Forty Mile he was now ahead of his second-half schedule. The dogs were running well.

There were several cabins at Forty Mile, but only one suitable for habitation. The exterior of others had been restored to preserve their historical value but the cabin marked "General Store" and adorned by a set of moose horns was where you would find people, along with warm water for the dogs and hot food for the musher. It has a door with no handles, just thick pieces of rope, knotted at each end and threaded through a hole. Pulling on the rope opened and closed the door.

The town site was a First Nation fishing camp before gold was discovered in 1886. Overnight the fish camp disappeared and by 1893, was a settlement of several hundred providing supplies for thousands of prospectors and gold miners in the district. Forty Mile was in turn abandoned almost overnight after George Carmack, one of the three men who found gold on Rabbit Creek on August 17, 1896, arrived in town to file their claims and buy a round for everyone in the saloon with a shotgun shell full of gold.

Newton decided to cut his scheduled rest time because the dogs were up and ready to go after a short nap. He would soon appreciate the warmth of the cabin he left behind.

The cold hadn't broken since the race started, with temperatures still hovering near -30°C. In the shadows cloaking the Fortymile River the cold deepened, approaching -40°C. Thoroughly miserable, the slog towards the American border was more of a demand on his mind than it was on his legs. The frozen air seemed to get heavier, weighing everything down.

When they stopped he would warm his hands by putting them into the pits under the dogs' legs – the warmest parts of their bodies. "You take care of your dogs. They take care of you," Newton said.

He noticed a pie plate on a stake beside the trail. *Alaska. 100 yards* it read. Further on there was a Canadian flag on one side of the trail and an Alaskan flag on the other.

Martin Buser had earlier noted the boundary marker with amusement, "I felt like I was entering the country of Alaska."

Finally the last steep incline off the river, up the escarpment, out of the extreme cold and into the merely cold, cresting the top, next to the tent with its fire. He rested, according to schedule, thawing himself out, and then set off across the top of the mountain. It was a perfect morning for a crossing. The wind stayed calm and all the elemental hazards potentially awaiting him remained passive. Only the side hills, several of which were dangerously icy and threatened to tumble the sled on more than one occasion, and the continuously rolling hills wore on him. Slithering, sliding, bucking and jerking, the team chewed its way across the wind swept terrain. His legs and arms burned with the effort of keeping the sled upright.

"It's a bastard trying to get those dogs over the hills," Newton said. "It's not fun."

An hour ahead of him, Colleen Robertia and Mark Sleightholme were traveling close together. Mark was in the lead with Colleen following his progress by watching his headlamp. She saw the light hesitate, then slip precipitously off to the left and come to a sudden stop. Then it started moving again and stopped.

As she approached she heard Mark call to her, "You might keep to the right here. There's a bit of ice."

When Newton started dropping off the summit, he had no idea how far he had traveled on the featureless landscape. It could have been five miles or 15, he didn't know. The road he was following entered the trees, starting to level off and now his muscles, after continuous hours of stress, could relax, aching from this simple effort.

The night before, Alaskan Dan Kaduce, driving his team in ninth place, took his attention off the dogs for a moment to adjust his gloves. "All of a sudden the dogs smelled or saw something and gave a big 15-mile an hour jerk and took me off the back (of the sled)." He regained his feet and started chasing the sled.

"They did that thing where they run just the exact same speed as you, to let you think you can catch the sled, but then right when you're running out of energy they just seem to keep it out of your reach." Kaduce stopped running and turned off his headlamp. The team, no longer seeing their musher behind them, stopped. He walked up, stepped on the runners, and the dogs started off again.

Newton sang to his dogs as they trundled through the woods. Dropping into the trees gave a psychological lift to the mushers. They felt less vulnerable. The exposed mountaintops and rivers provided very little shelter from the wind and cold. In the trees, it seemed warmer. There was shelter from the wind and firewood, in case added heat was required.

He wasn't the only singer on the trail. Normand Casavant also serenaded his team through the forest. "I sing to them a lot of songs. Canadian-French folk songs you know, so they really love that." His team also chased a moose down the trail for a mile or so.

Newton had no such encounter. The dogs trotted comfortably and finally the lights of Eagle shone through the darkness.

Newton, Miss Shelley, and Newton's sister, Ashley.

Miss Shelley

I think she's an angel. She'll want wings.

Newton Marshall

"The problem in Jamaica is not the people," says teacher, writer and philosopher Bertram Arnold, better known by his nickname "Scree." (Everybody in Jamaica has a nickname.) "The problem is mismanagement. The system is broken.

"We've done nothing about education since 1962. Jamaica wasn't ready for independence and the downhill trend started on the day of independence. It's taken this long to get where we are today, but it started in 1962."

Statistics and experience have shown that an educated workforce leads to a stronger economy. Workers with more training and education tend to make more money and have lower unemployment rates. Danny recognized the problem a number of years ago. "I think we've finally realized what we have done over the past 40 or 50 years in education is abominable. We need this to be a revolution in education, not just a change.

"Go into the street and meet some of the Jamaicans. They are smart people. Very smart people, but a lot of them never had the opportunity. Like

Newton didn't. He never had the opportunity and there are so many leaving the system who cannot read or write.

"We need to educate them," reiterated Danny. "It doesn't have to be rocket science. Right now the hardest thing is finding a good tradesman. Carpenters. Plumbers. It's all education. It is vital to our operation to have people who are dedicated and educated so they can grow with the company. They can improve their skills and go from being a guide, to the office, to supervisor, to manager. We are growing all the time. We need people who are educated."

"As much as there's an economic gap (the rich and the poor), there's an educational gap (the educated and the uneducated)," said Shelley Kennedy. I think we're dealing with illiteracy that goes back generations, especially when you get back into the hills." A former special needs teacher from Michigan in the United States, she instructs classes for adult employees of Chukka Caribbean, like Newton, who want to learn how to read and write.

Only one quarter of all Jamaican students graduate from Sixth Form, the British equivalent of Grade 11 and 12 in North American schools. Many graduates still can't read or write beyond a primary school level. The result is social dysfunction and economic distress that reaches deep into the Jamaican culture.

"There's no value placed on education in a lot of the poor families and neighborhoods. The older generations had no use for it and since it's grandmothers raising grandchildren, they're teaching the children today there's no value in an education," said Shelley.

"There are some top schools here (in Jamaica) but there are also a lot of 'bottom of the barrel' schools – and even they are not available to everybody.

"It takes a lot of money. You can't go to school for free in Jamaica. A family has to pay for uniforms, books, lunch and transportation. At the end of the day, the cost of sending one child to school equals the amount of money you can earn at work that day. If you have more than one child, you have to choose which one goes to school," said Shelley. For some families who do place value on education, both parents work seven days a week, at three or four different jobs, to earn the necessary money.

All students who haven't dropped out of school before turning 12 years of age have to write a test – The Grade Six Achievement Test – that will determine their future in education. "If you do really well on the test, but don't have any money, the government will pay to send you to a good school," said Shelley. "If you have money and do well, you'll obviously go to a good

Barb Thomson and Miss Shelley teaching at Chukka.

school. If you have money and do poorly, you'll still go to a good school. If you don't do well and don't have money, you're pretty much through right there."

Test scores can condemn a child to a low educational track, convincing them they aren't bright and damaging self-esteem. They begin not to care and learn to live with a low ceiling of expectations: "Me one can't do nothing!" Their teachers begin to believe the children will never rise above a certain level and fail to make any effort to enable them to try.

"Our social problems come back to the classroom experience," said Althea Laing, a teacher, mother and grandmother in Mandeville, a city in the southern mountain ranges of the island. "In the general school system there are still teachers who speak into children's lives so much negativity that they fail. We, as teachers, write off students too early. For you to get results, you have to be passionate about children. I drew on my skills in personal development to empower my students and to build their self-esteem. When children believe in themselves, you can get them to do almost anything you want them to do."

Schools are underfunded. Teachers are poorly paid and there aren't enough of them. Educational materials are outdated, worn out or there just isn't sufficient to go around.

"There's not a lot of money and there's a lot of kids," Shelley explained, "huge class sizes. Teachers who don't have a lot of help and a lot of material. There are so many fabulous learning aids out there and they don't have any of them.

"You could have 60 kids in each classroom and you might have one teacher trying to teach her class, and the class across the hall because that teacher didn't turn up today for whatever reason."

Until now the system has continued to fail because…for most Jamaicans that's the system. It can't change so "it doesn't make sense troubling it."

In the late 1990s Danny had an idea for Chukka Caribbean Adventures. So many of his employees were illiterate and that limited both their potential and his. He wanted to provide in-house adult literacy education but wasn't sure about how to go about doing it.

It sat on the periphery of his mind until a dinner party at his villa in 2002 for the BC Polo Club where he indulged in some horse lesson bartering with his new neighbor, Brian Kennedy, a former civil law attorney from Bay City, near Detroit, Michigan.

Brian and Shelley Kennedy had been traveling to Negril, Jamaica, for Christmas each year since 1979. "It was a nice getaway. A honeymoon. It was like going to camp. You didn't need to think about anything." After 15 years they reached the point where the staff would line up to greet them when they arrived and line up again to say good-bye when they left.

Over breakfast one morning Shelley glanced up at Brian, "I think this would be a great place to retire."

Brian wasn't terribly interested, "Yeah maybe. I don't know. I can't imagine I'm ever going to retire."

He had been practicing law for 26 years, starting out as a district attorney prosecuting career offender and multiple homicide cases. After four years he switched to private practice in criminal defense "because that's what I knew." Eventually he made the transition into civil litigation. He loved the law and the idea of not working with it just didn't seem feasible.

But he indulged Shelley's suggestion. They looked at property around Negril, but it was "too rural." On one trip they decided to visit a former colleague of Shelley's, Barb Thomson, who had retired to Runaway Bay. When she heard they were looking for property, she introduced them to a woman who had four acres for sale, right on the ocean in a place called Chukka Cove. For a decade, they did nothing with it until Brian's father died in 2001 and they started to reevaluate their lives.

"That caused me to realize I probably wasn't going to be immortal either," said Brian. "I had done it all. Prosecuted criminal cases. Defended criminal cases. Won multi-million dollar verdicts. Lost multi-million dollar verdicts."

"I didn't have to work. When you reach the point where you don't have to work, you have the freedom of choosing what you want to do rather than having to keep your shoulders in the traces every day.

"I'm a baseball fan. My boyhood hero was Al Kaline (a former player for the Detroit Tigers who played from 1953 to 1974 and was inducted into baseball's Hall of Fame in 1980). Al left the game when he could still hit the ball. He got out while he was still able to play. And that's what I wanted to do. I had a couple of my best years ever and that's why nobody could figure out why I would retire."

He told his partners he was going on a sabbatical for a year. Knowing Brian was a workaholic, the staff set up an office pool, betting on how many days it would be until he returned. He doesn't know who won because he never went back.

He swims every morning – leaping from the rocks into the clear water of the cove, plays golf and writes books – courtroom dramas. "I write about what I know." His first book, *Improving Lies,* was published in 2007. He loved it when he discovered his postal address was going to be "Laughlands." "If you can't be happy here, where can you be happy?"

It was while their house was being built that Danny invited Brian and Shelley to that dinner for the BC Polo Club.

During the course of the evening, the conversation drifted around to the social problems affecting Jamaica. Danny started talking about education and illiteracy and how it was handicapping the country – including some of his own employees. I wish there was a way to deal with it, he stated.

"Oh," responded Brian, "my wife can do it."

He and Danny worked out a deal. Shelley would teach the employees. Brian would get riding lessons. Now all Brian had to do was explain it to his wife.

Shelley's first job as a special education teacher had been working in a youth detention center, when she and Brian moved to Bay City after he completed law school. "At that time, if you were locked up, you were considered to be emotionally impaired. It's ridiculous. You're locked up. You're going to have emotional problems, but it doesn't mean you're emotionally impaired. I loved it. It turned out adolescents were the type of population I should be working with."

For 10 years she worked inside the system, watching the "revolving door" where children were incarcerated for crimes and then paroled on condition they attend school. The kids would eventually quit going to school so they would get locked up again for violating parole.

"But they weren't committing crimes. They just weren't attending school." She asked them why they had quit. The teachers, they told her, didn't want them back and, frankly, were glad when they did leave the class. Shelley and another teacher proposed a plan to the justice system to stop the "revolving door." They set up a pilot project in the detention center that allowed the kids to attend class and go home at night instead of being locked up.

When the State of Michigan cancelled the program, Shelley and her partner set up their own school for kids who needed an alternate approach to education, the Bay-Arenac Community High School. They expanded past "court kids" to include children with drug and alcohol problems and teen parents.

"We taught parenting to pregnant teens. When the kids were in daycare (also provided in the school), we had classes for the moms on how to do things better. Then we had the kids who didn't fit in. Kids who got kicked out or dropped out of traditional schools. They were bright enough. They just had other issues."

One of her first contacts with illiteracy came while she was handing out books at the beginning of the class. One young student stood up, tossed the book back at her.

"You're just like all the other schools I've been in. They hand you something and tell you to read it! Well, I'm out of here!" and he left the classroom.

Shelley followed him and stopped him in the hallway. "What was all that about?" she demanded.

"I can't read," he admitted, "that's why I'm here. To learn how to write and read."

They set up a special arrangement for him. Every morning, before regular classes started, he came in to learn how to read. When he graduated, they decided to have a congratulatory dinner. Instead of hosting it at their home, Brian and Shelley took him to a restaurant where he could read the menu and order from it.

After they'd moved to Jamaica, Shelley wasn't sure what she wanted to do but she contacted Barb in Runaway Bay, who had started a pre-school, the Glen Preparatory School in Discovery Bay. Shelley went there once a week to help and her involvement grew, including being elected the chair of the board of directors for the school.

As Brian filled her in on the deal he had struck with Danny, she barely blinked before agreeing. The challenge was irresistible.

Danny and Devon screened the Chukka employees and selected three for Shelley to work with. They provided her with an outdoor schoolroom – an unused porch attached to the back of the washroom – with chairs and a table. Shelley had a limited supply of the basic needs like pencils and paper, but immediately she saw students sneaking pencils into their bags to take to someone else at home.

"It's hard. You have to balance counting pencils with the need to help spread the benefit of education."

The biggest surprise for her was that she had to learn how to teach them even as they were being taught. The fundamentals were mostly the same as she was used to but while the differences were subtle, they were significant.

"When you deal with teaching, there are different channels of learning. Visual. Auditory. Kinetic. Tactile. And there's any possible combination of those. For Jamaicans, visual doesn't work very well, but auditory, kinetic and tactile do.

"I can trace a letter on somebody's back and they can tell me the letter. But if I show it to them, they can't tell me what they're looking at. They can feel it, but they can't see it."

She had to use the basics of teaching English as a Second Language (ESL) to start them off. Jamaicans may speak English, but they don't think in English. Their first language is Patois, the common speak that every Jamaican learns from birth.

It is a dialect of English, combined with various African words, developed when slaves were used to work the sugar plantations and enabling them to carry on discussions that couldn't be understood by their owners or overseers. Since slavery was abolished Patois has crossed social lines and everybody born or raised in Jamaica speaks it.

When they hear a question in English, they translate it to Patois, develop an answer in Patois and translate it to English. Sometimes something is lost in the translation.

Occasionally they interpret words slightly differently. If during a conversation a Jamaican says, "yes" to you, it doesn't mean he agrees with you. It means he's listening to you.

"Part of the language barrier here is you think that you're dealing with someone who has the same experience as you," said Shelley.

"I'm trying to get them to identify the sounds of a letter, so I'm using pictures where they can see the letter. In the book I'm using, the 'O' sound is identified with an owl. I show them a picture of an owl, use the letter 'O' and go to say owl – and they say to me, 'patou.' Because here they call owls, patou. So for them, the 'O' sound turns out as the 'P' sound.

"So I used olives. I made everyone eat an olive. They all said 'Ohhh' and I said that's exactly the sound the 'O' in olive would make. But they hate olives and every time they see one, they make the 'Ohhh' sound.

"When new students come they all tell them how wonderful olives are. If the new student hasn't had an olive, they tell them, 'Oh. You must eat an olive.' Then they pretend they love olives and they sit there watching the new student put the olive in his mouth. Then they break out in laughter and point at him when he reacts and spits it out."

At first other students were added by Devon, and then more just started arriving by themselves. Eventually, people who weren't Chukka employees started to attend. With students turning up when they could classes were held between three and five in the afternoon. One night a week turned into three. Some of her students took taxis from their towns and rode for an hour or more or walked for 45 minutes to be present at class.

One learned about her classes from his friend Mike. Another was told of them by Devon. For some of them the classes were part of the requirements to keep their job. For others, it was a desire to learn.

One man was motivated because he wanted to be able to read to his children and didn't want them to know he couldn't read. Another woman was there because she wanted to become as good a reader as her daughter, who was in fourth grade.

One day a man drove down from the hills to meet Shelley. "I live up there," he pointed back toward the mountains. "Thank you very much for what you are doing."

After a short time the people of St. Ann's Parish no longer called her "Miss Kennedy." She became popularly known as "Miss Shelley." In the hills and in the coastal communities when someone spoke that name, everyone knew who was being discussed.

When her students saw her walking to and from the school, they would go out of their way to escort her and carry her books. They made sure she had the best chair at the table and would hold an umbrella to keep the sun or wind off her during class. If anyone got out of line, it was the other students who reprimanded him or her.

"They are extremely respectful of me at all times. Sometimes that's very different than what I experienced (from students) in the States. The more educated this age group becomes, the more educated their children will become.

"I wish I could just open up the top of their heads and pour all this knowledge in...but unfortunately it doesn't work that way."

Another former Michigan teaching colleague of Shelley's, Mikke Kilts, arrived in Jamaica for a short visit. The two of them went down the road to the Blenheim Gliding Club where they took turns taking flights. While Shelley was flying, Mikke chatted with the young man who operated the winch that launched the aircraft.

"Do you go to school?" she asked him.

"No ma'am."

"Well, you should!"

When Shelley climbed out of her glider, Mikke walked over to her. "I got you a new student," she declared. "This is Newton Marshall."

Newton had heard of the classes. One of his best friends, Ardeen, worked at Chukka and was one of Miss Shelley's students. He had suggested that Newton come to one of the classes with him, but Newton had always found an excuse not to go.

"I was scared to go. I never really liked to go to people. But I really wanted to learn. All my life people told me I was slow and stupid. I wanted to show people I could achieve something. That I really wasn't stupid."

Shelley asked him if he really wanted to go to her classes.

"I said, 'Yeh ma'am.' She told me when I should come over on Monday and she would see what I don't know. So I went to class. I came to class every time I could. The first class was weird. I didn't know what to expect."

After work each Monday, Wednesday and Friday Newton would go out to the highway and find a taxi to take him to Chukka or ride his bike down from his grandmother's house. He became a familiar sight, running each evening up the driveway toward the outdoor school while Shelley sat waiting for him, swatting at the mosquitoes that came out every day just before dark. "Lots of times we used flashlights so he could read."

"I went to school when I lived with my grandmother (his mother's mother)...now and then," Newton recalled living in Mount Olivet, in the mountains above Runaway Bay. "Used to go to school in St. Ann's Bay. They didn't have a bus to carry school kids unless you go to a private college. I would walk from Mount Olivet to Runaway Bay then take a taxi to go to school. That was a few miles."

Newton's grandmother never went to school. Neither did his mother. When it came time for Newton to go to school, she would find chores for him to do in the yard.

"Instead of the value being placed on school," said Shelley, "it was placed on – we have things for you to do here. Dig yams. Watch the younger children so the parents could go somewhere else."

"When I was at school I used to get bullied," Newton regrets being denied an education, but he doesn't resent it. "One of the kids wanted me to write his homework for him. So I would take his books and I would write down what the teacher wrote on the blackboard. I was just copying. I wasn't learning how to write or what it meant.

"The teacher never asked me if I knew what I was doing. They would tell me what to do and write it on the blackboard for me to copy.

"I was a pretty slow learner because I missed a lot of school. There was nobody there to check up on me and make sure I was doing the work.

"I can only remember this one time when my father took up a book and he was trying to teach me, but he was beating me at the same time. He got this stick and gave it to my sister. If I didn't know a word, she was supposed to use it on me. He wasn't teaching me very much.

"When my other grandmother (his father's mother) read a book to me I feel like I want to learn more. You pick up a book and start reading it to your kids. The stories are so interesting, your child is going to learn to want to read that story.

"I picked up a book and I tried but there was nobody there to help me. I didn't know what to do. So I never learned.

"I think I would have been better educated if my aunt hadn't died. She was the only one who would read to us at night and make us pull books out. She was very bright and was respected by everyone. She sang in the church choir. Organized kids into a group to read or play games." Newton's Aunt Lisa died of cancer in 1992.

In 2005, Newton was still living with his grandmother. However, when his mother made one of her infrequent returns from wherever she had been, he was told to leave because there wasn't room for everyone. Not knowing where he might end up, he told Shelley he might have to stop going to class.

Shelley knew Newton was well on his way to earning his "surfer ticket" (graduation certificate) and didn't want to see him stop. She and Brian invited him to live in the extra room they had in their staff quarters beside the house.

The next spring he traveled to Minnesota to train with Rick and Nettie and make the *Sun Dogs* documentary.

Fall from Grace

To err is human, to forgive is canine.

As said by Carole Melville

Summer, 2006

Rick was getting ready to leave Chukka. He and Devon were taking one final walk through the kennels. He was giving instructions on what to do when he was gone. "We need to do this" or "We need to do that." A couple of times Rick mentioned something that Newton would have to learn how to do.

Finally Devon, who had been unusually quiet, stopped walking and looked down at Rick, "I don't think Newton is going to be a part of the program anymore."

"What?!" Rick wasn't sure he had heard correctly.

"I don't think he's going to be a part of the program anymore."

"What do you mean?" Rick stammered. "The whole program is built around him. He is the program. Without him, this isn't going to work!"

"He stole Mr. Matt's car last night and totaled it."

Rick stood stock still, his mouth hanging open. The rest of the walk was completed in a daze. Rick not knowing what to say. Devon not really listening anyway.

When Danny's personal driver, Dale, turned up to drive Rick to the airport, the reality of what had just transpired hit him. Rick sat in the passenger seat and tears welled up in his eyes. He and Nettie had developed an emotional bond with Newton during his time in Minnesota. They had sat together for two hours last night, going over the to-do lists for the dogs and talking as if they were grandson and grandfather. Rick couldn't believe what Devon had just said.

"I felt like somebody had kicked me in the stomach." Nettie was going to be devastated.

From the driver's seat, Dale looked at him. "Don't worry Mr. Rick," he spoke with a soothing tone. "Newton will be back. It'll be okay."

Devon had still been at work in the Chukka yard just after nine o'clock the night before. He noticed the headlights of a car come out of the Kennedy's driveway and head down the road past the Polo field.

"I saw the car, but I didn't think it unusual." Devon went into his office and was working when the phone rang. He recognized the voice immediately. It was Miss Joy, the cook for the house next door to the Kennedys, and she sounded panicked.

"Mr. Devon! Oh Mr. Devon. They just robbed Mr. Kennedy's house!"

"What do you mean they robbed Mr. Kennedy's house?"

"Yes. Yes. They just robbed Mr. Kennedy's house and took his car."

"So where are the guys? Who told you this?"

"Newton."

"Where is Newton?"

"He's here!" she handed the phone to him.

"What happened?" demanded Devon.

"I was on my way out from Mr. Kennedy's house and there were two gunmen in the yard. They took me back into the house and asked me for money. They tell me if I don't give them money they're going to kill me! I didn't have any money so I gave them the keys to the car. And they took the car!"

"Where did they go? Which direction?"

Newton was crying into the phone and couldn't answer.

"Where are the dogs?"

"The dogs were there."

"What did they do?"

"Nothing."

Devon sat up a little straighter. There was something wrong, but it wasn't that a robbery might have taken place. The problem was Newton's story. The Kennedy's two guard dogs wouldn't have just stood by and let strangers into the yard and into the house, far less steal a car.

"Okay," he spoke slowly and clearly to Newton, "what you need to do is go to the police station and make a report." Then he hung up. The phone rang again a few minutes later. It was Bobsy, the Kennedy's caretaker.

"Mr. Devon. Nobody steal the car. It's a lie," he said.

"How do you know?"

"Nobody steal the car. Newton took out the car."

"Bobsy, where's the car?"

"I don't know."

Another phone call to Devon informed him that an autobody repair shop near Priory had a damaged silver sport utility vehicle (SUV) that belonged not to Brian or Shelley Kennedy, but to Brian's brother, Matt. The fender, hood and headlight on the passenger side had been smashed in. The windshield was shattered. He went over to the Kennedy's house and confronted Newton.

"Newton if you did this, I don't want to have anything to do with you. Is this the truth?"

"Yeh Mon."

"You're lying to me. You must tell me the truth."

Devon waited for a few moments, "Newton. What really happened?"

At the beginning of each summer the Kennedys traveled back to the States to spend three months at a cabin they own on a lake in northern Michigan. This year Brian's brother Matt, who owned one of the villas at Chukka Caribbean, had asked if he could leave his car in their garage. He felt it would be safer in a secure compound with gates and guard dogs than it would be parked at the empty villa.

Newton's Story

The Kennedys had told Newton he could use their phone to make overseas calls while they were away. That night he was in their bedroom making a call. The person he was calling, a friend of the Kennedy's daughter, was going to read him a phone number. Looking for a pen he opened an eyeglass case and saw two keys.

"That's how I found the keys." Bobsy, he said, had often talked about taking the car but "none of us had a license.

"On Friday night, I didn't have any money to go to St. Ann's Bay. My grandmother's sister called me and asked me to get some ice for her to rub on her feet. If I brought the ice to her, she would give me some money. Robb also needed a ride to where he lives. So I just took the car.

"I was driving pretty fast. Before I catch the turn to go up to Robb's place I didn't remember we were going up there."

"There," said Robb. "We're going up there."

The SUV had traveled too far and was going too fast. A more experienced driver might have slowed the car down and looked for a place to pull over and turn around. Newton tried to make the corner. The vehicle left the road and smashed into a rock embankment.

"I was really worried. I go around to Robb and I ask him, 'Are you alright?' I didn't know what to do. I started to panic. Other people stopped to help. A couple of taxi drivers pull up. I told them it wasn't my car and I didn't have a license."

One of the taxi drivers turned to Newton, "Boy, you in big trouble. You're gonna have to tell a lie."

Between them they concocted the story about two gunmen breaking in to rob Newton. Robb then went home. One of Robb's friends, a taxi driver, drove Newton back to Chukka Cove.

"You just leave the car and the key," the taxi driver told him.

The first person he talked to when he arrived back at the Kennedy's was Bobsy.

"I lied to him. I told him that somebody came and stick me up with a gun and took the car. The dogs didn't do nothing.

"I was crying because I knew what I did. Not because I was lying, but because I crashed the car. I went across to the house next to the Kennedy's and told Miss Joy. She was calling everyone and telling them."

"One song," said Danny, "How many rock stars have you seen who have one hit…one song…that makes it big and it screws up their life?

"I think Newton just got spoiled. Newton's background was such that he couldn't handle it. Some of us saw it coming. He wasn't working like he used to. We tried to warn him, 'Don't mess up a good thing.' Andrea (Stewart, director of *Sun Dogs*) turned him into a star and all of this was going into what was essentially the mind of an unprivileged child. He started to believe his own press clippings. He lost touch with himself.

"So he thought, I'm a star and he took the car…it wasn't that he took the car. It was the lie he told to cover it up. It made it worse to try and justify what happened by not telling the truth."

Devon's conclusion was similar to Danny's, "A lot of Jamaican kids when they start to get exposed to certain aspects of life – they change. They want to be seen more. And to be seen…is to be seen in a vehicle. To be seen driving something would increase your value in the eyes of your friends."

The consequences of his actions started as early as that same night. Bobsy called the Kennedys in Michigan and told them the story.

"Remove his stuff," ordered Brian. "He can't stay there anymore."

Shelley was dismayed but not completely surprised, "In the spring following his trip to the States he was slacking off at school. At his work. He was getting bigheaded. He had gotten a little bit of fame. Some extra money. A lot of attention. I think he didn't know how to deal with that. I don't think a lot of people around him saw that and how it was affecting him.

"The crash was an opportunity for everyone to just stop and say, 'What just happened?' "

Bobsy and another person emptied Newton's room. Newton went over to Miss Joy, who hadn't heard what had transpired since he turned up on her doorstep the first time. She allowed him to sleep there for the night.

He went to work as usual the next morning to find the story had already been heard by all the staff. Some of them tried to encourage or comfort him. Others simply said, "That should have happened to you a long time ago."

Then Devon handed him the letter. He was suspended from work and instructed to leave the property. "I don't want to see you on the property," added Devon, "Anytime at all. Anywhere."

"I just took off," recalled Newton, "I didn't care where I went. Suspension means you might not get back your life. I went and told Miss Joy what happened. People were calling my grandmother, telling her that I was going to kill myself. That I was going down to the shore to jump into the sea and kill myself. Some people actually went and searched the cove.

"It was the first time I was ever fired from a job. It wasn't nice. I didn't want to talk about it. I really loved my job. I loved the Kennedys. I couldn't believe that I really did something like that. I thought if I took the car they wouldn't find out about it. I wasn't going to tell them I used the car. I was going to drive it, put it back and leave it like that."

His day wasn't over yet. He was asked to go to the police station in St. Ann's Bay.

"They asked me to take off my belt. They emptied my pockets. I started crying because I heard what happen in those stations. I started to cry so hard the policewoman thought I was going to die. She came and sat beside me. She was very kind.

"I was trembling. I was scared. Police came in the back and tell me I mustn't go into the cells, 'don't worry. Bad things happen in our lives. This is your bad thing and I don't think you gonna be doing it again.' They called Bobsy and said, 'Come and pick up your friend.'"

No criminal charges were ever pressed by Matt Kennedy although he refused to ever talk to or have anything to do with Newton again after that night.

Newton moved back to his grandmother's house. "I was really down. I wasn't happy. I couldn't sleep most nights. I didn't go anywhere. I spent a lot of time sitting alone. I didn't want to see anybody. I didn't even want to see my grandmother I was so embarrassed. I felt like I should just hide in a corner and not come out. I didn't know what to do."

Danny's personal driver, Dale, who had taken Rick to the airport, drove up and found him sitting on the front step of his grandmother's house.

"Don't give up," Dale told him. "You will rise again. So don't worry yourself." As he left, he looked back at Newton, "I think that one day Chukka will take you back. You try and talk to Mr. Melville."

With Newton gone, the people whose trust he violated had a chance to evaluate what had happened.

In Minnesota, Nettie felt violated, but rather than disowning Newton she directed her concern toward the dogs. "What's going to happen to them? Because there are 17 dogs that need care and attention and Newton was such a huge part of it." Then like a grandmother protecting her young, "Most Jamaicans would take advantage of their position. I don't think Newton would intentionally do that.

"I don't believe Newton took the car with malicious intent. I think he took it to help Robb. To give Robb a ride home. He just wasn't competent to handle it."

They contacted Danny. "If this was your kid," Rick said to him, "and he made the same mistake, would you disinherit him? You can't just discard him because really – you need him more than he needs you."

Danny didn't disagree. He felt that he and Devon would get to that same point at some time in the future, just not now. "For me, it was a personal disappointment. Everyone was pulling for him. Everyone wanted him to go places…and he just blew it.

"Newton had some big lessons to learn about life. Not to take for granted what people like the Kennedys and Devon were doing for him."

"It was very difficult to know what to think or feel," Shelley could see all her hopes and Newton's aspirations evaporating into the tropical air. "Newton was part of our family environment and we felt very disappointed, angry, hurt, upset.

"It was just one of those dumb things that somebody does. The biggest disappointment was that he lied about it. He had everybody in the whole area upset because he told them a gunman had come into the yard, held him up and made him give them the keys to the car. Then it got messed up. He lost his job. He lost his place to live."

It was Devon who felt the greatest emotional impact. "It just ripped me up inside. Whatever he needed I had been there for him. I treated him like my own kid. That's how I looked at him. He was good at what he was doing, so I hoped it would be a wake-up call for him. I wasn't going to give him any chance until I felt I could trust him again, the way I did when I first brought him into the dogsled team. That I could put everything behind me.

"Then when I thought about how someone could be so heartless…is that someone you really want around you?"

Devon recalled the times he helped Newton grow a sense of responsibility. Like most young Jamaicans, he started working at Chukka with the bad habit of turning up late for work, then blaming the bus and taxi system. "There's a bus from here (Chukka) every day that will take you to work and it doesn't cost anything…what's the problem?"

When he worked with the horses it was a perfect world for an animal lover, but Newton wasn't the perfect employee. He knew people responded to his charm and thought it was all he would need to succeed.

Devon made the extra effort to push him a little harder, "Nothing is going to come easy. You want something, you have to work for it. This is the only job you have. If you want this job…then you have to make a decision."

By the time Devon selected him for the dogsled team, Newton had turned into a reliable employee, one that Devon planned would stick around and grow with the business. Now he had to understand the consequences of his actions. He had to accept the responsibility, take the heat and walk away with some self-respect.

Danny left the decision about whether or not to bring Newton back entirely in Devon's hands, but he was anxious. He wanted to know when it was going to happen. Over the next few months he kept asking, "When are you going to bring him back?"

Devon would shake his head, "Not yet."

For nine months it appeared that Newton had simply vanished into the hills to whatever fate awaited him there, but he hadn't. He was talking to Rick and Nettie on a regular basis. He was also calling Danny, only Danny didn't know that at first. When he answered the phone, Newton would hang up, "I felt so ashamed I didn't know what to say."

Finally he worked up the courage to tell him who was calling. There was a moment's silence at the other end of the phone and then Danny said he couldn't talk right now and would call him back – which he did a few minutes later.

"I thought he would forgive me if I apologized." said Newton. "I told him I was sorry. He told me how upset he was. He told me he had to feel I was different. He said he wished he could take me back – but the things I had done – the car and telling the lie. He didn't want someone like that working for him."

He called the Kennedy's several times before finally reaching Shelley and apologizing. Don't apologize to me, she responded, you need to talk to Matt. He did contact Matt but he didn't want to hear it and refused to accept it.

"It hurt, but I understood why he was angry and there was nothing I could do."

In a subsequent phone call Newton asked Shelley if he could return to class. Yes, she replied, but he had to get permission from Danny and Devon to come onto the Chukka property.

"Of course," said Danny. "If Mrs. Kennedy is willing to teach you, you can come back. But Devon must okay this also."

This was the call he wasn't sure he wanted to make. Devon had told him he didn't want to hear from him again.

"Yes," Devon responded, "you can come back for classes."

There were other conditions imposed on his limited return. He still couldn't go to the Kennedy's property. He had to bring $500J ($500 Jamaican dollars, about $10 U.S., one third of a day's wage in Jamaica) to each class to give to Miss Shelley. She forwarded it to Matt to help pay the storage fee for his car. It took months for the repairs to be made.

Brian agreed to meet Newton to talk face-to-face, outside the front gate of his home.

"I'm very disappointed in you," he greeted Newton, "How could you let us down like that?"

Brian recalled how miserable Newton was when they talked that day. "My face-to-face was probably easier because enough time had gone by and I had been through this with so many kids in my past – kids that had done bad things and disappointed themselves and me.

"A lot of what I felt was that this was the make or break for Newton. It was going to be a turning point for him that would either make his life worse or better. What I talked to him about was making it an opportunity to turn things around."

Shelley believes the real turning point for Newton came while he was sitting on the school steps waiting his turn in class. There are only two or three chairs on the deck area so people arriving for their lesson will wait until one of the students leaves and then take their chair. Much of their class time is spent waiting on the steps, reading ahead in their book or helping each other study.

"I think that, in the way we as humans think, he thought that because time had stopped for him, it stopped for everybody. So he hadn't really experienced the dogs since the accident. It was a very poignant moment, when he learned everything had gone on without him," she said.

Newton sat on the steps just waiting when Robb turned the corner with the team and raced right past in front of him.

"You could just see him gasp, like an 'Oh my!' Then he couldn't control himself. He was just sobbing and watching the dogs go," said Shelley. "I think for him it was another of those moments, 'I miss that. I want to do it again. I would like to have that back.'"

"That was really hard," it's one of those times in his life that Newton will never forget. "I had been with them right from the start. I accomplished

Shelley awards Newton the first educational certificate he ever earned, September, 2008.

everything with them. I knew everything that we needed to do. I loved driving the cart. Then to lose it…just like that. That was really hard."

He asked Devon if he could visit the dogs. Devon agreed. He could visit, help feed and clean the yard but he couldn't work with the dogs and carts.

"I had to know he understood what he had done was wrong," Devon was carefully watching Newton through each stage of his reintroduction to Chukka. "He needed to understand what it had cost him. I had to feel myself that he had changed. That I would be able to trust him. When I reached that point, I said, 'Okay I'm ready to bring him back again.'"

Newton was working as a tour guide at Dunn's River Falls when Devon called him.

"Come see me at the end of the week." Newton didn't go.

Devon called again, "Hey boy! You were supposed to come down here and talk to me."

"I didn't know."

"Come on Mon!"

"All right!"

Newton called Danny who told him to see Devon right away. Big plans were in the wind for the dogsled team and they wanted him to be part of it.

"I went upstairs (in the building he was working) and I leaped in the air. I grabbed the lady there and started dancing. 'Let me go! Let me go!' she say to me so I tell her the good news and she was happy for me. I was walking on water and smiling all the time. One man said to me, 'What you smiling for. Did you win the lottery?' "

While he was celebrating the Kennedys were having a family meeting with their household staff. Danny told them Newton was coming back to Chukka. Brian and Shelley agreed that they were prepared to give him another chance, but needed to be sure their staff was willing to welcome him back to live in their home.

"If you're going to do something you've got to be sure everybody is on the same page," Shelley explained. "They were good friends with Newton and they wanted him back. They had continued to be in touch with him, but you want to be sure there were no resentments that maybe he had done something wrong and gotten away with it."

Newton arrived back at the Kennedy's and Chukka Cove at the beginning of summer in 2007, almost exactly one year after he had been evicted.

"I love my job." Newton flashed his infectious grin. "I come to work really early at five and work until seven or eight at night. I do it because I want to be here. Anytime I even think about telling a lie or making an excuse for something I did or something that I didn't do, I think about the problems I could be in.

"I like listening to people. I listen to advice. But I learned how to know bad advice from good. I found out I'm a good person. I just had to find that out for myself."

Newton's Schedule

Eagle to Circle City

165 miles, 38 hours

"Don't expect too much," said Alaskan trail coordinator John Schandelmeier when he briefed the teams in Dawson City. "I can put in a good trail, but I'm not God."

His job was to oversee the breaking, marking, proofing and sweeping of the Quest trail from the U.S.–Canada border to Fairbanks. From Whitehorse to the border the trail had been built by the Canadian Rangers, Canada's northern version of the U.S. National Guard. With the exception of snowdrifts on top of American Summit and small amounts of overflow, the trail so far had been a super highway.

"The Canadian part (of the trail) was so perfect I slept all the way to the border," Martin Buser said. The biggest problem he had was falling asleep on the sled, then falling over and being rudely awakened as the team dragged him along.

The Yukon River from Eagle to Circle City threatened to make the ride to Fairbanks a lot rougher.

North America's fifth longest river, the Yukon is born in the mountain glaciers south of Whitehorse just 24 kilometers from the Pacific Ocean, then meanders for 3,680 kilometers through the central Yukon and interior Alaska before emptying into Norton Sound near Bering Strait. The river has one of the largest drainage basins on earth, being fed by rivers and streams from northern British Columbia, 70 percent of the Yukon and over half the state of Alaska. More water flows out of the mouth of the Yukon River than flows out of any other river in the world.

The river is fairly narrow and runs relatively fast until it passes Eagle, and then it spreads out into a braided series of slow-moving channels that can be as wide as six kilometers in some areas.

There are only two dams on the river, both of them close to Whitehorse. Five bridges cross the river, four for traffic and one footbridge – all of them in the Yukon. Traveling down the Yukon River is as close to true wilderness and isolation as a person can get. Both the Yukon Quest and the Iditarod travel approximately 200 miles on the winter ice but they may as well be on different planets. Further downriver, where the Iditarod runs, the river freezes in layers but is mostly flat with a limited amount of what river dwellers call "jumble ice."

The Quest, however, makes their longest run on the river just after the narrow section finishes. The faster current tends to take the ice as it forms and hurl it downstream to the shallower water and numerous sand bars just past Eagle. Large and small pieces of ice refreeze into a cubist nightmare, sticking out of the ice at odd angles, forming barriers eight to 10 feet into the air, blocks as big as houses or cars, or shards as sharp as broken glass. Jumble ice.

Quest musher and Eagle resident Wayne Hall described the freeze-up in front of Eagle as the worst he had ever seen. "The ice looks like a bunch of small cabins rolled all over the place. That was a month ago. It's changed some, but it's never really changed good."

Between these areas of jumble ice, there was glare ice. Glare ice gives the dogs and sleds no traction at all and no reference points – trail markers can't be set up, wooded river banks look the same going in either direction. If a sled started to spin on glare ice, it could disorient the driver so he or she could no longer determine the original direction of travel.

Many mushers estimate they spend six days a week in winter crossing rivers, streams or lakes while running their dogs. They know to both respect and fear ice. There is no way to know for sure, until you are on top of it, whether it will support the team or not. Many have broken through on occasion. Most have just gotten a good scare and very wet. A few have disappeared into the frigid water beneath.

Making the situation potentially worse was the lack of snow cover along that part of the river. A layer of snow could provide traction on the glare ice and cushion the bumps in the jumble ice.

"Go slow over this section," cautioned John Schandelmeier. "Go very slow." A short distance past Slaven's cabin (just over 100 miles down the river) the jumble ice and glare ice was buried under snow. The last 60 or so miles into Circle would be fast and fairly easy.

Basically the trail was "very good," he added, because – with the noted exception of a lack of snow cover – "of all the places that needed work, the local people have done a heck of a job."

The Alaskans hired John because the two-time champion had broken over 100,000 miles of winter trail and raced the same amount over trails others had built. He knew what was needed and how to get it done.

"In reality anyone can do what I am doing. They just have to connect with all of the people scattered in all towns and villages along the way and once they do that, the trail is in, and it's good. Many (of the trailbreakers) are more qualified than me. "

As the teams traveled to Eagle, John's river trail got the snowfall it needed. It wouldn't be perfect but it would be a lot better than expected.

The town of Eagle, a collection of hand-built shacks and homes, historical buildings and gravel roads, sits on a bend in the river, hemmed in by mountains. Across the bend from the town is the 300-meter-high Eagle Bluff – a triangular rock that is one of the most recognizable landmarks on the river.

The road the teams travel is open only during the summer months. For eight months of near-winter and winter, the residents are virtually isolated. Many of the older structures are unoccupied and either falling down or already in a heap on the ground. It has a motel, a bed-and-breakfast, a pool hall, a Laundromat, two landing strips and a new schoolhouse. It takes about five minutes to walk from one end of town to the other.

There's a monument behind the motel, a silver globe perched atop a small pedestal that honors Norwegian Arctic explorer Roald Amundsen. He arrived in Eagle in 1905 to broadcast to the world by telephone that the Northwest Passage, the all-water route across the top of North America, had been conquered.

The town itself started as a trading post set up on a nearby island called Belle Isle in 1874. It grew because some prospectors weren't fond of Canada's mining rules and regulations so, rather than living at Forty Mile or in Dawson City, they settled at Eagle – six miles inside American territory. In fact, they didn't really like any kind of rules and laws other than those they enforced themselves.

Jumble ice.

Eagle has continued to attract the self-reliant and socially discontented. Most of the free-spirited residents work and play uninhibited in the northern wilderness, unencumbered by the social limitations of modern civilization. Many are former cabin dwellers, who were born and raised in wilderness camps along the river but forced out when the United States Bureau of Land Management took over administration of the Yukon-Charley Rivers National Preserve in the late 1970s.

More than any other community along the race route, Eagle symbolizes the way Northerners look at life. Outside the box. Off the beaten track. Just different. It's why people choose to live in the North in the first place. They don't want the frenzy of city life, with its social pressures, mob mentality and crime. They want to live a slower pace, in a world where nobody needs to lock their doors, where everyone knows your name, and they're willing to sacrifice personal comforts to accomplish that.

The Quest is their major event of the winter – possibly of the entire year. As far as the people of Eagle are concerned, the Quest is not just a race in the North, it's a race of the North. Dog teams are what opened the North up, making their lifestyle possible. There are only about 120 people living there but every one of them is involved. Musher Wayne Hall's wife, Scarlett, is checkpoint manager.

"The Yukon Quest is a big happening here, because nothing really happens in the winter time," she said.

Most people drift into the checkpoint, which is located on the north side of the town in the old white schoolhouse with its gable-topped entrance. Picnic tables circle a massive bonfire blazing merrily night and day.

The mushers are met by a customs officer, who conducts more of a conversation than an inquiry and checks passports. When Newton finished bedding down the dogs and doing his chores, he stumbled (most mushers stumble everywhere they go because their Neo boots or Bunny boots are so big they snag on everything) past volunteers, trail breakers and their snow machines, locals warming up at the fire and keeping an eye on the comings and goings, on his way into the schoolhouse.

Unlike most checkpoint people along the trail, Scarlett wasn't surprised to see a Jamaican dog musher. She had met Newton a year earlier when he turned up in Eagle during the Percy DeWolfe Race, one of the two qualifying races he had to complete to qualify to even enter the Quest. What she did find interesting was the black stamp-shaped spot on the tip of his nose, the result of frostbite. Every once in while he would reach up and rub it until the skin came off. But, in the -30°C temperatures, it just kept coming back and kept getting bigger.

She recited the menu to him: chicken and rice, chicken potato and gravy, chicken Alfredo, pancakes and ham....

"No Mon. No ham," said Newton, "I don't eat nothing from a pig. No ham. No pork. No bacon."

...biscuits and gravy.

He selected the chicken and rice, sat down, and then asked, "Have you got any hot sauce?" Scarlett handed him a lot of salt and pepper packets.

After the meal he headed to the bunk beds in the back of the schoolroom and laid down for a short snooze. He'd discovered that two-hour catnaps worked better for him than longer sleeps.

The Yukon River between Eagle and Circle City is possibly the most strategically important part of the race for most teams. On the ice most mushers will finally recognize the limitations of their teams or realize they don't have any. By now they've had a chance to evaluate the other teams and decisions must be made that could mean the difference between winning and losing.

It was on the river to Circle that Alaskan Bruce Lee tracked down the "phantom musher" Quebec's Andre Nadeau in 1998, and Joe Runyan erased the 12-hour lead held by Alan Stewart's mentor, Scotland's Rick Atkinson, in 1985. Both men went on to win the race.

To most observers William Kleedehn seemed to have the race well in hand. His times between checkpoints were fast. The team that appeared to be his most serious challenger, Hugh Neff, was matching his speed but not making up any ground. Hugh, almost two hours behind, started cutting rest times to try and close the gap but not even that seemed to help.

William Kleedehn and Newton.

The rough trail on the ice was taking a toll on William. His prosthetic leg was causing him pain and made it hard for him to balance on the sled. It put added stress on his wheel dogs. While crossing one ice ridge, his sled tipped precariously and started skidding toward a shelf of ice hanging over the trail. He laid the sled down on its side to avoid being jammed under the ice. A couple of glare ice patches caught him by surprise because there was just enough snow on it to disguise it until the dogs lost traction and the sled started to spin. "There's only so much fun that can be had on the Yukon River with all this bad ice," he was thinking.

In most sports William would have been placed into a special category because of his leg. However, there are no such distinctions in dog mushing. All – men, women, young, old, black, white, one leg, two – compete as peers. No matter who they are or what problems they may have, it is that unqualified equality that attracts so many athletes to the sport.

The leg had only been a factor once in all the years William raced the Quest, when he fell and broke the bone above the prosthetic. Instead, it was that other indeterminate factor that every champion needs that had consistently let him down – luck. There is no such thing as an unlucky champion and in the years when he could have won, circumstances seemed to conspire against him.

"If you're trailing the leader and can't catch them with speed, the only way to catch them is if something happens that is unforeseen," John Schandelmeier has had his fair share of luck, both good and bad. "You don't concede until the Finish line. I bet you William is not thinking he's got it made until he crosses the Finish line (first)."

William already knew he didn't have it made. His wheel dogs were exhausted. He had dropped a dog at Slaven's cabin and knew he was going to have to drop two more before the final run into Fairbanks. He didn't have enough dogs to stay ahead of the teams chasing him.

Hugh's dogs were running fast. They had that magic carpet feeling to them. He also dropped a dog at Slaven's. If he cut rest, maintained the pace and didn't make any mistakes, he felt the race was his to win or lose.

An hour behind him, and slipping a little further back at each checkpoint, was Jon Little. Jon was trying to stay in touch with the race in front, but in Eagle he had suddenly become aware of the threat from behind. He kept expecting a dog team to bump into his rear end any time. "Don't anyone underestimate Sebastien (Schnuelle)," Jon cautioned. "He says he's not racing, but he just happens to be right up at the front."

Brent Sass and Sebastien were running together almost seven hours behind Jon. Brent knew he was short on dog power and was aiming to hold his position.

Sebastien did seem to be just having a camping trip. He had a schedule and stuck to it religiously. The two of them stopped to snack their dogs in the middle of the river near Glenn Creek. Normally, by this time most mushers are thinking of the race in terms of "Oh God, we still have 500 miles to go."

"But Brent and I, we were talking about 'Are we ever lucky to be here!' and 'How awesome it was to just be out here….' This is what we live to do. It's sunny and bright. We're camping out with our dogs," said Sebastien.

Then Sebastien called up his dogs and blasted off down the river. Brent's mouth dropped open as he watched them vanish. He realized that Sebastien had been holding his dogs back. "Man," he thought, "that guy could win this race.

"I never told him but I thought all along he had the strongest team out there," added Brent.

Martin Buser was starting to move up in the standings but knew he had waited too long. The race was out of his reach.

All along the river there were cabins that came to life just once a year – when the Yukon Quest rolled by. Trout Creek cabin is a six-hour run from Eagle. It lies within the national park boundaries and hadn't been occupied full time for a number of years. Each February it was opened by its owner, Karl Sager, to provide a warm place to sleep and dry off, warm water for the dogs, and a bowl of hot soup for the musher.

Halfway between Eagle and Circle City one can slide back 50 years in time. This isn't history you can just touch. It's history you can sit in, eat a meal in, sleep in. Biederman's cabin used to be a popular stop on the trail but the distance from Trout Creek is too short and most teams now just go right by. Those who do stop abide by the only rule that dictates how a visitor is to treat an empty cabin. When you leave, leave things as they were when you arrived.

Biederman's cabin was built in 1916 at the junction of the Yukon and Kandik Rivers, the midway point for the longest mail route in the United States Postal Service. Ed Biederman, and then his son Charlie, delivered the mail to the people who lived on the river by dogsled until 1938 when airplanes finally took over the business.

In winter the dogsled mailman was the sole link with the outside world for communities from Dawson City to Circle City. The last dogsled mail contract was cancelled in 1963. The hickory sled that Ed and Charlie drove up and down the river was enshrined in the National Postal Museum in Washington, D.C. in 1995, shortly before Charlie died.

The last of the Canadian mail carriers delivering by dogsled, Ed Whitehouse, died in 1996. He delivered the mail upriver from Dawson City in the winter of 1928-29. It is their trails and histories the Quest follows each winter.

The river itself is part of an even older world. Not far from the river, in Alaska and in the Yukon, is evidence of the earliest encroachment of man from Asia across the Beringia land bridge to North America almost 15,000 years ago. The Yukon is the continent's oldest highway for human travel.

"A lot of times this race is talked about as being a reflection of the past of dog mushing," reflected William. "I met one of those people who live along the river and run dogs. It was one of those old toboggan sleds, pulled by big dogs. He got off the trail so I could get by. He looked like one of those guys from the past.

"Those guys who live along the river and run those big dogs – they gotta have big balls. There's no way I could run a team with a strong dog team like that on jumble ice.

"This race doesn't just reflect the past of mushing. It reflects all the people who have ever lived along the river," said William.

Slaven's cabin is the official dog drop on the river. It's a two-story building, restored as a heritage building in 1993 by the Alaska Parks Service, where the mushers can climb up a ladder staircase to a second floor sleeping room. Downstairs they can chat with the vet or eat the best chili on the river. It was built in 1932 as a whistle stop for riverboats in the summer and a roadhouse for dog teams in the winter.

Each Quest the cabin is staffed by Park wardens, but not Alaskan park wardens. Spending Quest week at Slaven's is a sought-after bonus for personnel from other U.S. National Parks. In 2009, they were from: Everglades (Florida), Glacier (Montana) and the Grand Canyon (Arizona).

Newton's run to Circle started off easy enough. The dogs cruised. He was singing, doing a little dancing on the sled. "Grooving on the runners" as he called it. He thought the dogs might appreciate it since long runs on river ice or across lakes bore them and they tend to lose focus. The dogs kept trotting along while he sang, occasionally throwing a glance back over their shoulders at him. He wondered if they were running for him or from him.

"I wasn't making up songs, but I was only singing parts of songs because I didn't know all the words:

Today. Today you're down (da-owe-n)
Come tomorrow.
Chances of rising again seems hollow
Doubt may be in your mind
But give it time
And all will be fine (fa-ine)
If you cannot make it
But you can
You'll find life in the darkest of night
Your feet might be weary,
But not your mind...."

Then he hit the jumble ice and his vocabulary changed. "Bumba Clot! Rass Clot!" (Jamaican curses).

The dogs had no problem on the rough trail, but the sled bounced off the ice ridges and blocks, at times actually tossing him into the air behind the sled. For 80 miles the river punished his body and mind. He was sore from one end of himself to the other. Even catching a couple of hours of sleep at both Trout Creek and Slaven's didn't help. His eyes were bloodshot from lack of sleep. He was tired of being tired.

"I'm not feeling so good now. This is very hard. You have to keep telling yourself 'I want to do this, I want to do this,' I'm telling myself that. I'm trying to sing positive songs to motivate myself."

He kept checking his hands. He was traveling with Mark Sleightholme and Colleen Robertia, who had frostbite on their fingers. The skin had cracked and split wide open, their fingertips bled into their mitts.

"When you have frostbite and cracks on your fingers, it is so hard to open anything, to do anything," said Newton. "It is painful and your fingers are so stiff."

His hands were fine. In fact, Newton didn't feel cold at all despite the refusal of the weather to warm up.

The sun had been down for a couple of hours when the dogs found the boat launch in front of Circle City and turned gratefully off the ice for the short trot to the fire station where the checkpoint was located.

"They told me (at Slaven's) that (the trail) was really good. It was the best it had been in a long time." He mentioned to the checker, "I don't want to see it when it's bad!"

Sebastien had been elated when his team steamed into Circle City. "After hearing all the horror stories of glare ice and jumble ice," he exalted, "it snowed the perfect amount and made the trail a perfect trail.

"I know John isn't God, but I'm beginning to wonder if he isn't related to him."

Colleen Robertia and Mark Sleightholme.

Dick

Grass callaloo grow weh mi nature tek.

Jamaican patois: Things grow under the right conditions.

February, 2007

As rare and off-the-wall as the idea of a Jamaica Dogsled Team may seem, Danny Melville was not the first person to think of it.

That distinction goes to Dick Watts, a Whitehorse optometrist who came up with the idea in 2000 – five years before Danny had his moment of epiphany.

At the time Dick was co-chairing the joint board of directors for Yukon Quest International. The race, as usual, was struggling for media recognition to entice major sponsors to get involved. They had just terminated a sponsorship contract with Fulda, a German tire manufacturer, which had given the Quest tremendous television coverage in Europe, but made no inroads into the American marketplace.

Like Danny, Dick has never been one to find his imagination confined by practicality.

He thought back to his time as a volunteer at the Calgary Olympics in 1988. He was one of the workers at the bobsled venue and recalled the media excitement when the Jamaican Bobsled Team made its debut.

"It was interesting to see where the media was. You had all these highly placed athletes at one end of the media room and this bobsled team at the other. And most of the media were talking to the Jamaicans.

"I just thought it would be a good idea to come up with a Jamaican dogsled team, sort of a spin-off from the bobsled team."

He bounced the idea off former Quest champion Frank Turner, who liked it.

"We'd probably have to find somebody to train for two or three years," he suggested. "Lease them a team since they probably wouldn't have one of their own."

Dick had been traveling to Jamaica since the early 1980s with Canadian Vision Care (CVC), a charitable organization dedicated to provide eye care to those who couldn't afford to pay for it. It started out as a joint venture with the Lions Clubs of Jamaica in Montego Bay and expanded until he and his colleagues from Calgary were conducting clinics in every corner of the island.

If there was one thing about Jamaica Dick grew to love, it was the "edginess" of the country. "I like the culture shock you get there. The warmth of the people. The vibrancy. Their pride in country. Their passion about who they are. And the potential…it's unlimited if unleashed.

"The crime. The drugs. The negative parts. That's all part of it too." Never one to shy away from going where angels might fear to tread, he had a mixed bag of experiences.

He and a colleague rented mopeds in Ocho Rios, against all sensible advice they received from the Lions Club there because it was a time of political violence and headed east along the coast, looking for Dick's Bar, a drinking establishment in Port Antonio. They could hear the bar a block before they could see it.

The two of them walked through the front door and the place went dead silent. It was a dark room and all he could see were eyes looking at them from the interior. They were the only two white people there. They looked at each other, telepathically decided, "Okay. We've come this far," went to the bar and ordered a beer.

The bartender asked, "Where you from?"

"Canada."

"Oh…You're from Canada!" The beer arrived and everybody wanted to talk to them.

In 1998, he and four other optometrists were riding in a van through Spanish Town, the former national capital city west of the current capital, Kingston. It was an area noted for violent crime, the type of area CVC tried to avoid because it was hard to navigate the streets and dangerous.

"You make a wrong turn in Kingston or Spanish Town and you could be in trouble," said Dick. They made a wrong turn and a gang of young Blacks rushed the vehicle, throwing rocks at them and slamming against the side, all the time shouting, "Whitey! Whitey!" Then another group who knew who was in the van charged the gang. There was a lot of yelling and pushing, then suddenly everyone was gone and the danger was over.

"It's not an experience I would care to repeat, but we can't stop our activities because of something like that," said Dick.

While Dick was in Jamaica in 2000, he talked to members of the Lions Clubs about the dogsled team idea. There was some interest but nothing ever came of it. When he returned to the Yukon, his term on the Quest board was coming to an end so the idea just got dropped.

All he had to show for his vision was a stack of T-shirts – one of which hung on the back wall of his office in Whitehorse. He mentioned the idea occasionally to people who shared his passion for the Yukon Quest. One of those people was Stephen Reynolds, the newly hired executive director for the organization, who heard about it while having dinner with Dick in the summer of 2003.

It wasn't something that Stephen thought about until he received an email from Andrea Stewart in February, 2006. She was making the *Sun Dogs* documentary and looking for video footage of the Yukon Quest to be inserted into the film. A couple of hours later he started to wonder if Dick knew about the JDT.

Stephen phoned him, "Are you still involved with the Jamaican dogsled team?"

"No," Dick was surprised, "I dropped that idea a long time ago."

"Well, something's happening. We've had a request for film footage for a film being made about the Jamaican dogsled team. Do you want to look into it when you go down to Jamaica?"

Dick was enthralled, but wasn't scheduled to go with the CVC for a couple of months. He suggested that Stephen put one of his T-shirts into the package with the film footage – a suggestion Stephen acted upon, placing the shirt on top so it would be the first thing seen.

"When they opened the package," described Stephen, "that they thought was just media content, there was this T-shirt from four or five years earlier promoting a Jamaican dogsled team that obviously had never seen fruition, but was definitely in the conceptual phase."

Danny and Dick.

The contract sent to the Quest office also contained an interesting clause: Andrea couldn't portray Chukka's Jamaican dogsled team as being part of the Yukon Quest unless they actually came to run the race, "which at that time we didn't think to be very realistic."

A second T-shirt intended for Jimmy Buffett was hand-delivered to the Margaritaville Restaurant in Montego Bay in April, but there was no indication it ever reached him.

In a subsequent trip to Toronto, Stephen decided he wanted to meet Andrea. She informed him that Danny Melville, founder of the JDT, was also in Toronto and they agreed to meet for a beer.

"We quickly realized we had a lot of common values and aspirations for what dog mushing could bring to the rest of the world, and for (what) the JDT could bring to the world of mushing."

Stephen invited Danny to come North and check out the Yukon. In September he got a call from Danny. He was in Victoria visiting his mother and decided to accept the invitation. He was intrigued by the fact that someone else had the same idea five years before he did and wanted to meet him.

"Danny Melville, the owner of the Jamaica Dogsled Team wants to come up and see the actual Quest trail." Stephen asked Dick, "Could you line up a plane for him?"

It was a perfect autumn day for a flight over the trail from Whitehorse to Carmacks. As they passed over Braeburn the pilot, Gerd Mannsperger, started chatting on the radio with another pilot flying nearby, Bernard Stehelin.

"I'm just flying back to my place," said Bernard. "Why don't you guys drop by for a coffee?"

Twenty minutes later the floatplane landed on Coughlin Lake and taxied up to the dock in front of a fishing lodge.

"I couldn't believe it," Danny was overwhelmed because the whole experience was so far outside his sense of reality. "I had never done anything like that before. One minute we're flying. Then we're in a lodge on a lake in the middle of the bush. Have a cup of coffee. Then we take off again. If they can do that, they can do anything!"

"We had no idea that Danny's visit in 2006 would result in a Jamaican musher running the Quest two and a half years later," said Stephen, "It was just reaching out to another person from another country, saying we share a love for dogs. Come up and be our guests.

"I think it was that drop-in coffee on Coughlin Lake that really inspired Danny to pursue the idea of a musher running the Quest," Stephen concluded.

A meeting with the Yukon government's tourism department resulted in a suggestion that Danny bring Devon up to watch the 2007 Yukon Quest and spend time driving a team in winter conditions.

Danny with Hood – a Northern shelter dog with a new life.

The purpose of the winter trip would be to educate Devon.

"In Jamaica, if a musher falls off his sled in Jamaica, he could easily walk back to the kennel. If you fall off your sled in the middle of the wilderness, you will probably die," said Stephen. "Devon needed to learn that sense of dependency between the dogs and the musher, that most traditional mushers are aware of, but which he probably never needed to develop in Jamaica.

"The dogs (in Jamaica) are totally dependent upon the kennel for their lives, food, shelter but don't provide an essential service to the musher. The musher has no dependency upon them.

"And that co-dependency is the essence of dog mushing," Stephen explained.

On his next trip to Jamaica Dick not only visited Danny, he purchased the villa next door to him at Chukka Caribbean. It would give the CVC a base to operate from in Jamaica, he justified to his wife Gabrielle.

Gabrielle was used to Dick's penchant for acting on impulse. They moved to the Yukon in 1994, following a fishing trip he made with another optometrist from Whitehorse. Dick wasn't planning on moving to the Yukon, knew nothing about Whitehorse, but he "fell in love with the place."

He and his business partner wanted to make changes in Calgary, where their practice had grown to the point where they had become administrators rather than optometrists. When Dick did something there was no such thing as a half measure. His idea of change was to leave Calgary and move to Whitehorse.

His passion for the Quest was kindled at three o'clock one morning as he and Gabrielle stood at the Finish line waiting for the first-place team to arrive.

"When he crossed the line his wife and two children rushed to him," said Dick. "You know they hadn't even seen him for 10 days! And one of his daughters just headed for this one dog that was just going crazy because he was so excited to see her. That was one of the most amazing things I'd ever seen.

"That this dog that had just run a thousand miles could hardly wait to see this little girl. At that point I realized there was more to this mushing than just a musher and his dogs."

He joined the Quest, went straight to the top of the organizational hierarchy and co-chaired the Alaska-Yukon joint board of directors for three years. Even after stepping down from the joint board, he continued to sponsor individual mushers and help with various fundraising events. Until Danny turned up in Whitehorse in September, 2006, he had been gradually reducing his involvement in the sport to focus on other community activities.

Before Danny and Devon arrived in Whitehorse in February, 2007, Dick was up to his neck in the JDT. He still loved the Yukon Quest and just couldn't resist seeing his oddball idea become a reality – even if it wasn't he who did it.

The Start Banquet in Whitehorse: (L to R) Danny, Yukon Minister of Tourism Elaine Taylor, Newton, Dick.

Danny vaguely remembered seeing the Quest name when he did "Dogsledding 101" in 2005. It was, he knew, one of the two biggest races on the dog driving calendar. Everyone in the mushing world gave that extra measure of respect to people who completed either the Quest or the Iditarod. He decided that to connect the Chukka name with the Yukon Quest could do nothing but good for the JDT. He wasn't seriously considering running a team in the race but conceded it was probably lurking somewhere in the back of his mind at the time. The major obstacle was money.

"It was kind of crazy," Danny remembered. "I had enough money to do Robb's thing in 2007 (his training in Minnesota with Ken Davis), but I had no money to do anything more. Jimmy Buffett's sponsorship was generous, but I couldn't ask him for more. My sons weren't happy with the JDT because it was a drain on the company and didn't generate enough income, so I had to do it all myself."

He decided that he and Devon would go to Whitehorse in February to attend the Start Banquet, watch the start itself, travel to Dawson City to see the teams go through and have Devon do an overnight dogsled trip in true arctic conditions. While there he might explore the possibilities.

Although Devon wasn't even an entrant in the race, he was the darling of the media. The novelty of a Jamaican dog musher being so close to the heart of the dog mushing world was too much for them to resist.

His overnight dogsled trip along Lake Laberge, a 50-kilometer long lake just 32 kilometers north of Whitehorse, with Quest veteran and winter tour operator, Ned Cathers generated almost as many news stories as the race itself. It was Devon's longest dogsled ride and his first time sleeping in any wilderness.

"When we pulled up at the overnight camp area I thought I would see a cabin. But Ned just stopped in this clearing with nothing in it and said, 'I think this is a good place to stop.' I thought he was joking. 'Stop to do what?'

"He said, 'I think we camp here.' And I'm like, 'Oh my Gosh! The ground is all covered in white. And there's no hammock!'"

Within a half hour Ned had the two teams bedded down, fed, a tent erected and fire going.

"It was the most incredible night of my life. It was the best sleep I had while I was in the Yukon."

While Devon drove a team into the snow and cold, Danny was thinking about the future. "Could this be done?" he asked. "Why not?" was the answer. "How would we go about doing it?" "How much would it actually cost?"

"There's an incredible amount of wilderness training involved because you cannot take somebody out from Jamaica and have them frostbitten," said Danny.

Stephen, seeing the media feeding frenzy over Devon, directed him to one of the Quest's top mushers, a transplanted Austrian and three-time Quest champion, Hans Gatt.

Danny didn't talk about entering a team in a Quest during that dinner meeting. He could see the potential, but there was always that lingering doubt. "When you have to hire a Hans Gatt. Accommodation. Leasing dogs. Feeding. Training. This is big bucks!"

When he returned to Jamaica, Danny approached the issue with his sons from a sentimental side. "Horses and dogs are similar. My family has been a horse family for three generations. Horses love to run. They are born to run and run fast. They want to win!

"That's what this is all about. That's what the Jamaica dog team is all about. Winning."

That led into his business angle, "What is the value of the dogsled team in the scheme of Chukka Cove? Unquantifiable because it's public relations. It's a great loss leader. Every time I go to the United States or Canada, all I hear about is the Jamaica Dogsled Team. It gets you in the door. Then you can sell the rest of the package… all of the other tours."

Then the patriotic pitch, "It is to give young Jamaicans like Robb the opportunity to travel the world and bring their experience home."

And finally, the last resort of all parents – the guilt trip. "I reminded my sons about all the things they did when they were younger that I had to pay for. Now they had to pay for the things I was going to do."

For the most part it worked, except funding did get temporarily cut at one point due to unrelated legal bills and a hurricane.

Devon – the darling of the Yukon media.

The partnership was roughed out in five minutes over a bottle of Grey Goose vodka on Danny's patio in April, when Hans traveled to Jamaica for the official launch of the dog tours. The details were ironed out over the next five months.

"One of the reasons I wanted you here," admitted Danny, "was to give the whole idea some credibility."

Devon would spend two winters training with the goal of entering and completing the 2009 Yukon Quest. Devon paraphrased Mount Everest conqueror Edmund Hillary when asked about why he would do it, "Well, if it's there, why not give it a shot?"

"My first reaction was 'you can't do something like that!' It was a crazy idea," said Hans. "My second thought was 'but I've always been up for crazy.' Riding motocross. Moving to Canada. Becoming a professional dog musher. Running the Iditarod. Running the Quest. Training a Jamaican musher… Yeah sure. Let's do it!"

The publicity was also beginning to generate excitement in the sporting world. Danny was invited to be a panelist in the closing session of *Dog Power 2007*, the annual general meeting of the International Sled Dog Racing Association (ISDRA) in Reno, Nevada, June 15 to 17, 2007.

“Jamaica is a huge brand. We’ve brought a high profile to a sport that hasn’t had one for a long time.” He and Carole saw “a doggy trade show,” met Rachael Scdoris, the first legally blind person to complete the Iditarod, and Rob Downey, who had just won the North American dogsled sprint championships in Fairbanks, Alaska. A special showing of *Sun Dogs*, which had just debuted at the CineVegas Film Festival, was combined with a raffle for tickets to Jimmy Buffett’s “Bama Breeze” concert tour stop, with all the raffle proceeds going to purchase supplies for the National Disaster Search Dog Foundation (NDSDF). The NDSDF rescues shelter dogs and trains them for search and rescue operations in disaster areas.

On the panel with Danny at the last session of the conference, “Future Vision: Working together to plan a positive future for our sport,” were ISDRA Executive Director Dave Steele, Quest-Iditarod champion Lance Mackey and Arctic explorer, dog musher John Stetson.

“I had no business being there,” Danny laughed. “If you want to know about sponsorship I can help you. If you want to talk about dogs, I know very little.

“They had some Arctic explorer (Stetson), he was really out there. Well thought of by the mushers, but really out there.”

When the show was over, it was IFSS president, Tim White, who was left shaking his head in wonderment at the fanfare. "You've done more for sleddog racing," he told Danny, "than anyone in 20 years."

As November approached, the month Devon was due to head north, Dick started to get more apprehensive. He had met Devon a number of times by now and wasn't convinced that he was the right person for the job. In Jamaica for Danny's birthday party, Dick suggested meeting over lunch with Danny, Hans and Devon to talk about what was going to happen.

Hans gave a brief description of where Devon was going to be living and what kind of a training schedule he would be expected to follow.

"You do understand what you're getting into?" Dick pointedly asked Devon. "Do you understand the commitment necessary to make this work?"

"Yeh Mon," he exuded confidence. He knew where he had come from and what he had accomplished with his life and this was just one more thing that had to be done.

"I respect Devon. I like Devon. He's very good at Chukka Caribbean but I didn't think Devon could do four months up there in the winter." Dick wasn't convinced, "I don't believe he ever really understood what was going to be expected of him. It just wasn't for him."

Hans greeted Devon at Whitehorse International Airport on November 13, 2007. It was cold for November, already close to -25°C. They moved him into his accommodation – a converted Airstream travel trailer.

The next morning he took Devon on a 14-mile run with the dogs using a four-wheel all-terrain vehicle – there wasn't enough snow for a sled yet. Devon was unusually quiet. When the ride was over, he walked around the dogyard for a bit, then lost it emotionally.

"I can't do this," his ego withered in the face of the evidence. "I just can't do this."

Hans wasn't sure how to react, "I guess he was so shocked. No cell phone. Devon is addicted to his cell phone because it's his lifeline to his work. No television. No stereo system. (Devon has a massive stereo system in his home that could entertain the entire north coast if he turned it up.) I think he believed he would still have all that. For him to imagine a lifestyle without them was impossible. The more he thought about it, the more it shocked him and he just collapsed."

Damion Robb.

They talked briefly inside the trailer, but it was obvious to Hans that Devon was in over his head. He drove him back to the airport and put him on a flight back to Jamaica on November 15.

Danny was furious. Robb was racing the sprint circuit but the plan called for the 2009 Quest to be the centerpiece for the JDT. It was the race that was truly going to give Jamaican mushers credibility.

Financially, quitting the Yukon Quest made sense but for Danny that wasn't an option. It would have reflected poorly back on Chukka Caribbean and on Danny himself. The Quest had to happen, but how?

Robb was already committed. Newton had just been hired back to tend the kennel while Devon and Robb were gone. Danny's options were few and there was very little time to make a decision, although he did have an inkling about where this was going to end up. The media coverage on Devon's Quest had been extensive and it wouldn't be long before someone called looking for a follow-up story.

His first conversation, with Dick, helped to calm him down.

"I'm not sure exactly how the publicity will impact on the project," cautioned Dick. "Let's not make a big issue out of it until we've got plan B figured out."

His second call, to Rick, provided him with some firm direction, "What should we do?"

"Call Newton. Ask him. He'll do it."

"Are you sure?"

"Yes, I'm sure Newton will do it."

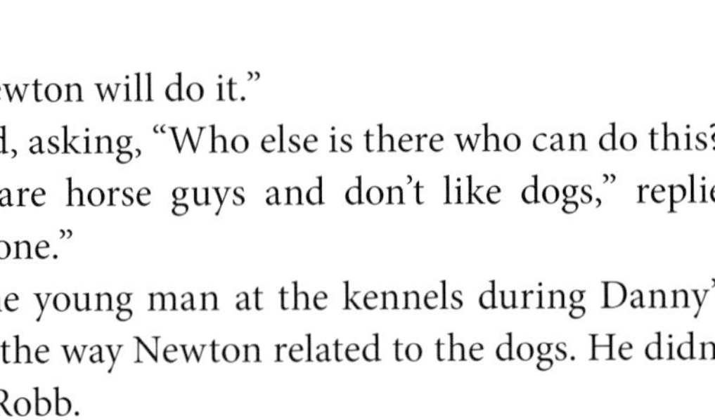

Then Hans called, asking, "Who else is there who can do this?"

"Most of them are horse guys and don't like dogs," replied Danny. "Newton's the only one."

Hans recalled the young man at the kennels during Danny's birthday party. He had liked the way Newton related to the dogs. He didn't have the same feeling about Robb.

“I don’t know Newton.” Hans liked the gut reaction he felt, “I know you’ve had some problems with him in the past. But I think he’s the guy we need. If we want to proceed with this, then we need to get him here right away.”

Newton was at the Kennedy’s when Danny phoned him.

“Newton, Devon isn’t working out up in Whitehorse. Do you want to go up to Canada to run the race?”

“Yeh Mon.”

“Are you sure you want to do this?”

“Yeh Mon. I want to do this. Is this going to be like Minnesota?”

Danny didn’t pull any punches. Newton had to be sure of what he was getting into. “No,” Danny said, “Hans is gruff, rough and tough. It is going to be hard. He’s a professional. He’s unforgiving and has very high standards. That’s why we want him.

“He’s one of the best. He’s a taskmaster. And he has to be because one mistake could cost you a finger. A foot. Or your life. It’s not about being nice. It’s about being tough. You’re not going to go up there, then quit on me?”

“No Mon. I won’t do this. I won’t quit.”

He saw it as a way to thank Mr. Melville for giving him a second chance and to help his grandmother. “They’ve both always been there for me. They’ve given me so much.”

However, even after Danny’s explanation of what he could expect, he still didn’t fully understand the job he had just accepted. Newton thought it would be a sprint race, like Robb was doing in Minnesota. Only much later, when the race was described in detail to him, did he realize the magnitude of the journey he was about to take.

“Oh Jesus,” he moaned, “What have I got myself into?”

Danny called Hans, “I asked Newton if he wanted to do this and he said he would pack his bags tomorrow.”

The press release stated that Devon had decided to step back from the race when faced with the reality of being separated from his six children in Jamaica for the next two winters. It voiced everyone’s certainty that Newton was the perfect replacement. The media bought into the story and a public relations disaster was averted.

It was -22°C when Newton stepped off the plane in Whitehorse wearing nothing but a “hoodie,” jeans and carrying a daypack. Dick, Hans, Susie and Moira were there to welcome him. For a few minutes they waited for his luggage.

Hans Gatt and Danny at the Whitehorse Visitor Information Centre.

"How many bags do you have?" Dick inquired.

"I have no luggage, this is it (indicating the day pack)."

Dick was nervous about Newton, "I had apprehensions about Devon and Devon was a lot more worldly than Newton ever was. Devon had traveled and had been around a lot in the United States and Canada. Newton had never been off the island other than his trip to Minnesota. I knew how different this was going to be for him."

Newton's first reaction to the North told Dick a lot about what he might expect to discover about the young Jamaican.

"It was amazing. He didn't turn around and go back. The first thing he did when he walked out of the terminal into the cold was laugh," said Dick.

Planning session with handlers in the home of Hans Gatt and Susie Rogan.

Hans

This is the law of the Yukon, and ever she makes it plain:
Send not your foolish and feeble; send me your strong and your sane.

Robert Service

December, 2007

A dog musher's lifestyle combines the intense training of the Olympic athlete with the commitment and work schedule of a farmer, a career that Hans Gatt claims is good training for a budding dog musher.

The day usually starts long before sunrise when musher and handlers cook up a meal and feed the dogs. Then they each take a team for a two- or three-hour run or longer – eight or 10 hours, sometimes two or three days. The time of day isn't important – during the night or day – as long as they run every day. They practice passing. Dog care on the trail. Switching leaders and moving dogs around in the team. They train so dogs and musher both know how to handle breakdowns.

They all conceptualize conditioning in different ways. Some think it's like a ladder going straight up. Others view it as a series of plateaus, blockages, ceilings. Many believe it is a geometric spiral, with most spins of the circle taking the team a different distance upward, and some of them taking you down. Regardless of the path, the goal is the same for both dogs and mushers. The trail is a substitute for the Olympic training center.

Newton at Gatt Kennels.

Then they water the dogs, clean the dogyard, remove snow from the driveway, clear a trail or head into town to buy supplies. If time permits, an evening run with those dogs who didn't get a chance in the morning. A second feeding. Then to bed sometime long after dark.

Seven days a week. There are no holidays. No long weekends. No regular weekends. No vacations until the winter racing season is over – and even then, although the dogs are no longer racing, they still need to be run, watered and fed every day.

"There were times when I wish I was back in Jamaica doing some of the things I like to do." Newton worked seven a days a week with the dogs at Chukka because he wanted to. In Canada at Gatt Kennels he worked seven days because he was expected to.

"Someone has to feed the dogs, run the dogs every day. There are no days off and I find that very hard. I get angry sometimes that I can't do what I want to do. I have to do something all the time that someone else tell me to do. I have no freedom."

Reminded that he chose to be in the Yukon, he nodded, "I'm not blaming anyone else. I promised Danny I would do this race and that is what I will do."

The musher's home is team headquarters. The sole topic of discussion is dogs. There is usually a dog or two hanging around inside. For the majority of mushers, almost every dollar they earn either racing or as a wage goes into their dogs. They are driven individuals. Not only will they invest all of their money and time, they are willing to race themselves to total exhaustion. It is not just a lifestyle – it is their life.

Why they do it is a much more complicated issue.

Some, very few, are professionals. They make their living running dogs. It is the competitive nature of the business that drives them. Sponsorships, endorsement contracts and prize money combined enable them to continue although the term "professional" almost seems like a contradiction in terms.

While dog mushing is one of the most demanding professional sports in terms of training, costs and time commitment, the top mushers are some of the lowest paid athletes in any discipline. A star football player, hockey player or soccer player earns almost as much in one game as a top musher will earn for the entire season – and he doesn't have to feed dogs!

For the others, the competitors and up-and-comers who don't yet have sponsorships or endorsements, the recreational musher who seeks adventure, it is the challenge of co-existing on a higher level with the land and environment.

They choose to live at the edge of civilization, where nature is stripped of any constraints. In a cruel winter habitat that is anything but benign. When that cruelty is exposed to them, many living-with-the-earth wannabes collapse and weep, praying against whatever horrors the earth would turn on them. There's no place to hide. No way to fake it. No deals to be made. It is not a world that everyone can live with, but it's why the mushers, even the ultra-competitive dog drivers, became mushers in the first place.

Yet, along with the challenge and brutality, there is an ethereal beauty to the dogs and to the land that makes it worth drawing breath on the fringes of civilization.

Perennial Iditarod contender DeeDee Jonrowe is awestruck by long wintry trails through virgin wilderness. The sound of dogs panting, their feet padding, their lines softly jingling, runners gliding softly over the snow, the shadows of mountains cast by a full moon in the frozen silence. "I marvel at God's great creation: the people, the dogs and the unspoiled landscape. It's not just pretty, but powerful. Bigger than big."

No one can worship in a cathedral of sunsets, sunrises, the Northern Lights dancing and circling the sky, as well as they can from a prone position on top of their sled, perched atop a mountain peak or ridge in the middle of nowhere.

1998 Quest champion Bruce Lee of Denali Park, Alaska, believes "somewhere back in time there is a place that has ties with our bond to work with animals and travel across wild lands."

During a training run early one morning Newton stopped his team in a clearing just a few miles from the Gatt kennel. He looked at the mountains spilling out around him and down the Yukon River valley in wonder, picking up handfuls of shimmering snow and tossing them into the air to watch the crystals twinkle in the golden glow of the sunrise, asking himself, "What did I do to deserve this?"

Hans Gatt started out life as a farmer so long days and short wages were part of who he was long before he got into dogs. Because he was the only boy in a family with five children living in Ellbogen, a small town near Innsbruck, Austria, "I was raised, both in childhood and as a teenager, in preparation to take the farm over.

"Which was, at that time, a real thorn in my side. I wanted nothing to do with it. I was really into sports and I had other ideas about life. But that's the way it was and I kind of accepted it, but I didn't like it."

Hans was always a runner and a skier and persisted at it despite a lack of support for any sports activities from his family. His uncle gave him a bicycle when he was 12 and that started him on the path to racing professionally as a motocross rider for 10 years.

"It was totally insane. I got so addicted to it. That's all I was thinking and breathing about, motocross. That caused a lot of conflict – especially with my father. He could see where it was leading and it wasn't leading to the farm.

"In hindsight I would do it all over again. It was one of the best times I ever had in my life. It still gives me butterflies in my stomach when I watch a motocross race or when I start up a bike to take it out for a spin."

In 1987 a friend of Hans started running dogs and suggested that he come and watch him race. Off they went to Fischach, a town near Salzberg, and Hans found himself captivated. He returned to watch the next weekend.

He acquired a couple of dogs, which he used to pull him back up the hills after he had skied down them. He kept going to races and started studying the sleds, then built one himself. A third dog was bought because two weren't enough for pulling the sled. Near the end of the winter of 1987-1988, he traveled to Pasa di Nali (sic) in Italy and competed in a dogsled race for the first time. He finished in the top half of the field and, encouraged by that result, decided to get serious.

By the beginning of the next winter he had a kennel of a dozen dogs and started his own breeding program. "It wasn't any different from breeding dairy cows and I was good at that. I knew about genetics and what to look for. Getting into dogs was just a different animal, but the basics were the same."

Hans leased out his dairy cows, gave up being a farmer and moved to Fischach because it was a better place to train dogs. During the winter of 1987-1988 he won eight straight 3-dog races including his first European championship "and that, of course, did it. I was 100 percent into dog racing."

He and his wife, Herma flew to Edmonton, Alberta, in 1989, and drove up the Alaska Highway to watch the Open North American Sprint Championships in Fairbanks, Alaska.

"It was impressive and shocking," Hans said. "When you come from Europe, to drive from Edmonton to Fairbanks. The size of the country. It was like nothing we had expected. It just blew me away. I was fascinated. Herma was so shocked she couldn't get over it for weeks.

"People don't understand how mind-blowing it is to come from Europe – where everything is so close together – and then Canada is so immense! I fell in love with it immediately. For me there was no question about whether I would move."

In 1990, the year he moved to Canada, he shocked the people of Ellbogen by giving the farm to one of his nephews. "You just don't do that over there. It's so traditional. If you inherit the family farm you just keep on doing it," said Hans.

He had partnered with his brother-in-law, Ernst Danler, to manufacture dogsleds under the trade name *Gatt Sleds.* When Hans moved to Canada, Ernst changed the name to *Danler Sleds.* Danler sleds are still the most popular sprint sled in the world. Hans brought Gatt Sleds to Canada and is one of the top long distance sled manufacturers in the sport.

It wasn't easy at first. A dairy farmer who barely spoke English, starting life in a country where even its size was unreal to him, trying to succeed in a sport jealously guarded against interlopers like himself.

He still had sponsorship responsibilities in Europe, so he traveled there each winter until 1992 to race in the European championships, winning everything he entered. He stunned the mushing community by winning the 1992 IFSS World Sprint Championships – beating his mentor and friend, Fort Nelson, BC's Terry Streeper. "There was nobody out there who could beat him then," Hans said. "He was the king of the sprint world at that time."

The next year he quit sprint racing and entered his first long distance race, the Yukon Quest.

"We had moved to Atlin, BC, and in the Yukon, sprint racing just didn't get any recognition at all," Hans recalls. "Which kind of pissed me off because there is a lot of effort and time invested in it. People would say, 'Yeah, that's nice. But those dogs couldn't do the Yukon Quest.' Never tell me I can't do something. Because I'll figure out a way to do it."

His first Quest, by most measures, was a success but Hans didn't see it that way from the back of the sled. He had a team of sprint dogs, made rookie mistakes and still finished seventh although the team was probably better than that. At the Finish line he swore to Herma, "I'll never do this again. I'll go back to sprint racing, but I'll never do the Quest again."

He switched to middle distance races, between 100 and 500 miles in length but money was becoming an issue. His European sponsors had dropped him because he wasn't racing there anymore and he had to rely on sled sales, race purses and building log cabins to survive.

He borrowed some money and headed to Wyoming in 1996. There was a new 550-mile race down there using a new format – the first world-class stage race. Only 30 teams were allowed to enter and the real attraction was that it was the richest middle distance race at the time. Hans finished second behind five-time Iditarod winner Rick Swenson, earning enough to pay off his debts and set him up for the rest of the season. He ran the Wyoming Stage Race six times in total, winning four of them, finishing second twice. Not only did the purse money help, his success brought him sponsors.

The first year that he didn't race in Wyoming, 2002, he triumphed in the Copper Basin 300 – Alaska's toughest middle distance race – then entered the Yukon Quest for the second time and won it, the first of three consecutive wins. In 2006 and 2007 he finished second to Alaskan Lance Mackey.

Herma returned to Austria in 2003. "She was very close to her family and even after all these years in Canada," Hans said, "she never got over being homesick. She had given dog mushing 110 percent for all those years and didn't feel she could give any more. But without her we wouldn't have had the success we did."

Hans moved to Whitehorse in 2005, purchasing a log house in the countryside just south of the city, set up his 72-dog kennel, kept racing. When Newton arrived in December, 2007, Hans also had a new partner, Susie Rogan.

The trailer that Newton spent his first Yukon winter in was about 15 meters from the house. Susie showed Newton his quarters, gave him a heap of clothes, showed him how to layer the clothes so they would keep him warm and demonstrated how to adjust his winter boots.

"Come over to the house for dinner in about an hour," she told him as she left.

When he turned up at their front door he was wearing every piece of clothing she had given him.

"All he had to do was get from the trailer to the house," Dick laughed, "but that's what he had been told – 'This is how we dress in the Yukon' – so that's what he did. Even if all he had to do was go 10 feet, he was going to dress properly.

"He had no experience with a lot of things. The weather. A different social environment. Different food. Lifestyle. Clothes. Things we take for granted, that he had never experienced before. He probably firmly believed he would freeze to death on that first trip from the trailer to the house without all that clothing."

The biggest shock was discovering that his trailer had no plumbing. He had to go to the feed shed for a shower or just to get water and use an outhouse. "People in Jamaica didn't believe that such things actually existed," Newton still recalled the shock he experienced during his first usage. "When I told my friends about going to the outhouse in winter, they say 'me lose me appetite for shit.'"

One thing that surprised Newton about a cold climate was the number of times he had to pee in a day. In the tropics, a person just perspires out their moisture. In a cold climate, a person urinates. In both it is vital to drink a lot of fluids each day.

Susie, who had as much to learn about Newton as he did about his new life, discovered early that he was a hard worker. "If the fire went out in the main house, he would get up without being asked, go split or carry in a pile of firewood and start a fire. He loves doing things for people. He really does. He's really good at taking care of people."

Lisa, another handler working for Hans over the winter of 2007-2008, discovered Newton's sense of humor. On a rare evening off, all four went to a party being held by a neighbor. They stood around a massive bonfire and Lisa started to get too hot. Removing her jacket she looked for a place to put it.

"I can hold that for you," offered Newton, then with a grin, "And any other clothing you want to take off, I can hold them for you too."

Newton's illiteracy became a hurdle early on in the training. He misunderstood directions because his English was literal and common phrases used in Canada may have been obvious to Canadians but not to him. For example, the phrase "to put your foot down" is used in reference to imposing a limit on something. To Newton, it meant simply to take a step. He was expected to keep notes on the dogs and records of what occurred on his runs but wasn't able to.

"He's got all the words," Susie acknowledged, "but he can't write as fast as he can think." The solution was making use of Theresa, another handler working for Hans. She would walk through the team with Newton, and write down the notes for him as he spoke about each dog.

When Hans went to discuss a future run with Newton he would pull out a map, but Newton had never seen a detailed map before and couldn't read one. He had no concept of north, south, east or west. Like most Jamaicans, it was easier for him to take someone to a destination than it was to tell them how to get there. Hans would trace the route on the paper but it meant nothing to him. The main source of information for Newton was the verbal description of the trail.

"I just use common sense. Someone tells me there's something out there I need to be worried about…I watch for it," Newton said.

Despite his experience with the dogs at Chukka there was still a line that Newton wouldn't cross. One of the relationship building techniques Hans suggested was to have Newton take one of the sleddogs into his trailer each night and let it sleep under his bed or by the door. At first, Newton wouldn't do it at all. Then he started letting a dog in for a few minutes but would take it out again. It was apparent he didn't like having dogs in his house.

"It's not that he didn't like the dogs," observed Susie, "but there's that Jamaican thing where there's a limit to where dogs should be… and dogs shouldn't be in the house."

As much as Newton was on a learning curve to become a northern musher, Hans found himself on one as well. He was a demanding taskmaster,

Newton crossing the snow during the Carbon Hill race.

a dictatorial perfectionist who knew what to do and set severely high standards for himself, but had limited experience teaching others how to do it. His challenge was adjusting his approach to suit what Newton needed to know.

Even Newton recognized Hans' limitations, "He's a good trainer, but he's not a good teacher."

Hans didn't delay getting Newton into his first race, entering him into a local 32-mile sprint race, the Carbon Hill, just two months into his training. It proved to be an interesting experience for both.

By that time Newton was essentially doing 90 percent of what he needed to do correctly about 90 percent of the time, but he still needed direction and constant reminders.

"You tell him to do something it gets done," Hans wasn't finding Newton's passive approach to mushing easy to accept, but he understood it. "But if there's no one there to tell him what to do, then he doesn't do anything. It's tough to come out of a culture where you've been exposed to a lifetime of being told what to do and how to do it – to here where you need initiative and you need to know how to think your way through. Once you're out there, you're on your own. You need to be able to make decisions."

It was a beautiful morning, with a robin's egg blue sky – much like a Jamaican morning, but instead of sand and palm trees it was snow and jack pines. The temperature was -20°C. The cold didn't bother Newton. He strolled around the marshalling area, greeting other mushers he had met over the past two months. They all wore hats and gloves. Newton had bare hands and nothing on his head. Long-time Northerners just shook their heads in astonishment. They felt cold, why didn't he?

His inexperience showed up early. Newton was entered in the 8-dog class but could only find seven dogs in the dog truck. He had left one dog behind at the kennel. So he started one dog short.

When he thought he was ready he summoned an official to go over the mandatory gear checklist. Twice he threw his hands in the air and ran back to the dog truck to locate the missing item. He had everything, with the exception of that one dog. It just wasn't terribly well organized. It was an easy introduction to racing since this was a recreational race where those mistakes could be made. His next race was an essential component in the project and wouldn't be so forgiving.

To qualify just to enter the Yukon Quest, Newton would have to complete two long distance races for a total of 500 miles within the 12 months prior to the start of the Quest. The qualifying races served to weed out the individuals who weren't capable of doing it but tried to enter anyway.

Hans had originally planned to enter Newton in the Percy DeWolfe Memorial Mail Race between Dawson City and Eagle, Alaska, at the end of March, and in the 340-mile Dagoo, between Eagle Plains, a highway lodge about 200 miles north of Dawson City to Old Crow, a native village well north of the Arctic Circle. Unfortunately the Dagoo was cancelled late – too late for Hans to find an alternate 300-mile race for Newton this season. He would have to race in "the Percy" and finish his qualifying the next winter.

The Percy was named after the *Iron Man of the North,* Percy DeWolfe, who carried the mail between Dawson City, Yukon, and Eagle, Alaska, from 1910 until 1949. If there was a mailman who delivered on the code of postal delivery despite "rain, hail, sleet and storm," it was Percy. He made the trip regardless of temperatures (-58°C was the coldest recorded trip he made) and whether or not the ice on the river was frozen. During thaw and freeze-up he would shift his team from ice flow to ice flow. In 1935, King George VI of England honored his accomplishments with a silver medal. Delivering the mail was life to Percy. Two years after his last contract was terminated, he died.

The race in his honor was started in 1976 as a fun run for local mushers. It is still a small race in the world of dog mushing – in fact, it's hard to be much smaller – but as close to pure dog mushing as one can get. Over the

Start of the 2008 Percy DeWolfe in Dawson City.

years it's developed into one of the most enjoyable events on the mushing calendar and has attracted most of the Iditarod and Quest champion dog drivers.

But it's not a cakewalk for anyone. "It isn't that easy," Hans warned, "It's 200 miles and you only get six hours of rest in that."

The trail to Forty Mile, a vet check and dog drop for the racers, followed the Quest route. Where the Quest swings up the Fortymile River to American Summit, the Percy continues downriver on the Yukon to Eagle, where the teams rest for six hours before starting the journey back up river to Dawson.

In years where the Yukon River freezes fairly flat, it's not considered a difficult race. There are no hills to climb, only one short portage. There's glare ice and overflow. In years where the river doesn't freeze flat, it can be brutal on the dogs and musher. River valleys also act as funnels for wind and there are few places colder or more unpleasant than being on a river during a tempest.

The greatest danger is when a team goes onto or off the ice. Pressure cracks are usually along the banks of the river and a dog stepping into one could seriously damage a wrist, elbow or shoulder.

The Percy represented Newton's first major step towards the Quest and his first challenge, not just as a dog race but also as a shift in his own personal culture. Until now, with the noted exception of the Carbon Hill race start when Hans let Newton make his rookie mistakes, Hans had dictated what to do and how to do it. Newton hadn't been expected to make decisions because he didn't have enough information to do so.

Before the race Hans sat with Newton and emphasized what was going to change. The Percy, Hans warned, was going to be his "wake-up call." In the North, he reminded him, Mother Nature was not as forgiving as in Jamaica.

"Newton, you need to start taking control. You need to start…not just making decisions…but making the right decisions at the right time." Hans was also racing so they would see each other on the trail, but he would not interfere with Newton's race. "If I do that then you're not running your own race. If I pull you across (the Finish line) what's the point of qualifying? We've given you everything you need to make the right choices. Now all you have to do is use the information you've got."

"In Jamaica there's nothing to be gained by making decisions." The responsibility of being without guidance on the trail was daunting for Newton. "You make a good decision and nobody notices. You make a bad one and you get fired. So the best thing to do is not make any at all."

Hans wasn't sure how to answer that. "With the dogs," he responded, "not making a decision is making a bad decision. You have to make decisions. The lives of your dogs depend upon it. Your life depends upon it."

There were four teams from the kennel in the 2008 Percy: Hans, Susie, Newton and Alan Stewart's son, John, also training with Hans to run the 2009 Quest. The two rookies had an ongoing friendly dispute about which was better for the dogs – Reggae or Bagpipes.

"I play bagpipe music for the dogs," John insisted, his highland blood coming to the fore. "They're marching songs. Reggae's too slow."

"I sing fast Reggae," countered Newton. "It makes them go quicker."

The two of them continued their banter as they encountered each other along the river toward Eagle, agreeing only on one thing – they would need to know a lot of songs to go 1,000 miles.

The plan was to run the entire 105 miles to Eagle, then take a stop at Forty Mile on the return journey. As darkness approached Newton started to get nervous. He had done long training runs at night but those were on trails the dogs knew or he was familiar with. The river with its glaciation, overflow and missing trail markers was a different challenge. He found himself zigzagging back and forth across the ice looking for the trail. One patch of glare ice, just before he reached Eagle did spin him around.

When his team rolled up the riverbank into Eagle for his six-hour mandatory layover before heading back to Dawson, the residents took a collective gasp of shock. They knew there was a Jamaican in the race. It had just never occurred to them that a dog musher might be anything other than white or native. Then they turned on the hospitality.

"They bring me a lot of food (curried chicken, added to the menu just for him). I got a little sleep, but I didn't feel tired."

When he left Eagle the Northern Lights were putting on a display for the ages. One delicate band of color alone or in concert with others, flooded the jet-black dome of the heavens with a muted, trembling brilliance, making the stars seem pale and far away. Newton could hear them singing to him. Snapping and crackling with bad temper, rippling like running water, sighing like a gentle wind through the trees or purring like they were the contented custodians of some sacred secret.

Finish line at Percy DeWolfe race.

Science tells us the *Aurora Borealis,* the Northern Lights, are a solar light storm seen on earth as slithering, shimmering, prismatic bands of color. For Eskimos along the north coast, they are torches held by the spirits to guide the souls of those who have just died. For indigenous peoples who live on the lower reaches of the Yukon River, they are animal spirits.

One French Canadian musher once described his reaction to the Northern Lights as "you fall on your ass…but you're still standing up!"

John was bedazzled. He saw them in Scotland but nothing like the green and white sheets with bits of rainbows along the ragged bottom, hanging like a chandelier from the heavens. He had little time to appreciate them fully.

"I was busy watching the dogs and watching the ice. Then I lost the trail. So I went to this side. Then to that side looking for it. I could hear the ice pop and snap under the runners. It made me a little nervous."

The only things in Newton's experience he could compare them to were rainbows and "sundogs"– large atmospheric halos around the sun that make it appear as if there is more than one sun in the sky.

"This is like a dream," Newton enthused. "I never once thought I would be doing anything like this. The Northern Lights were just beautiful but I couldn't get lost in them. I had too much to do to keep the dogs from stepping in cracks or slipping."

He tried passing a team and the dogs got tangled up with each other. He lost the trail a couple of times and other teams kept catching up and passing him.

With just 20 miles to go he didn't like the way Eastwood, one of his wheel dogs, looked and loaded him into the sled bag. When he pulled up over the dike onto Front Street in Dawson, Eastwood sat comfortably in the bag with his front legs daintily crossed in his lap.

"I'm impressed," race head veterinarian John Overell was approving of his actions. "For a rookie to turn up with a dog in the basket is pretty impressive. You did the right thing. When you're questioning whether a dog should be in harness or not it's best to err on the side of dog safety.

"You should be very proud of yourself. For someone in their first-ever distance race you finished well and took care of your dogs."

Newton was the seventh team across the Finish line and John Stewart was right behind.

The race was experimenting with new tracking technology that had been tested by selected mushers in both the Iditarod and the Quest. Small and unintrusive, it sent up a signal every 10 minutes, enabling race fans to follow the teams on their computers at home. The tracker, on loan from the manufacturer, didn't always work that well. At one point it had Newton miles ahead of competitors who were actually miles ahead of him.

At the Finish line, the communications manager for the Percy, John Bryant, approached Newton. "First of all," he said, "do you have your tracker?"

"I think I lost that," replied Newton deadpan. There was a stunned silence from John. Then Newton grinned and reached into his sled bag, pulling out the tracker.

"I can't believe I fell for that," gasped a relieved John.

At the Finish Banquet that night one fan wanted to trade a "hoodie" for Newton's Reggae Boyz soccer shirt. "You're the best thing that's happened to the Percy in a long time!" the fan gushed, "You're the best thing that's happened to mushing in a long time!"

Newton was voted the Sportsmanship Award.

Air temperature at the start of the 2009 Copper Basin was minus 48.

"This is the coolest award because it's voted on by everyone by what they've seen on the trail," explained race marshal Mel Besharah. "It's the person they think is the best out there. The most fun out there. The most helpful."

Before Newton left Jamaica in December, he and Brian Kennedy had a long conversation. Newton still had doubts about this job and expressed concern about whether or not he would make it.

"Do you know the word 'perseverance'?" asked Brian.

"No."

"What it means is to have the determination that, whatever it takes, I'm going to get through this. I'm here. Here's my goal on the other side. I will persevere to reach my goal. That's the measure of a man.

"Anyone can do something that's easy. Those who persevere are the ones who mark themselves as a man and make it through. That's what you're going to have to remind yourself up in the Airstream trailer in the Yukon," advised Brian.

The day Newton returned to Jamaica he gave a triumphant grin. "Mr. Kennedy," he said, "I persevered."

But there was another season to go. The honeymoon period was over and his second year in the Yukon would be marked with progress and marred by conflict.

Newton being interviewed by the press.

An Issue of Trust

Relationships of trust depend on our willingness to look not only to our own interests, but also the interests of others.

Peter Farquharson

November, 2008

Susie stopped trusting Newton at Christmas the previous year.

He had flown back to Jamaica before Christmas but on the return journey snowstorms in Dallas, Texas delayed his arrival into Vancouver by eight hours, too late to make his connecting flight. According to Newton, the Air Canada staff told him it was unlikely he would get a flight to Whitehorse in the next couple of days because of the backlog of passengers.

The airline provided him with a free room at the airport but he never checked in. "I didn't know anybody at the hotel," Newton said.

Instead some Jamaican friends who had moved to Vancouver, whom he had called from Dallas, were there when he cleared immigration and they took him to their home.

There were open seats on the flights to Whitehorse the next morning but Newton didn't return to the airport for two days. Claiming to have lost their phone number, he didn't call Hans and Susie to explain what he was doing.

When he arrived in Whitehorse they drove directly to Atlin for a training run. At the end of the run Hans took a look at the paws of Newton's dogs. Five had injuries that were usually the result of not using booties on the trail. He asked Newton if he had bootied the dogs.

"Yeh Mon."

Hans lost it, yelling at Newton, picking up the paws and spreading the toes to expose the redness, "I know you're not telling the truth on this one. I can see the dog's feet!"

"I checked them," replied Newton, "I checked every foot."

Susie didn't buy it. Just as she didn't believe he was being totally honest about his extended Vancouver stay.

"For us the implications (of missing the next flight in Vancouver) were much larger," she explained. "More than just missing three days of training, it was 'How can we trust this guy?'"

When he gets angry, Hans has a hair-trigger temper, but his anger passes as quickly as it comes. Susie, on the other hand, is a skilled tongue-lasher. Her way of dealing with an issue is to confront it directly. The conversation over dinner that night took a nasty turn. Susie challenged Newton, both about Vancouver and the dogs' feet.

"So Newton," she got sarcastic, "Is there anything you did wrong? Anything?"

He didn't respond, just sat and stared down at the table.

"Oh, so you're completely blameless!"

Newton, misunderstanding the word, reacted vehemently, "You're calling me brainless!! You can call me anything you want. I can't take this abuse anymore!"

"It's not easy (living here)," downcast as he recalled it later. "It's tough. They might swear at you. Get cross. Angry. Miserable. It's very hard to please them."

Susie still gets upset when she thinks about how their relationship started to deteriorate that night. "My respect for him was at an all-time low. Honest to God, it was horrible. I didn't even want to look at him for the next week and a half.

"I didn't want to abuse him! But he almost pulls it right out of you. He grew up with parents who beat him. In a society that to kids is dismissive and abusive, I can yell at him and it doesn't mean a thing. He knows how to deal with it.

"I think that is the Jamaican culture. You play dumb to get away with it. When people can't get what they want by asking for it, because they don't have the power, then they manipulate to get what they want.

"He's a manipulator. It's a skill set in Jamaica. It's not a negative for them. It's unfair the way that culture is set up. Manipulation is a craft. An art. It greases the wheel in Jamaica because I don't see the people in charge wanting to change it. They (the employers) are trying to provide employment so people will have food on the table. Maybe he's not doing it consciously, but it's a pattern of behavior.

"It's easier for the managers or employers to accept a little white lie and drop it rather than having someone tell them, 'I know I told that, but if I had told the truth, you would have said no.'

"That is honest. Newton did eventually say that he hadn't bootied the dogs to us and the world didn't screech to a halt for him. He didn't get fired. It was, 'Okay. We can deal with that.'"

From that night onward, Newton tended to be sullen and withdrawn in most of his dealings with Susie.

John Stewart didn't return for his second year of training with Hans. He later stated that, while he respected what Hans had accomplished and his knowledge of the sport, he didn't like Hans' approach to teaching and also had personal differences with Susie.

Dick could see the erosion of the relationship but felt it wasn't his place to come up with a solution. Newton and Susie had to sort this one out on their own.

"Newton's a charmer," observed Dick. "It's a natural charm. He's got this great infectious grin. Easy to laughter. Polite. Naïve. The girls love him for it.

"Unfortunately the relationship with Susie started to deteriorate because of that. Susie didn't trust the charm. She started to believe the charm was a cover for lies and deception. I think she always thought he was trying to get away with something.

"In Jamaica you have to lie to survive. I think they don't think of it as lying. They see it as a way to manipulate life so they can survive because everyone else isn't telling the truth either. If you do something wrong…even something minor…you deny it. I think that's just part of his nature. A kid from the streets. That's the way it is," Dick explained.

"Hans had the advantage of being able to recognize the 'little white lies.' He would get angry but wouldn't necessarily challenge it. He would find a way around it. Let Newton know he knew it wasn't right and this is what really happened.

For his second year Hans built Newton a log cabin.

"Susie never mastered that. She just challenged it as lying. And all that did was make Newton defensive."

There was a glimmer of hope when Newton returned for his second season. In an email on October 29, 2008, Susie wrote: "Newton just arrived in the yard. It seems the quad must have died because he came in running beside it and is now stripping off his Canada Goose heavy-duty parka, his mitts and hat. Looks like he had quite a jog.

"Anyway, it is fabulous to have Newton back. I can't convey how enjoyable he is to have around. Last night he was talking to Havanna (one of Hans and Susie's retired sleddogs) and I said, 'Ya. She's getting old.' Newton said to her, 'When the moon get old, she light just shine brighta.'

"He's always saying and doing nice things. He sees me carrying a load of wood in one arm and pail of wood in the other, and he runs over to grab something. He's in the kitchen talking and just picks up a rag and starts cleaning countertops while he talks, or picks up the broom and starts sweeping. It's all so natural to him to just help out while laughing and being a nice person."

The hope lasted until their first conflict and then the suspicions, distrust, animosities and resentment boiled up again.

However, Hans and Dick both noticed a marked change in Newton.

"The biggest thing I noticed with Newton was self-confidence," Dick was impressed with the difference. "In his mind, in Jamaica, in terms of self-esteem and personal self-achievement, he had nothing. I don't think he looked at his background – looking after his sisters, learning how to read – as accomplishments at all.

"I think it was when he started to do things and found he could do them well. He never really talks about it, but you can tell he's starting to feel pretty good about himself."

During the summer accommodations had also improved. Hans built a small log cabin for Newton with a small wood stove, an eating and reading space and a proper bed – but he still had to use the outhouse.

"He has matured," observed Hans. "It's like night and day. He has more confidence and he's not afraid to make decisions." However, there were still some concerns.

"I've never worked with anyone like him before. One day he'll be perfectly responsible and say 'from now on, no more mistakes. I'm really going to be on the ball.' Two weeks later, something comes completely out of the blue.... He forgets about something you thought would never be an issue again.

"I don't understand it. I can't get my head around it. When he does make a mistake he still always has an excuse ready. Never takes responsibility or says 'I made a mistake.' He just won't do that...it's not Newton's fault. It's conditioned into him. Self-preservation in the world he comes from – but which has no place in the mushing world.

"When I look back, it's amazing what he learned in a short time. Most people take years to gain that knowledge. If we can get him past that then he'll be a very good musher."

The first race of the season for Newton and Hans was the Sheep Mountain Lodge 150, held in the mountains 113 miles (181 kilometers) northeast of Anchorage, Alaska, on the Glenn Highway. Organized by Iditarod and Quest regular and lodge owner Zack Steer, the goal of the race was to provide mushers with a well-marked and safe trail for early season distance training.

There were three legs of approximately 50 miles (80 kilometers) each with a five-hour mandatory layover at the end of each leg. Both Hans and Newton had a schedule, not to win, but to match. Their individual goals were to complete the race at the time they predicted they would finish. Newton was precisely on time – coming across the Finish line in 21st place out of 48 teams, in just over 20 hours. Hans stuck to his schedule until the final leg and then uncorked the team and raced to a third place finish.

One race vet was impressed with Newton's performance. "He had his checkpoint routine down almost perfectly. You could tell he was having to think, but he didn't miss a thing."

Hans knew what he and Newton needed to find out during his second and longest qualifying race, the Copper Basin 300. “That’s what these races are for. The problems we find here are the problems we’ll have on the Quest.”

The two main questions he wanted answered concerned Newton’s ability to deal with sleep deprivation and dog care. It wasn’t necessary to find excuses for not completing the 300; the race itself would supply those in abundance.

“For two years we’ve been trying to work on coping with small amounts of sleep,” said Hans. “When he’s sleep-deprived, he slows down and some of his decisions are not great. He knows all of the technical stuff – the equipment, the dogs, the trails. It took awhile to get across that dog care is the main priority. But his ability to maintain control depends entirely upon his ability to cope with sleep deprivation…and that has me concerned.”

Hans wasn’t sure of the answers he would receive, but there was only one way to find them. As much as anything else, technology, skill, organization, Newton would need his share of good luck.

The Copper Basin, known in the mushing community as “the toughest 300 miles of hell in Alaska,” is notorious for being cold. In 2001, the race was cancelled when temperatures hit -57°C.

2009 was no exception. When Hans and Newton drove into Wolverine Lodge on Lake Louise on January 8, 2009, it was -48°C. “Wicked cold, Mon! Cut into me like a knife.”

At those temperatures there is no moisture in the air. Your senses seem sharper. Vision is clearer – everything you look at is rendered in ultrasharp contours. The snow is so dry it doesn’t squeak under your foot but you can hear the metal on the vehicles grow brittle and the wood in the trees split. There is the sense of not being able to smell anything – the air itself is odorless. Everything that can freeze is frozen.

Writer Jack London described the northern environment as “a foe to be contested.” For those who are in it, it’s the only thing they can talk about because it invades even the warmest places and spaces. At first it’s possible to keep warm or heat a room but eventually the cold seeps into everything and once in, it’s almost impossible to get it out.

“We’ve been cold,” the Start Banquet master of ceremonies stated. “In fact, we’ve been hammered by the cold.” Eight straight weeks without the temperatures rising above -40°C.

They hadn’t been the only ones. All of Alaska had been in a deep freeze since the beginning of December. The teams had trained but it had been only to maintain conditioning – no gain was made. Lance Mackey ran figure eights on top of the mountain where he lived outside of Fairbanks. Temperature inversions, where warm air higher in the atmosphere traps colder air at the lower elevations, meant it was 20 degrees warmer up there than it was in the valleys below. "No way I was going down there," said Lance.

The trail itself was the worst under the toughest conditions imaginable. Long stretches of sugar snow – loose granular snow so dry it doesn't set into a good trail, like trying to run in sugar, loose and unstable. Mountains to climb. Open water on the rivers. And, of course, the cold. Cold that eats away at your spirit.

"The Percy is an easy 200-miler. The Sheep Mountain is an easy 150-miler," said Hans. "But this…the Copper Basin. It's as hard a race as you can find. This is Newton's first real taste of what the Yukon Quest is like."

Newton drew the number one starting position and one of the first things he did after leaving the Start line was lose the trail. "I was looking in my sled bag and the dogs went where they thought they should go and the trail went off to the right. After awhile I didn't see any other musher, so I stop the team and go look at the trail. There's been no sled go ahead of me so I knew I made a mistake. So I turn the team around and we go back to where I make the wrong turn."

In the town of Glenallen, 49 miles down the trail, two of his competitors approached him as he bedded down and fed the team.

"You're the favorite choice of everyone as our most popular rookie," said one. "Of course, the higher you finish the better it'll be. You could be the first Jamaican to win the Copper Basin. You'll be the first one to ever finish. Hell, you're the first one that ever entered!"

"Thanks," responded a frosty Newton, "I need to finish because there's no more race."

"Good luck," the other musher nodded. He understood why Newton was racing. This was his last chance to qualify for the Quest. "I'm real glad you're here."

The 59 miles to the next checkpoint at Chistochina took him onto the Chistochina River where massive open leads in the ice momentarily panicked him. "I was really scared when I saw that," said Newton. "We had to go so close to it. It was cold, cold and there was black water open in the ice, running under the ice. Would we go too close and the ice break? I had to not think and I had to get by it."

He successfully negotiated the U-turn on the top of Gakona Hill. Failure to do so would have sent him on a final, life-ending descent down a steeper, more direct route to the river below.

Stay a little longer at Chistochina, Hans had instructed him, because the hardest part of the race would be the next 72 miles to the mandatory eight-hour layover at Paxson. Hans had written a schedule out on paper and plasticized it for him so it wouldn't be damaged if it got wet. Newton had studied it but knew he wouldn't have time to try reading it during the race. He memorized it, could verbally recite it back when asked, and the paper remained in his sled for the duration of the race.

The trail zigzagged across the river again, then climbed up towards Paxson through hills so steep and slippery that Newton had to run behind the sled, pushing it uphill to help the dogs. "I take a deep breath and the cold air, it hurt my lungs. I still feel it a bit but only when I laugh." He got mild frostbite on his nose and fingers.

The sugar snow started to take a toll on the mushers on the final two legs, 60 miles to Sourdough Creek and the last 59 miles back to Wolverine Lodge. Everyone was thoroughly miserable but refused to surrender to the elements.

Finisher's certificate for the Copper Basin qualified Newton to run the Quest.

Chad Lindner, son of the 1984 Yukon Quest champion Sonny Lindner, had his team quit on him 20 miles from the Finish line. He camped for six hours, tending to the sensitive wrists rubbed raw by the snow, hoping the extra rest would enable his team to recover sufficiently to trot into Wolverine. He ran out of food and other mushers passing by gave him what they had left. Finally he said "enough is enough." He hitched up the team, took his leaders by their neckline and led the team through the deep snow. It took him 17 hours to wallow his way to Wolverine.

Up ahead, Lance opened a substantial lead and then hung on to beat Hans to the Finish line. Brent Sass made the final run interesting but faded to third. Newton crossed the Finish line eight hours behind Lance, in 13th place.

"Congratulations," said Whitehorse musher Ed Hopkins, "You're now qualified to be just as crazy as the rest of us."

"Anyone else in your family mush dogs?" asked Lance as he shook Newton's hand.

"No Mon. They think I'm a mad man. My friends tell me I must be sick in the brain."

"Don't worry," laughed Lance, "There's a lot of that in this room."

When presenting Newton with his share of the purse for finishing in the last paying position, the race marshal stated the opinion of many in the room, "A Jamaican…I wasn't expecting much. What an attitude he has. I

wish every rookie out there could have his attitude. Is there anything that could get that smile off his face?"

"It was fun," responded Newton, "But the cold and the mushy snow. That part not so much fun."

"The Copper Basin is the toughest 300 mile race...period. And this year was no different," summed up the Finish Banquet master of ceremonies.

Hans shared the moment with Newton when he received his Finisher's certificate and unconditionally qualified for the Quest, but hadn't gotten all the answers he wanted.

"That's something I thought I had drilled into him and I thought it would never be an issue again. Always run the dogs with booties, especially in bad snow conditions. There shouldn't be one foot without booties. And when he comes in, he has four dogs completely without booties and others had booties missing.

"I'm not sure how to approach this. I have to figure out a way to deal with this. I know he didn't bootie the dogs, but I can't yell at him. It doesn't work. How do I get him to understand?"

He had bootied the dogs, insisted Newton, but they kept tearing them off. Hans countered that defense by describing that Newton knew he was close to the Finish line. He was tired. It was cold. It had been a tough race. He decided Newton made a decision not to bootie the dogs because they were so close to finishing.

Eventually, Newton admitted he could see the lights of Wolverine across the lake and made the call. He had just misjudged the distance.

"I don't doubt his mind will get him through the Quest," Hans had been hoping for a clearer vision of the future. "That's why most people drop out. They have a fantastic team, healthy team and they scratch because they don't believe what they are seeing.

"His ability to deal with the cold. His technical skills. He knows what to do. But I'm worried about his ability to deal with sleep deprivation. If he can't get by that, his dog care suffers.

"He may want to continue, but the vets may decide otherwise and force him to withdraw. He needs to stay focused on what's important. For the first time I have my doubts that he will finish the Quest."

Back in Whitehorse, Susie added the incident to her deteriorating opinion of him. She understood that Newton was not yet the master of his own destiny. That he was the child of circumstance, difficulties and struggles. His problems had sculpted him and his newfound talents and abilities would continue the process. But she put little faith in his ability or desire to truly change.

"This is the thing I think he needs to realize and nobody can tell him this. He's been given an opportunity to step into adulthood. Step away from that subordinate role. Whether he realizes that's the door that's open in front of him I don't know.

"I don't think he does. You can tell them (Jamaicans) things and they don't even know what you're talking about. Like 'grow up' or 'take responsibility'…who knows what that means?!" She never found how to communicate effectively with or motivate Newton.

From his own perspective, Hans struggled with how to reach Newton and finally did find a way in Dawson City although he probably never realized it.

The clues were always there during "Happy Hour" – the time each afternoon when Hans let all the dogs run loose in the kennel. The dogs made Hans part of their socializing, coming up to greet him. He, in turn, responded with affection showing each dog he cared about them.

"There are people who can get results from dogs in different ways," Newton observed. "There are still people who use a heavy hand with their teams. But their teams don't last very long. They need a new team almost every year.

"Hans' love for his dogs is obvious. They love him right back and will do everything he asks of them and do it year after year.

"Hans had to be hard with me because he wanted me to be a good musher. Susie…there was no need for Susie to be the way she was."

Despite her distrust and misgivings about Newton, Susie did harbor a certain level of empathy for him. "It's sort of a curse," she said, referring to his experience in the North and expressing concern about his future in Jamaica. "If you learn too much you don't fit in anywhere anymore."

She compared him to George Bernard Shaw's Pygmalion. "His life's experience is so far removed from Jamaica he may have trouble fitting in. But if he learns how to read and write he could go as far as he wants. He's a good guy. We would love to see him make something of this opportunity."

Susie could never say any of this to Newton because it was too late. Newton had stopped listening to her.

Newton eats a steak dinner beneath the standings board at Central.

Newton's Schedule

Circle City to Central

80 miles, 15 hours

"There's a Jamaican in this race," the radio in someone's car blared out.

"Name's Newton Marshall. I was a bit concerned he might be in over his head on this one – conditions here being somewhat different than there.

"But he's hanging in there. If you want to know which one he is, just look for the team of dogs with dreadlocks."

The children of Circle City were excited. There was a Jamaican musher coming to town. They had never seen one before and might never see one again. It would be like one of them turning up in Jamaica and, to a child, how likely was that? Most had never been outside of the Central Mining District. Their world was framed by the Yukon River to the north and the White Mountains to the south.

Despite their differences in environment and culture children of isolated northern communities are kindred spirits to the young of the Caribbean.

Many of them spend their entire lives without leaving the Yukon River Valley, just as many Jamaicans never leave their island. Most of those who do leave always yearn to return but probably never will.

Whenever they could they crowded around Newton, chattering at him, asking for autographs. He smiled at them, teased them, scratched his signature painstakingly out on whatever they handed him to sign. One girl kept returning to the checkpoint looking for him, but he was always asleep when she turned up. Finally she left her e-mail address for him and a note asking him to e-mail her. She couldn't know that while Newton knew what e-mail was, his illiteracy prevented him from using it.

As they do every year, the school kids of Circle City decorated the checkpoint with massive, hand-painted posters cheering on individual mushers by name, wishing all of them the best of luck. Their artwork transformed the community fire station, complete with fire truck, into a welcoming montage of color. There were long tables laden with food. Cots set up in an isolated room for the mushers to sleep on. There was a communications room off to one side that had a computer showing the current standings.

Newton's paper plate bent under the weight of the pancakes, corn-on-the-cob, and beans and wieners heaped on it. ("There's no pork in these is there? I don't eat pork.") At first he stood with Mark Sleightholme looking at the computer. He wasn't sure what it meant and wandered back out into the main room. Asking a journalist to use a newspaper and explain what he was looking at, Newton was startled when Susie pushed between them, snatching the paper.

"You don't need to bother with that," she said. "Eat and get some sleep."

"Susie, I am eating," he responded.

Earlier Hans, Susie and Danny agreed that Newton needed to minimize his distractions at the checkpoints. Hans had returned with his team to Whitehorse but called each checkpoint to talk to Newton about what he needed to do to improve his competitive position. Danny, in Fairbanks, had sent an e-mail instructing everyone, the documentary film crew and writers, to keep away from Newton. Susie's job was to act as his personal checkpoint distraction bodyguard.

As she left Newton muttered to the journalist, "I don't know why she's doing that. I did just fine on my own in Eagle and at Slaven. I don't want to do this again (run a long distance race) if I have to go through this. They keep treating me like a kid. Susie always whispering in my ear, 'You need to go to sleep.' I did pretty good in the part of the race where I didn't have anyone telling me what to do."

At one point she talked to him about the difference in his competitive positioning and that improving his standing just one spot was worth $500 to him. His eyes glazed over. He obviously wasn't paying attention.

Later, she approached the same journalist asking him if he had the correct time.

"Ten o'clock," he responded.

"Oh my God," she started adjusting her watch, "I'm still on Yukon time (there is a one-hour time zone difference between Alaska and the Yukon). They've put the times on the (standings) board down in Alaskan time. I thought Newton had been here for hours and he had just arrived. I thought he was just wasting time talking. I'm sorry."

When Newton decided it was time to sleep he started looking for a place to lie down. He didn't like the designated sleeping area in the back of the building.

"Go up on the fire truck and lay down on the fire hoses," suggested Susie. "Lance Mackey did that last year and he said it was a comfortable place to sleep."

As Newton clambered up the side of the truck, he paused and looked uncertainly back at a volunteer serving food to the mushers, "This thing isn't going to move is it?"

"Only if there's a fire," she cheerfully responded.

Mark had already laid claim to the front seat of the fire truck and Newton settled down on top.

"It was pretty good. I sleep not too bad at all."

Mushers arrived and departed as he slept. Whitehorse musher and Quest veteran Kyla Boivin, who had started the race with high hopes of being competitive, finally pulled into Circle. Everything that could go wrong for her race had gone wrong. She was depressed and looking at the standings board listing the mushers ahead of her didn't help her mood.

"Shit!" she shouted.

"Who are you chasing?" asked a handler standing beside her.

"I'm just running a dog race," she snapped back. "But I don't know if I'm running a dog race anymore." She scratched the next day in Central after dropping her main lead dog.

In 1896 Circle City was the largest log cabin city in the world. Gold was discovered on Birch Creek in 1893 and prospectors from all over Alaska flocked to the Central Mining District, making their temporary homes there on the banks of the Yukon River. They mistakenly thought the town was on the Arctic Circle and named it as such, but the circle itself is about 100 miles further north.

At its peak it had an opera house, two theatres, eight dance halls, 28 saloons, a library, stores and trading posts, a newspaper, a U.S. Customs station and the first official post office in central and northern Alaska. It was the end of the road north from Fairbanks. However, gold seekers being gold seekers, when word of the Klondike reached the community it emptied overnight.

Even the original town site is gone, washed away in the 1930s by the annual spring floods and high water of the Yukon River.

The current location has a store, a restaurant and four-room motel, a small post office, a fire station and a school. A large hotel that had been built on the Yukon River looked abandoned. Only about 100 people live in the community. A few dozen log cabins and houses made up the residential area.

Circle is also the home of the Perry Davis Pain Killer Thermometer – a temperature gauge that consists of four bottles set outside a window during winter. If the first bottle, containing mercury, freezes, it isn't too bad. If the second, whiskey, freezes it isn't great but it's bearable. If the third bottle, containing kerosene, thickens – now a person should hesitate before going outside. The fourth bottle contains the Perry Davis Pain Killer – a strong tasting, but totally useless medication hawked by charlatans to innocents heading north to the gold fields. If that one solidifies, there isn't anyone going outside.

The Central District is notorious for cold weather. This year, with temperatures hovering around -30°C, it wasn't bad at all. Not even the mercury had frozen.

The trail to Central followed Birch Creek, a meandering stream, wide in some places, so narrow and tight in others it sometimes appears the teams are doubling back on themselves as they follow its coils. It is usually rife with overflow, but there was none of that this year. At one point along the creek the teams are just 12 miles from Central but it twists again, taking them in the wrong direction. Following the trail they would still have 20 miles to go to reach the checkpoint.

When it finally left the creek, a few miles from Central, it passed along the end of the airstrip at Circle Hot Springs (one of the original Quest checkpoints, now closed to the public), where the steam from the mineral pools can be seen rising into the sky. Then it traveled through willow trees before emerging and following alongside the road for the last few miles into Central.

The team set a good steady pace and Newton was content to just let them go, only occasionally stepping off the runners to help. His schedule called for him to stop for four hours at Cochrane's Cabin, a quiet, sleepy cabin on the banks of the creek almost halfway between the two checkpoints. Trapper Carl Cochrane has made his cabin one of the most comfortable hospitality points along the Quest trail since it was first run in 1984. Even the competitive mushers stop in to say hello and have a coffee before continuing their race.

Newton glanced up the trail to the cabin as he approached and just kept gliding along at a good clip. "The dogs were running good so I decided to keep going." He knew the dogs were more than capable of making an 80-mile run with just snack stops and it was an opportunity to catch some of the teams ahead of him. He settled into the half-conscious neutral state of mind a musher gets when the dogs are performing well. He began to get the feel of the country. Its size and emptiness appealed to him as did the flat, sweeping corners of the creek. He imagined it would not prove unfriendly to a man with respect for the natural order of things.

The dogs were covering a good deal of ground at a uniform, reasonably efficient traveling speed. For them the sensation of pulling was not unlike riding some kind of minimalist vehicle, one that traveled at a steady though unspectacular pace and would take them just about anywhere they wanted to go. It was perhaps that feeling that inspired them to enthusiastically and willingly embark on 100- or 1,000-mile runs.

Many of them had been on this trail before. Psychologically, it's easier for a dog to run a familiar course than a new one so they seldom went exploring for changes of scenery. Seldom, but not always. Occasionally they too could get distracted and wander from the marked trail.

As they closed in on Central, the dogs decided to take a detour from the trail into a farmyard. Newton jammed on his brake, called "whoa!" and, when he finally got them stopped, set the ice hook in the snow. He looked behind himself but didn't see any trail markers.

"This doesn't look like the trail," he said to himself. He made sure the team was securely anchored, walked to the farmhouse and knocked on the door. The man who opened it seemed surprised to find a musher standing on his front porch and a dog team parked in his driveway.

"Hello. I'm Newton Marshall and I'm in the Yukon Quest. I think I've lost the trail," he said. "Can you tell me where the trail is?"

"It's the road," the man responded.

"Thank you," said Newton. He returned to the team, turned them around and headed back to the road.

He wasn't the only one with trail problems on the final stretch into Central. One of the fundamental rules in a close race is to keep yourself as mistake-free as possible and hope the people in front made one that you could take advantage of.

Hugh Neff, trailing race leader William Kleedehn by just a few minutes, had also strayed off the trail after passing the airstrip near Circle Hot Springs. Once past the airstrip, the trail travels on the road for a couple of hundred yards before swinging into the woods again. For almost six miles he drove his team along the road rather than the trail.

Members of the media along the trail reported a team traveling on the road and Race Marshall, Doug Grilliot asked Hugh about it when he arrived in Central.

Hugh admitted he had traveled on the road despite suspecting it wasn't the right trail. He had seen dog poop on the road and ran on the better surface for almost 40 minutes. When he saw William's team running on the bush trail he dragged his team off the road. The officials assessed him a two-hour penalty, to be served when he reached the final checkpoint at Twin Bears.

"This is very inclusive of sportsmanship," explained Doug when asked about the severity of the penalty. "It not only hurt the team ahead of him, it also hurts the teams behind him. This is very different from accidentally getting off the trail for a certain amount of time, dragging your dogs back onto the trail that is very well marked and continuing.

"That happens to everybody at some point in the race. A willful act like this to enhance your own position is not acceptable."

William turned around and saw Hugh on the road rather than the trail but lodged no official protest.

The mistake put Hugh into a contemplative mood. He would have to gain a substantial edge in the mountains past Central if he wanted any real chance at winning. William had a reputation for finishing fast over the final 50 miles.

"If it comes down to the last day and we're neck-and-neck, I'll lose," Hugh moaned about his two-hour penalty. "I really don't want to be in that situation but it could very well end up being that. We'll have to see what the dogs do in the mountains."

Jon Little, still in third place, was almost three hours behind. "You never give up but he (William) is several hours in front, so I don't know that (catching up) could happen. He's got a really fast team." He was still looking over his shoulder, waiting for Sebastien Schnuelle to catch him, but Sebastien never showed up.

Sebastien was an unknown amount of time behind him. Because of his schedule and camping out of the checkpoints it wasn't clear just how far back he really was. The rest of the teams were starting to lose touch with the leaders.

Jamaica's three mushers: (L to R) Damion Robb, Devon Anderson, Newton Marshall.

An Honorable Legacy

The lure of the Arctic is tugging at my heart. To me the trail is calling. The old trail. The trail that is always new.

Matthew Henson, first explorer to reach the North Pole

Black dog mushers have either been poorly documented or were very rare. There are few written accounts of them but the records that do exist are full of accomplishment and set a high standard for those who follow.

For the most part, however, Black history in dog mushing is anecdotal.

Rick Johnson remembers a Black woman from Florida entering the 6-dog class in the John Beargrease race.

The Beargrease was the preeminent middle distance race in the lower 48 of the United States, starting and finishing in Duluth, Minnesota. The trail runs north along the coast of Lake Superior to a turnaround point in the Superior National Forest, just south of the U.S.–Canada boundary. Teams will take four days to complete the route, which is famous for extreme temperature swings, heavy snow or rainfall and severe storms blowing in off the lake. It follows the very rugged mail delivery route run by native dog musher, John Beargrease between 1879 and 1899.

She didn't finish, he says, in fact, nobody was really sure she even got out of town. "As far as we know she had never run dogs before and had never run them on snow," said Rick.

In those years there were no qualifier rules for the difficult races because organizers never thought that inexperienced people would even attempt them.

There are photos of, but few details about a Black prize fighter, dancehall mascot and dog handler known as "The Black Prince" in Dawson City during the Klondike Gold Rush. History doesn't even record his real name, where he came from or what happened to him.

Lucille Hunter was a 19-year old pregnant girl when she and her husband traveled by boat, foot and dogsled to reach Dawson City during the Gold Rush. She was apparently the first Black woman in the North and was definitely the first Black female ever seen by the Interior natives.

Retired nurse, Barbara Hillary from Arverne, New York, the first African-American woman to reach the North Pole, took up cross-country skiing, dog mushing and photographing polar bears when she reached her 70s. Her goal was to celebrate life since she had beaten cancer in her late 60s.

Prior to Newton entering the 2009 Quest, Barry McAlpine had been the only Black musher to start a long distance race. He was a "Pioneer Musher" of the Iditarod, having run in the inaugural race from Anchorage to Nome in 1973. He scratched from the race but had apparently never given up entertaining the idea of trying it once again. He died at age 71 in a fire at his cabin in Alaska's Chugiak-Birchwood region on June 3, 2007.

Two men charted the path for Black dog mushers in the early part of the 20th century.

George Gibbs from Rochester, Minnesota, was the first Black to set foot on the Antarctic continent in 1939. He served as a dog musher with Admiral Richard Byrd's third expedition to the South Pole, one of only 40 men selected from over 2,000 applicants for the job.

History took a long time to properly recognize Matthew Henson as the first explorer, Black or White, to reach the North Pole. It wasn't until 2000, a decade after his death, that he was awarded the National Geographic Hubbard Medal, the highest honor an explorer can receive celebrating "distinction in exploration, discovery and research."

Robert Peary and Henson spent seven years in the Arctic and drove over 9,000 miles on dogsleds in the 1890s, attempting to reach the North Pole.

They tried again in 1906 and a final time in 1909. With 24 men, 19 sleds and 130 dogs they traveled between 30 and 60 miles per day and reached the Pole on April 6, 1909. Leading the advance team by foot and breaking the trail across the treacherous ice pack, Henson arrived first with two Eskimos and 15 dogs. Peary and two more Eskimos were a couple of hours behind him.

Peary thought because he was the leader of the expedition that he should have been the first to arrive, and the fact that Henson was there first rankled him. Although history books acknowledged the expedition leader as the discoverer of the Pole for the next 60 years, their 20-year friendship ended that day on the Polar ice pack. Eventually, historians unraveled the truth and now generally accept that Henson, his two Eskimos and their dogs were the first to reach the Pole.

Henson was elected a member of the exclusive Explorers Club in 1937 and received a Congressional medal in 1944 for his work on the Peary expedition. His most prized award was a gold medal from the Chicago Geographic Society.

He wrote one book about his Arctic experience, *A Negro Explorer at the North Pole* (1912) and an autobiography, *Dark Companion* (1947, with Bradley Robinson). A stamp issued by the U.S. Postal Service in 1986 gave his accomplishment equal footing with Peary for their Arctic exploration.

Writer Cheryl Hannah, in her children's book, *Snow on Snow on Snow,* uses repetitive word play to tell the story of an African-American boy who loses, then finds his dog while sledding.

So many dog mushers who weren't born to the sport credit pulp cowboy-northern novelists Jack London, Rex Beach and poet, Robert Service with kindling their interest in the North and luring them from their homes to run dogs on the world's final frontier. In the early part of the 20th century, filmmakers also recognized the appeal of dog mushing as a theatrical device.

Driving dogs turned up early in Hollywood movies from silent films and early "talkies" that in their time were popular hits, like London's *Call of the Wild* (1903) and Service's *The Shooting of Dan McGrew* (1924). Black mushers didn't appear in the films but one, Harry Boone, worked on the movie sets as a dog driver with a former Alaskan musher by the name of William "Caribou Bill" Cooper. Boone and Cooper claimed to have mushed from Seattle, Washington, to Saranac Lake, New York, in the Adirondack Mountains in 1910. There they established a ranch where most of the scenes in the silent film era were shot.

Boone apparently quit the dog business, went to New York City to work as a callboy in a Broadway theatre, and then simply vanished from history.

Dog mushing films continue to be a draw for film fans, but only two recent pictures feature Black dog mushers as their central characters.

Snow Dogs (2002, Disney Films, staring Cuba Gooding Jr. and James Coburn) is a comedy that takes place in a remote Alaskan village called Tolketna. The climax is a dogsled race that pits estranged (and strange) White father against his never-should-have-come-here Black son.

A made-for-television movie titled *Glory and Honor,* documenting the adventures of Matthew Henson, was aired in 1997.

Until *Sun Dogs* and *Underdogs* were released, there were no documentaries that featured the accomplishments of Black dog drivers.

Eagle Summit.

Newton's Schedule

Central to Twin Bears

90 miles, 17.5 hours

It's where promises to God are made and dreams are lost. More races have been lost and won, more mushers broken, more dog drivers christened in the 30 miles from Central to the isolated buildings at Mile 101 on the Steese Highway than on any other similar stretch of any race on earth.

The approach looks easy enough – 15 miles of trail winding through the willows, crossing the highway in some spots, traveling briefly on it in others, a few miles on Birch Creek, a gradual ascent through trees that become more stunted the higher you climb.

Eventually the musher can see through the trees the notch in the mountain up where the old Winter Road to Fairbanks runs. Scattered here and there are remnants of machinery and mining operations that once tore up the floors of these valleys seeking gold.

Then you break into the open. Snow clothes the mountain slopes, producing great sweeping curves that soar upward and make the whole setting appear as an enormous porcelain bowl. Everything is white. There are no rocks or trees breaking through the solid cap of snow.

For the first time, you can see the climb to the first summit and beyond that, a wall of ice and snow. In the background, there is a roar like surf breaking on the shore but it's just the wind playing its tune amongst the rocks high above on Eagle Summit.

Gazing at that desolate, wind-scoured waste is enough to drain the strength from the limbs and the will from a musher's mind. The mere sight of the wall can stop a dog team dead in its tracks. A series of tripods leads across the surface, marking the trail as it climbs steadily and seriously to the bottom of the final ascent, a 150-yard almost-vertical crawl to the summit.

The dogs look at the markers, the wall and back at the musher. They know where this is headed and the driver can read their minds, "No way are we going up that!"

The musher is sorely tempted to agree. This place is a meeting point for nature's furies: a spot where man is not wanted nor long tolerated.

It's not the highest point on the Quest trail or the longest climb – but Eagle Summit is the ultimate challenge for man and dog. If there was any one place on the trail that could shut down Newton's Quest, this was it.

Three years earlier, military helicopters had to lift six teams and their drivers from the top because they could advance no further, nor retreat in gale-force winds and neck-deep snowdrifts.

Over the years it has repelled many experienced and skilled mushers who lost faith or had their dogs just stop walking and curl up into a bundle that couldn't be moved.

In 1995, Larry "Cowboy" Smith had his team balk. If they had climbed the wall, once on top they couldn't have been caught by his pursuers and Smith would have had the championship he chased for so many years. As they sat motionless on the slope 200 yards from sure victory, his lead evaporated and four teams passed him.

Others seemingly performed miracles to coax their team up the hill – unbelievable displays of the strong the bond between driver and dogs.

Frank Turner stalled midway up the final ascent in one of his final races before he retired in 2008. He crawled on his hands and knees in the snow ahead of his team, stopping every few feet and calling or whistling to them. It was a tremendous gamble on his part, relinquishing any semblance of control over the team and investing all his faith in his relationship with his dogs. They could have turned and headed downhill and he would have been powerless to stop them.

Years earlier, he had watched as another Quest musher, Linda Forsberg, had put all her confidence in the love she shared with her dogs. The image of her walking ahead of her team and calling to them so they would climb stayed with him for over a decade. Desperate times call for desperate measures, so Frank decided it was time to test himself and try the same approach. Responding to his gentle summons they lurched up and over the hill one step at a time.

Other mushers got over because they unloaded the sled, carried everything to the top, before taking their leaders by their necklines and leading the dogs and an empty sled up the slope.

Once over the top, there is a long, gradual drop down over rough terraces and mountain gorges, through an exposed trench that seems to gather all the winds from the south that want to go north and funnel them into the faces of the teams coming down.

The dog drop at 101 is a collection of small shacks built originally for a mining camp and retrofitted for the Quest. One of them has food, drying racks, a radio and veterinary help. In the back is a sleeping area for the mushers.

After cresting Eagle Summit and arriving at 101, a musher might be forgiven for thinking they are homefree, downhill all the way to Fairbanks – but they're not.

Once away from 101, the trail drops below treeline again, runs for 10 miles or so along a wide valley that, in a bad year, could be full of overflow, then starts climbing over rolling hills for a long time. Again they emerge from the treeline and travel across the long, bare four miles of windswept, exposed Rosebud Summit. But it's not the getting up Rosebud that's the hard part – it's the getting down.

At what seems to be the highest point on the lofty ridge, the expansive view of the southern valleys of the White Mountains is simply spectacular. At night the lights of Fairbanks can be seen in the distance. This is not the place to be distracted by the panorama. The trail takes a sudden sharp, left-hand turn and descends abruptly for about 200 yards.

There are only two things a musher can do to prevent the sled from running over the dogs – ride the brake all the way down or, if the whole thing starts to get out of control, tip the sled on its side to increase the drag and slow down the dogs. Tipping the sled is a drastic measure since the potential for damage to equipment, musher and dogs is high – but more than once on this stretch, sleds have been dumped because it seemed safer than keeping them upright.

Once at the bottom of the killer hill, the trail descends gradually to the Chena River Valley floor, wends its way through the trees and along the river itself to the final checkpoint before Fairbanks – a campground named Twin Bears.

The race changed at the wall, in the middle of the night, on the north side of the summit. Hugh Neff was the first to arrive in 40 to 50 mile-per-hour winds and drifting snow. He walked to the front of his team and led them partway up the mountain then lost the trail. "I got to the last reflective marker (I could see) and that was it. There was no markers. The tripods have dinky markers on them you can't see at night."

Jon Little walked his team up beside him and parked. Together they crisscrossed the mountain, struggling through the knee-deep snow looking for the trail in the dark before digging out their sleeping bags and settling down to wait for daylight.

"I got some frostbite on my left foot and was getting a little hypothermic but if you can't find the trail, you weren't going nowhere," said Hugh. "Jon and I helped each other over that mountain....That's the Quest. We're racing each other, but we're also helping each other out."

Below, close enough to see them but unable to do anything about it, was William Kleedehn, who had his own troubles. One of his female dogs, Breeze, went into heat and the males went insane trying to get at her.

"One dog doesn't want to go…they all don't want to go. Then the hormones started to flow and I lost connection with the team. I could get them to go forward but they would be looking around, trying to chase the female, everything but focus on their job." Combined with the dog power shortage William already knew he had, he realized his chances of winning were starting to dwindle, "I couldn't go up the hill because I had no leader to put up front."

He tried two more times by himself then tried following Jon up the hill – but nothing was working. He turned the dogs downhill and started heading back to Central to scratch. Then Sebastien Schnuelle turned up, got him straightened out and most of the way up the hill just as dawn was breaking.

Eventually Sebastien glanced up the hill and was shocked to spot Hugh and Jon. They were getting their teams ready to finish the climb. Yesterday, he had been eight hours behind them, now they were right there in front of him. He had decided the race was out of reach and even stayed an extra two hours in Central.

"I wasn't even in race mode. Then things changed coming up to Eagle Summit and there they are. All of a sudden they're close, so that was too tempting. I turned to William and was like, 'William. You're on your own now!' "

Sebastien stayed for another 30 minutes as William's team crept closer to the top, then, with an apology, headed off to chase the leaders.

Finally Brent Sass rolled out of the trees and saw the team stuck on the hillside above him. His lead dog Silver pulled the team to the top where he parked them, then walked back down the hill to William.

"I don't think anyone would have passed William up there. It was on the steepest of the steepest part where he was stuck. When I came around the corner and saw him, it was heart-wrenching. I just knew I was going to help him over the top and we would both get into 101.

"Once I got on the front and pulled the leaders and he was pushing his sled we just hiked right up.

"It was just one of those things that I know…if any of my competitors out there or anywhere came along the trail…that they would do the same for me too. That's what it's all about. We're out there to help each other."

Hugh never stopped at 101, blowing right past the buildings. Jon stopped for a cup of coffee and a quick feed of the dogs. Sebastien turned up 20 minutes later, stayed six minutes before he too zipped off toward Rosebud, where he finally caught and passed Jon. However, no matter how hard he pressed, Hugh never appeared on the trail ahead.

Two hours later Brent and William limped in. Brent kept on going. William took a one-hour break, hoping his team would get its brains back. They didn't and he continued a slow, unfocused run toward Rosebud.

As the drama unfolded on Eagle Summit Newton was polishing off a steak at Central. He leaned back and flashed a grin at the waitress removing his empty plate.

"Thank you so very much," he rubbed his stomach, "You save a life. Ma belly full."

Formerly a Circle-to-Fairbanks trail roadhouse called Windy Jim's, there has been a stop at this crossroads since the 1890s. Originally the crossroad was simply a hub of a network of trails to various mining operations on the surrounding creek. The name changed to Central House when the Steese Highway passed right by and a connecting road was built to Circle Hot Springs.

The restaurant itself was named Crabb's Corner, after it's owner Jim Crabb, who was one of the Quest's biggest supporters in its early years. In addition to being a hospitality stop, then an official checkpoint, Jim used to fly his friends and neighbors to Dawson City to greet the teams during their 36-hour layover.

There's a restaurant-bar, a small store where local craftspeople and trappers sell their wares, an Atco Trailer with single beds in rooms and no indoor plumbing. There is an outhouse behind the restaurant. In the restaurant, hanging on the wall above Newton, was a large white chart detailing every musher's location along the trail.

The schedule called for Newton to rest here for eight hours before tackling Eagle Summit, but he was rested. He had grabbed a couple of hours sleep, had a full stomach and was feeling pretty good. The dogs had been fed and also had a good sleep. After only a few hours they were standing up, ready to go. He decided to cut his rest time. He couldn't see any good reason to stay. Normand Casavant wasn't that far ahead. Mark Sleightholme and Colleen Robertia were running about the same schedule as he was.

"I didn't start competing until the last half of the race. There were a few little mistakes I made (in the first half of the race) that I think now I shouldn't have made. Yeh, I didn't know I get that feeling. That drive. Just like a horse."

Colleen trailed Newton for a long time out of Central. "He was my best lead dog." Finally he pulled over.

"Colleen, I think you have the faster team. Why don't you go ahead?"

She looked at him wondering what he was up to, thinking, "No way I have the faster team, but if you want I'll do that." She pulled ahead of him and saw what he had seen, the climb to Eagle Summit. "All of a sudden we're going straight up."

She climbed for awhile, then stopped. Mark passed her and she followed him to the first summit "not the real summit. Just the first one." Looking back they didn't see anything of Newton in the fading daylight.

"Have you seen Newton?" asked Mark.

Colleen glanced down the hill. "No. I'll go back down and see if I can find him." Then they saw him climbing a short distance below. They waited.

His team crested the summit and he called out, "Are we at the top yet?" Colleen laughed. It was now dark and Newton hadn't seen the wall in front of them.

He repeated the question, "Is this the top?"

"No," she replied. "I haven't done this before but I'm betting that the fact that we're still moving up means we haven't reached the top. It's not even the climb to the summit yet I don't think."

They dropped down from the first summit, then Newton, at the back of the line, saw Colleen and Mark's headlamps start to climb.

"Jesus Christ," he exclaimed, "Another hill." Then as their headlamps went straight up instead of forward and up, "No Mon. This can't be the trail...." Ahead of him he could hear Mark's voice urging on his dogs, "Up... Up...Up!"

Then Colleen's headlamp faltered. Her dogs had dithered and her sled skidded back down. "My dogs want to go every direction and my leader wants to quit," she said to Mark who was just ahead of her.

Mark looked back at her. His team seemed to be doing well. "If I get over the top I could get away and make some time on these guys," he thought to himself. He did want to beat them and he knew that Normand was within reach. He had caught up to him earlier in the day and saw his headlamp high above them on the climb.

Then he remembered his own journey to this place. He had been a dryland sprint racer in northern England. A chance meeting with Libby Riddles, the first woman to win the Iditarod (who also happened to be Sebastien's partner) brought him to Canada in November, 2008.

Mark had never driven a 14-dog team until he arrived in the Yukon to train with Sebastien. At first he had planned only to run a 300-mile race, but Sebastien had a different vision. He got Mark qualified for the Quest without Mark realizing what he was doing, then suggested, "Things are going pretty good for you. Do you want to step it up and go the 1,000 miles?"

By all rights, someone with his limited experience shouldn't even be here. Now was the time to show he belonged in the Quest. Besides, Newton had loaned him some dog food earlier in the race and he owed him something. "So maybe we'd better help each other up here," he suggested.

"Yeah," agreed Colleen, "Let's do that. Newton's back there breathing somewhere."

Mark chuckled, "I thought he would be the fit one of us three. He's the young one."

Newton took control of his team and Colleen's. Mark's team was the first one taken up.

Colleen came down to get her dogs, but they weren't ready to go yet.

"We'll leave them," she suggested. "Take yours up and come back for mine."

Partway up the hill one of Newton's dogs slipped his collar.

"Just a moment please,' he said, wrestling the dog back into line. Then they toiled to the top. Back down the hill for the third time to get Colleen's team.

"I have to catch my breath," said Newton as they reached Colleen's sled. "I have a pain in my ribs (a stitch in his side)."

As they rested Colleen tried to drink from her Gatorade bottle but it was frozen solid. She pried out a chunk of ice and sucked on it. "Oh God, does that ever taste good."

They started pushing the sled up the hill, slowly placing one foot in front of the other. Their backs ached with the stress, but to waver meant everything accomplished would be undone. Their joints throbbed. Every step became a separate entity – a major task demanding a maximum of effort.

"It wasn't like you could dig your feet in." Colleen spent most of the time crawling on her knees trying to get some leverage on the sled to help the dogs. "They just kept sliding out from underneath you."

At the top, the winds started to pick up and strong gusts rocked the sleds. "We've got to get the hell out of here," shouted Mark. "It's getting bad."

As they drove their teams down the far side Newton leaned over his handlebar, exhausted. His body felt like shutting down. He was barely able to speak or form a coherent thought. "I don't ever want to go back up there again," he muttered.

Six hours after they crossed the summit the storm was in full force battering other teams into submission. Jason Mackey returned to Central and scratched, unable to climb in the face of a whining maelstrom of abrasive particles of snow that seared the flesh and with two dogs in heat.

Russ Bybee detoured off the trail, went to the Steese Highway where he loaded his dogs into a truck and drove to 101 to scratch.

Yuka Honda did make it over the mountain but it took her over 20 hours to flounder through 30 miles of snowdrifts from Central to 101. She attempted to leave 101 after a long rest, but the storm had taken its toll on her dogs. Her leaders, rebellious since they left Pelly, stopped cooperating with her. She turned back and scratched.

Their mood, when Newton, Mark and Colleen reached 101, was jubilant. They sat in the cabin, eating, teasing, laughing, like survivors who had stared their fate in the eyes and lived to talk about it. Pushing past the pain wasn't easy, they agreed, but laughing helped.

"The trails have been excellent," Mark observed. "The weather has been just about perfect. This has to be one of the easiest Quests ever!"

"It may be easy for you," Newton disagreed. "It isn't easy at all for me." Susie was there and tried to convince Newton to get some sleep but he wouldn't listen to her. Finally she left the cabin, frustrated.

Outside snow was beginning to fall in big, lazy, fat flakes. To the north the storm could be seen over the mountains. To the south were clear skies.

The mushers got special treatment at 101 this year because of the Doug Grilliot Rule.

When Jon Little had stopped to feed his dogs, he burst into the kitchen area looking for something to eat but kept insisting, "I don't have time! I don't have time."

Doug offered to make him a sandwich and bring it down to him at his sled as he was leaving – which he did.

However, pointed out the dog drop manager, the Quest rules dictate that everyone had to be treated the same. "What are you doing? Now we have to deliver a sandwich to every musher at their sled." (Prior to that, if a musher wanted a sandwich, they had to go and make one for themselves.)

Now every musher was greeted at the checkpoint with a bacon and egg sandwich, except for Newton, who got chicken salad because he didn't eat pork.

Inside the cabin, the adrenaline rush from completing the crossing finally starting to subside, the mushers went looking for sleeping spots.

"In the light (see you in the morning)," Newton waved as he headed for the back room.

Outside Susie was still fuming over being ignored by Newton. "As far as I'm concerned," she said to a race official, "Newton can talk all night if he wants to, then he'll have to race tired."

The official looked at her in surprise, "Newton went to bed a long time ago. He's asleep."

Cutting his rest time short again, Newton was the third of the three out of 101 but he passed Colleen and Mark quickly. Suddenly the trail got confusing. There were caribou tracks everywhere on the ridge and drifting snow.

"I could see the trail. It was right there, but the dogs wanted to go another way. So I had to come up to the front and walk in front of them to the next trail marker." Colleen and Mark passed him again and vanished over the top of Rosebud.

They had heard the stories about the descent, but none of them had any idea of what to really expect. Colleen broke her brake on the rocks and spent the last few careening yards praying she wouldn't run over her dogs.

"That was a hell of a jump. There was lots of downhill," said Newton. "Straight downhill! It was the most frightening time on the trail. There was ice and rock and no control. Those dogs just kept running and I just hung onto the sled.

"My eyes were like this," opening his eyes wide in terror. "I didn't take my foot off the brake because there was a possibility the sled would go fast enough to run right over top of the dogs."

"There's one tree everybody hates," said Newton. Everyone bounced off it on the way past. Brent Sass had flown right over the top of it. Newton hit it head on.

He saw it coming.

"Whoa!" he called to the dogs, then more desperately, "WHOA!!" The dogs sped up. "Oh God!"

Then they hit, bending the brush bow and breaking a line.

The next time he saw a tree coming, he tipped the sled over and landed face first in overflow. Normally he would have reacted to the cold. This time, however, he was just plain thirsty. He had consumed most of his water before Rosebud and what was left was frozen solid. Finding himself immersed in water, his clothing soaked, he took the opportunity to bend down and get a drink.

As he rummaged through his sled bag to get some dry clothes while the dogs snacked, he came across his Bible. Newton wasn't a member of any organized religion nor did he often pray – although there had been one prayer in the outhouse before he started the race and at least one other during the day just past. All his life he carried a Bible everywhere he went. It was his comfort in times of duress. "It makes me feel better. I believe in God and Jesus," he said. "I can't read it but I know what it says."

He felt it in his bones. He knew just as he might know the presence of a greater being. This was almost over. He might survive it after all.

Sister Ashley, Miss Penny and Newton.

Newton

A gem is not polished without rubbing, nor a man perfected without trials.

Unknown

In the middle of an interview for this book Danny stopped talking and looked across the table at me.

"Did Rick ever tell you that Newton's father used to beat him with a stick?"

"Rick didn't," I responded, "but Newton mentioned something about it."

"Ask Rick," he advised, "He can tell you the whole story."

I never did ask Rick. There was no need to. Newton reluctantly spoke of it with me.

"I never talk about it because I didn't want anyone to think bad about them (his parents).

"Nobody cared about us. I feel like I was left out. I didn't get any love from my mother and father. I didn't know my father because I wasn't getting any attention from him. When you have a son, you carry him around. You play baseball. I didn't get any of that. My mother wasn't there most of the time, but I wanted her to be…I don't know why I wanted her there. I can't remember a time when my mother didn't hit me."

Newton's mother Diane.

(Back, L to R) Newton at age 13, cousin George, sister Ashley, (front) sister Cleone.

(L to R) Sister Melissa, aunt Lisa, Newton at age 5.

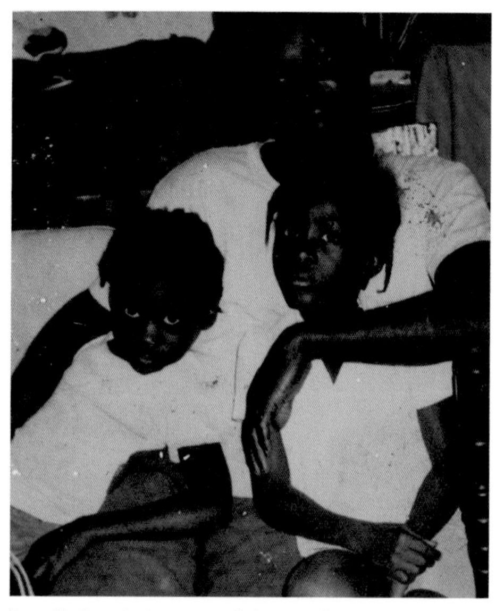

(L to R) Cousin Lorraine, father Wallace, sister Melissa.

"A lot of people thought I was very shy. Some of them called me 'stupid' because I was quiet, didn't talk much. I didn't socialize with people very well other than my family and friends. I didn't know what to talk about." Newton stopped talking for a long moment. He stared off toward the dog kennels, his eyes blinking rapidly as he struggled to contain his emotions.

"I was scared because a lot of parents used to beat their kids with whatever they can catch (get into their hands). First thing they can catch, they use it on you. If it was a stick with nails in it, they would use it," he continued.

"Anybody in the family – mother, father, uncle, aunt, grandmother – anybody could beat you because you must have 'respect' for others. If my uncle said something to me and I said, 'I'm not going to do that' he would beat me and I would have to do it.

"If you are walking down the road and somebody from the community passes you. If you don't say hello, you might get beaten by that person. Or they would go to your home and say 'your child walked past me and didn't say good morning.' You would get beaten again when you get home.

"I think people are learning. Not so much (beatings) now.

"A lot of kids used to run away from home. They would go to a friend or live on the street. Sleep in the bushes or somewhere. Then they would sometimes go back home.

I never ran away because I'm very dark and poor. My sisters. They ran away from home all the time.

"A lot of the time I thought about suicide because I was getting so many beatings for no reason. I just couldn't take it most of the time. I was angry at myself because I started to believe that maybe I was stupid. Sometimes I thought I just end my life somehow. I didn't want to die hard. I had to die slow and easy – no pain. I was trying to poison myself but it never worked out.

"I used to get insect sprays and spray them into a cup and drink it. It never did anything. It never even made me sick. Nobody know. I would just go to where I sleep, lie down and curse."

There are a series of highways that run the length of the north shore from Port Antonio in the east to Negril in the west. On the coastal side of the road system are the resorts and the cruise ship ports, where a large number of Jamaicans work. On the inland side and in the mountains are the townships where they live.

After slavery was abolished in 1834 freed slaves established plots in the mountains where they could be self-sufficient growing their own food. They had little education but were generating moderate wealth from agriculture. They didn't recognize the need for an education because they didn't see how it would profit them.

When the international market for their products changed in the late 20th century and tourism became the primary industry they were unprepared to take advantage of it.

"Newton" was born Oswald Marshall in St. Ann's Bay Hospital and raised between St. Ann's Bay, Richmond and Mount Olivet. Richmond was the sugar plantation that included the fields that later became Chukka Cove. His mother, Diane, worked at the plantation along with his grandmother, Miss Penny, and grandfather, Brother Lee.

His father, Wallace, worked as a handyman-gardener. "We didn't call him 'Dad' – he didn't like that kind of stuff." His parents never married. "A lot of people in Jamaica don't like the married idea because they say it has 'a tie-down' – because they can't do what they usually do."

Unless they can scrape together the necessary cash most Jamaicans will never own their own home. Interest rates are so high and the bank's requirement for collateral is so extreme that most Jamaicans can't qualify for mortgages. For those who can afford to build their own home it is an ongoing project that may take years to complete, if it's ever completed at all. A great number, like Newton's grandmother, Miss Penny, squat on property they don't own and many inhabit makeshift shacks with dirt floors. Miss Penny's home at least didn't have dirt floors.

The buildings are made of plywood or weathered concrete walls topped with rusting corrugated metal roofs, held down by cinder blocks to prevent the wind from blowing them away. If the wind does take the roof it's inexpensive and easy to replace. There's very little indoor plumbing. Many have pit toilets in the yard behind them. Indoor "cookie gas" and electric stoves are a new innovation.

Until only a few years ago, people cooked over open fires in the backyard. In the evenings, you could see cooking fires everywhere in any Jamaican town or hamlet, and smell the bittersweet aroma of burning wood and cooking foods. Newton's grandmother, Miss Penny, cooked on an outdoor wood stove fueled by material scavenged from the woods behind her house. There was a stove inside the house but gas is expensive and she used it only on rainy days.

"In the yard where I used to live," said Newton, "it was a big family yard with lots of cousins, lots of aunt and uncles. What they would do most of the time was get together, give money; they buy food to cook for everyone. 'One one coco full basket' (meaning everybody puts one item in the communal basket until it's full). Everybody tries to help each other.

"Sometimes it was hard and I think the cost of living wasn't so high when I was young. You could spend 50 cents and get a lot of things. Now you can't buy anything. Even with a dollar you can't buy anything."

Retail shops look much like the homes except they have metal doors and iron grates on the windows – no large plate glass windows full of displays like one will find in the tourist areas. What they sell isn't always going to be clear to someone who isn't local. A furniture store could be identified by a brown sofa painted on a chipped, blue and white wall. On the exterior the stores look run down but, inside, the products are usually good.

"Everybody just tries to get by," said Danny. "They do their own thing. They might have a job, but they'll sell clothes on the side or whatever. Everybody is enterprising. People operate outside the system because the system doesn't really work. They realize they can't depend upon the government to understand that."

"You get 100 Jamaicans in a room and you will get 100 different stories," explained ex-patriate Jamaican Joy Morgan, who lives in Whitehorse, "but all of them will talk about the community raising the children." Often it was because the parent had to leave the country to take advantage of economic opportunity abroad, as Newton's father did when he went to Canada to pick oranges and apples, and could not bring their families with them.

The community has always raised the children. Grandparents. Aunts. Uncles. All played a role if the parents couldn't. When he was 12 years old, Miss Penny, Newton's maternal grandmother, became the mother he didn't have.

Miss Penny lived near Mount Olivet, in a small three-room house overlooking the Chukka Cove, Runaway Bay coastline and shaded by a massive Ackee tree. There were beds in every room, even in the kitchen, so everyone might have a place to sleep. She wouldn't let anyone sleep on the floor. One time one of Newton's aunts turned up to stay and "there were five or six of us in one bed. You couldn't turn over unless everybody turned."

The natural beauty of the area attracted other people from the community to come up and "chill" in the fields or sit and talk under the tree. There was a breadfruit tree in the front yard, the pit toilet hidden in the bush off to one side and her outdoor kitchen was under the Ackee tree. She also had a small shop outside the front door.

Bob Marley memorabilia is still the biggest draw for tourists to Jamaica.

"She inspire me in many ways," said Newton. "She always wanted us to stay to help her because she used to have lots of goats. So we went to help my grandmother with cleaning up the yard, milking them. We used to have this big coconut field near us. My grandmother used to pick up coconuts and carry them back to the factory – where they used them to make soup and other type of stuff.

"It was just her way to make money to feed everybody. On Saturdays we would have to walk down here (to Richmond) on the road. My grandmother would have to go to Brown's Town (a township in the mountains) to sell coconuts to make money to buy groceries. We would have to walk with big bags full of coconuts to help her. They weren't light! We carried the bags on our heads and my neck was real thick! We would spend the whole day in Brown's Town. She used to take breadfruit, ackee, mangoes, limes. She would sell all those things."

Open-air markets are found near the center square of the town, usually identified by a large clock located near the middle of the square. The stalls are staffed mainly by women wearing baseball caps, headscarves, necklaces, strapped tops or loose-fitting cotton blouses.

"We would then walk home and spend time cleaning up the yard," said Newton. They used sticks to knock fruit off the trees, stuff them in their mouths by the handful and wipe the juices from their chin. Newton carried a knife to cut "jelly coconut" off the tree. Before a coconut gets hard, it's soft enough to cut open with a knife, drink the water, scoop out the slushy meat and eat it.

For the most part Jamaicans struggle through a life that, for the visitor, is unimaginable. They exist under circumstances that most people wouldn't want to even get up in the morning and face another day in. The average tourist spends as much on an evening of beer or wine as it takes many Jamaicans a month of hard work to earn. Wages in Jamaica are basically survival and not much else.

The workday starts before dawn and ends after dark. Most are at jobs seven days a week. The majority hold down two or more jobs because just having one won't cover the cost of their survival, let alone the cost of education for their children.

While Newton's grandmother didn't encourage him to go, if his chores were done and she had no need for him on any given day, she let him walk the four miles to the school in Runaway Bay. As he walked down the hill he found himself helping people. Climbing trees to fetch breadfruit or helping people to clean up their yards.

"All my life I like to help people. It's just in ma blood. Helping people. Understanding people. I try to make friends with people."

"They (Jamaicans) have a lot of values here you won't find elsewhere in the world," said Brian Kennedy. "The sad thing is that those aspects of being a third world country that are good are being corrupted or lost as the modernization of the country takes place.

"Old Jamaicans actually rue the arrival of cell phones and Internet because it means the end of the world in which they have lived for most of their lives," he added.

The cycle of poverty seems endless and the poor are hard-pressed to see a way out of it. Being born in a ghetto diminishes every opportunity – education, decent nutrition, social services, and human rights. Destitution is a terrible burden but the burden is much heavier if the condition seems permanent. One of the true indicators of poverty is that events conspire to keep you that way.

Unemployment is high in Jamaica, just under 20 percent. Many of the jobless, the majority of them men, are unemployable because they haven't been educated or socialized. For them it's a life lived in limbo. They have no goals and harbor few dreams. Many spend their days in apathy – watching television, smoking drugs, talking on their cell phones, playing dominoes in town centers, sitting on street corners or outside front entries to buildings and playing video games. Passive voyeurs of life.

Scree (Arnold Bertram) fingers greed and politics ("politricks" as the Jamaicans call it) as the other culprits in society's downfall. It is to the benefit of both the criminal element and the politicians to keep the people slightly above the starvation level.

Re-election for politicians depends on currying favor with the people at the local level. Creating a garrison constituency, a packet of housing erected with public funds, and screening residents so only reliable supporters would get a home, was one sure method of creating an unbeatable core of voters.

The lack of education, corruption, incompetence in policing and the money that can be earned growing "Ganja" (marijuana) has led to mostly petty crime against tourists along the north shore but to more serious drug gang extortion and turf wars in the mountains and southern cities, particularly Spanish Town and Kingston. More than one person has met their end at the tip of a machete and there is a form of Darwinian vigilante justice because the police can't be relied upon.

Newton's grandmother was particularly proud of the fact that he never got into "the Ganja." He was apparently the easiest of the five children to raise. "He was good," said Miss Penny, "Good to talk to. Stayed out of trouble…not like the girls." Her eyes sparkle and her grin widens as she glances up at Newton, "I love dis boy."

Newton did try "the Ganja" both in Jamaica and in Canada, but didn't like it. When Yukoners found out he didn't "smoke," they responded in astonishment, "You've got to be kidding me! Everybody in Jamaica smokes!"

The gun battles that erupted in Kingston in May, 2010, when the United States forced the police and military to attempt arresting a drug Don (boss), exposed the rest of the world to the role of government in creating criminal garrisons and the illegal drug trade. The gangs were established by political parties as groups of thugs whose role was to persuade voters to cast their ballots for the correct candidate. They still hold a powerful grip on society although they are no longer used for their original purpose.

The police force isn't trusted by the majority of the people who have affixed to them the Rastafarian word of "Babylon" (symbol of oppression). Both the people and the police rely on the Dons of the various gangs and

Miss Penny raised Newton when his parents walked away.

drug rings to perform the function of keeping order in the communities. The upside is local residents feel safer in their homes. The downside is gangs are free to operate without any significant interference.

There has been in Jamaica no enduring commitment, no vision of how to weave the less fortunate into a strong and humane society. It was left to the individual to do the best with what they were given while masking the truth of their existence.

Carole Melville is always amazed and distressed that she can visit a run-down shack, in the hills above St. Ann's Bay, and the face of the occupant is the well-dressed bank clerk you deal with, the secretary in the lawyer's office or the waiter at the restaurant where you had lunch. "They always dress for work and give you no clue as what their real home life is like," she said.

There are a few sources of enlightenment. Teachers in various locations who have opted to work outside the system. Corporations like Chukka Caribbean Adventures that have adult education programs for their employees. "If I was a Jamaican who wanted to improve my place in society I would work for a company like Chukka," said Dick Watts.

Long before he came to work at Chukka Cove Newton had recognized the problem lay not with himself and his sisters, but with his upbringing. "I still love my parents. What I hate is that they didn't do what they were supposed to do." How little can a parent give to their child and still retain affection?

Remains of Miss Penny's former home in Mount Olivet.

When Newton was still a small child his mother started vanishing for long periods then returning temporarily to see if she could get some money before disappearing again. Newton and his four younger sisters Camille, Melissa, Ashley and Monique stayed with his father in a one-room house with two beds in it. The larger one was for his father. The smaller one for the girls. Newton slept on the floor.

The family was constantly moving back and forth between Richmond and Mount Olivet, a small township in the hills above Runaway Bay. "My mother went away for a while again, then come back. My mother and father went to another place. They live there for a while, then my mother leave again.

"So my father just went back up to the house (at Mount Olivet). He wasn't getting along with my grandfather so we moved into my aunty's – who was trying to help with our situation because it was really bad."

Newton's father also started disappearing for longer periods, leaving the children either on their own or with Miss Penny. Five children were too much for his grandmother and she would send two or three of the girls to other relatives to look after. Only when one or both of his parents turned up were the children temporarily reunited. When they lost interest in being parents the children would be left to find their way to whomever would take them.

There were times when they had no money for food or clothing. Some days they had to drink water so their stomachs would feel full. They would forage for food from neighbors, on the streets and in the bush.

At one point the children decided to take matters into their own hands. "We tried to get some of us to stay with my mother and some of us with my father. So we went to the police but they said they couldn't help us unless they put us in a home. My father said 'no.' He tried to keep most of us with him. My youngest sister, she went to live with my mother in Negril. But it didn't last very long," said Newton.

Sometime during this aimless stage of his life, young Oswald acquired the nickname the world would eventually come to know him by. Everyone in Jamaica has a nickname. For some reason, he never understood why, people used to call him "yut man." One day someone called him "Newton" instead and it stuck.

Life was better with Miss Penny, but it wasn't good all the time – his parents kept coming back, thinking they might like to be temporary custodians of their children again.

"I remember one time when everything was bright. My mother and father used to have a shop and they used to sell a lot of stuff in it. It was a food shop up in Mount Olivet. They catered a lot of parties and made lots of money.

"My mother decided my grandmother didn't like her and she went somewhere. Left us with our father. My father started to have problems in that yard. Stuff went down because my mother wasn't in it any more to sell food. Things got hard because there wasn't much going on."

This time Newton and the girls didn't move back to Miss Penny's. She didn't own the property her home was built on and the landowner decided he wanted all the squatters off his land. She found another smaller shack in a different, not-so-nice area and didn't have the room to keep all her grandchildren.

Then his father went to Canada to pick oranges and apples. His mother came back to run the shop for a short time. One day she told Newton she was leaving. Look after the store, take care of your sisters, she said, promising to send money to help him, which never arrived. Instead she drained the bank account on her way out of town.

"I didn't know she had a business partner whom she had to pay every week and she had just purchased a fridge on credit. I didn't know how to run the shop. My mother used to credit her customers. She would sell them food on credit and when the customer had enough money to pay the bill or some of it, they would.

"But it was really hard to get that money (from the customers). And any profit you make had to go to the business partner."

Newton had earlier given his mother his life's savings to put in the bank for him. "I was too young to have an account so we kept it in an account in her name." As the shop ran out of supplies and the bills mounted, Newton went to draw his funds out of the bank.

"There's no money there," the bank teller told him.

"I have money in there! My mother said she wouldn't trouble it."

"Sorry. I can't do anything," replied the teller.

Newton walked out of the bank crying.

He found a job handling polo ponies for Dr. John Masterton, cleaning stables, exercising the horses and helping transport them to tournaments. At night he slept on the dirt floor in the back room of the shop.

"I tried to keep the shop going, but it was going to fail. I was still looking after my sisters. I was getting stressed about everything so I called my grandmother and asked her to help. She can't ignore my sisters. She called her sister and asked her to take Melissa because she lives close to the school. My grandmother take two of them. Camille stayed with me. Then I heard about the job at the airstrip (Blenheim Gliding Club).

"I went to work at the gliders and sent money to help Camille. She was running the shop but she didn't want to run the shop. She was so miserable. Nobody wanted to buy from her because she was so miserable. Since she couldn't sell it, she ate the food in the shop. Then she got pregnant."

A comment in the Toronto Globe and Mail in May, 2010, identified the absence of a father figure in the Jamaican culture as being one of its major downfalls – the "I like to spread my seed around" sign of a man's virility, to have as many children as possible, leaving the woman pregnant and alone. On the other side of the coupling, the woman has her baby, hands it off to her mother or grandmother and she leaves also.

"You ask them, 'Why are you having another baby?'" Cyd Miller just shakes her head, despairing the inability of too many young Jamaicans to provide even the basics of affection to their children. "'Because my mother told me I have to have another baby to show I'm a woman.'"

There's even a common phrase in Jamaica for it, "My brother from another mother.'"

Family upbringing is cyclical. "What you've seen in the past is the same thing you will do," ex-patriate Joy Morgan added. The difference between generations isn't what they do, but why they do it. "Young families are not

Newton at Chukka.

ready to take responsibility." What is still a positive way to raise children in the parents' absence is, for some, now a convenient excuse to dispense with them.

Newton's sister Camille was one of the girls caught up in that cycle. "She have her first baby when she was 13," he said. "When she was 22 she had four children. My grandmother raising all of them for her.

"No one know who the dads are. One of them is a cab driver who has nothing to do with his child."

Newton bought her birth control pills after her first pregnancy and told her, "You must take these." She didn't listen to him.

"Girl. This don't make sense," he pleaded with her. "What you're doing isn't getting you to where you want to go. Why you having all these babies?"

"I don't know," she replied, then went on her way as if nothing was amiss with what she intended to do.

"Having children young is common in Jamaica because they don't have parents around to guide them," Newton is often frustrated by his sisters. "The parents don't care. They think sex (at a young age) is a natural thing. They just go with the flow.

"I think now parents are starting to realize they don't want their children to have babies that young. But their children still go because their parents don't have much money. Maybe the boyfriend might be giving money to buy food and support his girlfriend. It's kinda tough.

"But most of them don't care. They find a girl, have sex, then leave, find another girlfriend. The girls are the same. They just give their children to their grandmother. They want to party. They want to enjoy life without thinking about what they want in life.

"It's starting to change…slowly. A lot of younger people who are in school are starting to realize there's a price. But there are still many who don't want to understand. They just want to have a baby. They just want to have fun. But they don't want to understand responsibility.

"A lot of people think that way. People force someone to get somebody pregnant. They tell them, 'You should go and breed the woman. Get them pregnant. It's not like you're having the baby. Go have fun and have kids.' A lot of guys boast about how many kids they have.

"I don't have any children because I had to look after my sister and I see what happen to her and her boyfriends. I don't want to have children until I have a roof over my head," said Newton.

For two years Newton worked at Blenheim operating the winch that launched the gliders into the air. The family shop shut down. His sister continued producing babies. He moved into Miss Penny's new house with its blue plywood siding and nylon tarps keeping the wind from blowing through the gaps in the walls. There was no bed or bedroom for him so he slept on the floor.

Newton rode his ancient black bicycle up and down the mountain every day but work at the glider field was starting to slow down. He started working for a friend of his father's, Solomon, doing yard work and painting houses.

Then Miss Shelley turned up at Blenheim and Newton started going to school at Chukka Cove. Newton had not only heard of Chukka, he had been there.

"When I was younger they used to have this big tent around Christmas time where they would have food, they used to have this thing called a 'grab bag.' You pay a fee to reach in and grab anything you could feel. You might get a toy. A chocolate. A T-shirt. It was for all the kids from St. Ann's.

"They had model planes on the Polo field – flying and you could hear this big noise. Everybody would get cleaned up just to be here. It was then I first heard about Mr. Melville but I didn't meet him.

"I didn't meet Mr. Melville until I started working at Chukka. I felt like asking him for an autograph but, because I was just an employee I didn't want to make any mistakes.

Santa Claus arrives by dogsled in Ocho Rios.

"They had people dressed up to scare kids. They would bark, come at you shaking their heads and all the kids would be running and screaming. There was a chariot pulled by a donkey with Santa Claus and Santa would get up on a stage in the field. All the kids would gather around and go up on the stage where they would get a plastic bottle with a T-shirt inside, a chocolate and a toy.

"It was a nice moment. Everyone was really happy. I remember looking forward to it every year."

As a teenager he had helped to clean up the Polo field following Carnival. "There were thousands of people. Every Jamaican wants to go to Carnival. They used to have Reggae here and other groups. It was the largest in Jamaica. Byron Lee and Mr. Melville (were) good friends.

"It was almost every year then they move it over closer to St. Ann's. We'd get jobs to clean up the place. We would work all night to pick up the garbage. People don't seem to care. They just throw their stuff all over the place and we had to clean it up before light up."

Jamaica's Carnival is a flurry of music and dancing.

To wrestle with the ghosts of your past one must use weapons that form no part of reality. Promises and dreams are all that are needed to start the process of healing.

When Newton started working at Chukka Caribbean Adventures, from washing buses to guiding on horseback to running dogs, it was like a dream come true. He had a job he liked. Was starting to get the education he had long before realized he needed. Lived with the Kennedys – in a room of his own and slept in a bed he didn't have to share with his sisters or find himself kicked out of because his mother had reappeared.

Now he could envision a future. One where he might be able to do things differently from his parents. A destiny with a house, marriage, children and in which the past would be nothing more than a distant memory. *Everting irie* (everything was fine).

However, while dreams have the power to promise and are guaranteed to please they come burdened with reality and all its dull and disagreeable facts. One mistake on the road to a tomorrow full of potential and you were on your way out of it.

When Newton was fired it was to Miss Penny's that he fled. It was on her front step, a board set between two cinder blocks, he at first wallowed in self-pity lamenting what might have been. His past kept confronting him. His father was somewhere else breeding another family. His mother,

Diane, turned up looking for money and then returned to wherever she went when she left. His sister turned up to drop her children off with his grandmother.

He remembered the times he had considered suicide. He'd imagined he had left that part of his life behind.

He watched his grandmother. What a life for a woman in her 60s, getting up before the sun each day and working until darkness fell to feed him, herself, her great-grandchildren and anyone else who happened to be hanging around. Her burden should have smothered her determination and overwhelmed her slight frame but she, like everyone around her, including Newton, had invented her own ways to survive.

He lived in a culture of daily surrenders demanded by society.

"Life was tough for me growing up," he realized the place to which he had fled wasn't where he wanted to be. "But it's tough for a lot of people growing up."

Here he could never regain any peace of mind after the car crash. If he stayed, the rest of his life would be a clash of personal dreams and collective reality.

There was a need within him to create a place in his life where he could be someone and accomplish something.

"I don't like to think about the past. I like to live the positive."

Newton and Marbles.

Dog drop at 101.

Newton's Schedule

Twin Bears to Fairbanks

50 miles, 7 hours

Twin Bears Camp in the Chena River State Recreation Area is smack dab in the middle of Two Rivers, a community of ranches and dog kennels tied together by a web of well-traveled sledding and snowmobiling trails. Two Rivers is considered the dog mushing capital of the world, since this is where the highest concentration of sleddogs on earth can be found. In the small area of the community there are over 50,000 sleddogs and approximately 5,000 people.

Twin Bears Camp is 12 cabins arranged around a small, secluded clearing in the forest. In the summer it's a lake. In winter, it's a flat place where dog teams gather, especially during the Quest. One of the cabins is heated, has lights and cooking facilities. It is packed with veterinarians, race officials, race groupies, journalists, sponsors, other dog mushers and handlers. Another has been set aside for the mushers to sleep in during their eight-hour mandatory layover.

The trail from Twin Bears to Fairbanks, Alaska's second largest city with a population of over 90,000 people, is hard and fast, running alongside the highway for part of it and along the meandering bends of the Chena River for the rest.

People start appearing on the riverbanks to cheer the teams on about 20 miles outside the city and their numbers intensify as the teams get closer. The early teams can expect their arrival to be greeted by hundreds of spectators on the ice or hanging from the bridge above the Finish line.

The banner that marks the end of the trail is on the river in the heart of what was once known as "Barnette's Cache" before it was renamed after U.S. President Theodore Roosevelt's vice-president, Charles Fairbanks.

It was gold that opened central Alaska just as it was gold that opened almost every corner of the North. Discovered near the Twin Bears site in 1901 by Felix Pedro, the resulting stampede benefited a small trading post set up the year before in the Chena Slough by riverboat Captain E.T. Barnette, who originally planned to establish a fur trade with the Tanana Indians.

Word of the gold strike was carried to Dawson City by renowned Japanese long distance dog musher, Jujiro Wada, who drove his team over the trail now covered by the Yukon Quest. When the gold stampeders who stormed into the region moved onto other discoveries, Fairbanks was established as a major supply center for the central and northern regions of the state. The construction of the Alaska Highway in 1940-1941 and military bases during the 1950s brought thousands of servicemen to the area, prompting the growth of service industries and a thriving business community.

The race was already over for the lead teams, who had passed through Twin Bears almost two days ago, and most of the crowd had gone home. But there was a small group of race fans waiting for Newton when he dropped out of the trees and crossed the clearing to where the veterinarians and race officials awaited.

One woman had been told by a friend of hers that a Jamaican musher was running the Quest. "No way!" she exclaimed before looking him up on the Internet, "and there he was and here he is!"

Another had seen *Sun Dogs* and wanted to meet Newton. She waited while he bedded down the team, fed them and talked with the veterinarians. Unfortunately, she had to leave to go to work before he was finished and missed her opportunity to meet him.

The atmosphere in the cabin was giddy, with Danny and Carole both giving Newton a hug as he walked in. Susie told him that Hans was on his way from Whitehorse to be at the Finish line. The smiles just got bigger the longer he stayed.

Newton and Danny at Twin Bears.

There were still 50 miles to go and there was already a feeling the adventure was over.

Nobody mentioned Brent Sass to him.

Arriving in Twin Bears in a solid fourth place, Brent was feeling pretty good about things. His team had exceeded all his expectations. They looked so good in the final miles into the checkpoint he hadn't even bothered to stop them for a snack break. When he was ready to go after his eight-hour layover, one of his lead dogs, Dude, balked.

Dude had led the team over Eagle Summit and Rosebud. Had performed admirably for 945 miles and now, only seven miles out of Twin Bears, he didn't want to go any further. Brent tried walking the team for a while but Dude's negative attitude was contagious and "spread like wildfire." Finally he stopped, pulled the team to the side of the trail and crawled on his sled bag for a nap.

Martin Buser came rolling up the trail. He could see Brent parked on the side of the trail ahead of him and started shouting at him.

"Hey Brent, you need anything? What can I help you out with? Do you need water?"

As his team trotted past he dropped a bag of fish snacks on the ground beside the sled. If a stalled team of dogs would eat anything it would be fish. Brent tried it. They weren't interested.

Michelle Phillips passed. He hoped they might get inspiration from her but "my team was totally oblivious."

William Kleedehn's team went by, looking unbeatable again. "These dogs," said William, "I got them back running and thinking about running and not just sex."

But it didn't help Brent.

Finally, after five hours stalled on the side of the trail, he stuck Dude in the sled bag, walked up to his lead dogs and started leading them. "I would have walked the whole damn way if I would have had to.

Martin Buser.

Brent Sass.

Normand Casavant.

Hugh Neff.

Michelle Phillips.

I was going to finish no matter what." As a last resort he ran in front of the team and, for some unexplainable reason, that seemed to stir them into action.

"We stopped once to snack and made it all the way." The final stretch tainted what had been a great run for him. While the dogs were physically tired, their decision to balk was purely mental. "But I'm proud of what we did. The whole race was great. I made some good decisions and I made some bad ones...and they (the bad ones) bit me in the ass."

Martin and Michelle started running together, jockeying for that little advantage that would secure one of them fourth place. For a short while they forgot to compete with each other as they loped down the Chena River into a bright crimson sunset that, according to Michelle, "almost seemed like it was made exclusively for us and us alone." As they edged closer to the finish chute, Michelle realized Martin's team had more steam left than hers.

"Age before beauty," she smiled, conceding the higher placement to the Iditarod veteran.

Hugh Neff knew he needed a two-hour edge when he pulled into Twin Bears. Because of the penalty imposed on him at Central anything less would put him at a disadvantage. With his team resting, he started watching the clock. The first hour crept past agonizingly slow. Halfway there. Another half hour.

Sebastien Schnuelle wins the 2009 Yukon Quest in record time.

Then the words he didn't want to hear, "Team coming."

Five minutes later Sebastien Schnuelle trotted out of the trees.

"Everyone else had a little issue with Eagle Summit," Sebastien explained to journalists wanting to know how he moved from fourth in Central to leaving Twin Bears in first. He would be able to leave 25 minutes ahead of Hugh but, he cautioned, winning would still depend upon running a clean race.

"I'm afraid one wrong turn or one wrong something, it's gone. So I am definitely not confident. We know who has the fastest team," indicating Hugh's team with his head. "If Hugh finishes 15 minutes behind me he still has the fastest team. That's all that counts in my books."

The two-hour penalty could cost him the race, Hugh conceded, but "just because I don't get a trophy or the money doesn't mean I don't think I was the winning team.

"I'm just happy the dogs don't have a clue of it. The dogs are having fun; they are eating well, running well. I know in my heart how good they are. They are a great team. I couldn't have asked anything more out of them."

Then he appeared to give up, slumping down in his seat, "The race is pretty much over with. I'm just going to go into town and have a beer somewhere. It's like I've been on this trail forever."

Sebastien didn't believe a word. As he headed out into the early morning, he glanced back over his shoulder for the first time. He would spend the next five hours wondering what was happening behind him, knowing that Hugh's dogs were chewing up the miles, whittling away his lead. "I could tell he was getting closer on the Chena River, so every corner I looked around to see if he's there."

Hugh began the chase 25 minutes later. On every bend in the river there seemed to be somebody with a watch. "People would tell me 15 minutes. Then 13 minutes. Then five minutes. But I never saw him. He was always around the next corner."

It was the closest finish in Yukon Quest history. After nearly a thousand miles and almost 10 days of racing only four minutes separated the top two finishers. The two men, competitors for a decade of racing, hugged each other at the line.

"I would have been fine either way (with first or second)," Sebastien set a new record of nine days, 23 hours and 20 minutes. "I was enjoying myself to the fullest. In all honesty I think that Hugh won this race. He would have been two hours ahead of me. He clearly had the better team. He knows that and I know that."

"It was easily my best Quest run ever," Hugh was looking forward to a beer and something he hadn't had for four days – a shower. "It was like living in a fantasy world for a week and a half."

Jon Little finished third, an hour behind the two leaders. "I'm amazed I've been able to be this competitive with the size of kennel I have. I couldn't be prouder. It's a really nice group of dogs."

Life couldn't get any better than this. The temperatures had finally warmed up. It was only -17°C. The dogs were loping and Newton could almost smell the Finish line. It was all peace and plenty. He was on top of the world, enjoying the run that after two years of work seemed only his due.

The adventure was almost over, but it opened the possibility of many more. This was a lifestyle he could live with, strenuous, but not unendurable.

"It's not an easy road out there," said Newton. "It's not easy by any means. If you put your mind to it, all things come ahead. But you have to want to do it. If you think it's too hard and you don't want to do it, don't try.

"You need to have a really strong heart to do this."

The bonfires, residential lights and shouts from random spectators along the riverbank didn't distract the dogs. They too could sense the end was close. Newton stopped twice to snack them, each time thinking, "I will never be here, with these dogs, in this place, at this time, again."

He sang to them, every once in awhile pausing in his song to break out into delighted laughter. Few ever experience how wonderful, delicious and life-giving it is to just stop at the end of such a race. After this Newton would have no excuses ever again.

A light snow started to fall as they trotted around what seemed like just another bend in the river and saw people mingled with bright lights in the middle of the river. The lights appeared to confuse the team and they started wandering from side to side on the trail. At the last moment, just as it seemed they were going to miss the chute, they corrected themselves and trotted under the banner.

Music with a Caribbean beat could be heard over the river. Doug Grilliott stepped forward and extended his hand. "Welcome to Fairbanks," he said.

"I don't believe it," Danny let out the breath he had been holding for the minute or so it took Newton to reach the Finish line. "Pinch me!"

Newton walked down the line of dogs, speaking to each one individually, "Thank you. You're a good dog. A special dog." Giving each a hug, rubbing their heads, holding them close to him.

"Sing them a song," somebody suggested but Newton just shook his head.

"I couldn't get here without you. Thank you."

"No matter how good you sound on the trail, if you put in a poor performance in front of a crowd, the crowd might throw rocks and bottles. If you sing poorly…you better be able to run quickly. I wasn't running no more that day."

There was as much media to greet him, the 13th place musher, as there had been for Sebastien and Hugh.

"Did your lead dog get you through it?" shouted a journalist.

"Everybody get me through it. The dogs pull like crazy. They're very good dogs. Very strong dogs. Very happy dogs. Our dogs in Jamaica, they couldn't handle this."

"Did you feel a lot of pressure on you with everyone telling you what to do? "

"Well, if it was the right thing they were telling me, it was good. Everyone was very encouraging. Everybody wanted me to do well," said Newton.

"I had a schedule and I stuck to it. I did some mistakes in the first half but it paid off because my dogs were good, running faster in the second half of the race." His elapsed time was 11 days, 19 hours and two minutes – 58 minutes faster than his original schedule called for.

The team that made it happen: Hans Gatt, Newton Marshall, Danny Melville.

"You said through the race you would dance at the Finish line."

"I didn't know for sure if this was the Finish line."

"Did you earn that black spot on your nose?"

He laughed and rubbed at his nose, "Yeh Mon. I earned it all through my life."

The media retreated, their curiosity sated for the moment. In the few moments everyone's attention was diverted from Newton, Danny came out of the crowd and wrapped his arms around him. Both men began to cry. This was more than just an athletic accomplishment. For both it was something bigger. It was about pride. It was about your reach exceeding your grasp. It was about changing their world. It was about those who aspire and thus inspire.

"I love you man," Danny spoke softly to him.

"Mr. Melville," responded Newton, "You give me new life."

Newton and 2009 Quest champion Sebastien Schnuelle at the Finish Banquet.

Respect

The first Black musher. The first Jamaican. And in Black History Month. This is truly exciting. I'll support this team wherever and whenever I can.

Lt. Marquis Marcellus, ex-patriate Jamaican and U.S. military officer stationed at Fort Wainwright, just outside of Fairbanks, Alaska

February 28, 2009

"It's a very important award," Doug Grilliot spoke deliberately, *"And we (the officials) do give a lot of consideration before we select the musher who will receive this."*

Doug spared the crowd at the 2009 Yukon Quest Finish Banquet the details about the debate held in the crowded SUV while the officials were still on the trail. A number of names were put forward, each official outlining the reasons for their recommendations. One name that was conspicuously absent from the discussion was Newton Marshall.

"I'll be the first to admit that when I saw his entry I didn't think it was much more than a publicity stunt."

Lt. Marcellus and son with Newton and Dick.

When his name was raised in the SUV, there was an initial silence.

"Put aside the public relations machine and corporate purpose behind him," his recommender stated. "Focus on what he has accomplished as a musher and an individual."

"Over the last 1,000 miles we've come to respect and admire his attitude, perseverance and the way he took care of his dogs."

William Kleedehn had already received the Dawson City Award, four ounces of gold to the first musher into the midway point who completes the race.

Martin Buser, despite his Iditarod record, was the rookie of the year. "My boys, who are in college, got so much fun out of their dad being a rookie again," he laughed.

Brent Sass, for helping William on Eagle Summit, was selected by his fellow mushers to receive the Most Sportsmanlike Award.

The coveted Veterinarian's Choice Award, honoring outstanding dog care on the trail, went to Michelle Phillips. "I had a beautiful team and I think it showed by the way they finished. It felt amazing to run behind them."

"This year's Challenge of the North Award is going to a musher that most definitely showed perseverance, class and grace under pressure."

Newton with the Spirit of the North Award.

Sebastien Schnuelle had several leaders in his team and he had to select two to receive the Golden Harness Award. Selecting Inuk and Nemo for their "loyalty, endurance and perseverance" he led them to the stage where they were each served the traditional raw steak. Nemo wolfed his down in record time. Inuk left a small chunk on the plate, which Nemo helped himself to.

"Nemo was the greedy one tonight," Sebastien was surprised once again by his dogs. "On the trail it's usually the other way around."

Iris Sutton received the Red Lantern, reserved for the last musher across the Finish line.

"Throughout the race, his smile and cheerful attitude never faltered."

The Challenge of the North Award was voted on by the officials and acknowledged the musher who best exemplified the "Spirit of the Yukon Quest," which compels mushers to challenge themselves and persevere.

"This year's Challenge of the North Award goes to Newton Marshall."

Almost lost in the prolonged applause and cheering was Newton's response, "I am quite surprised and a nervous wreck."

While the banquet eventually ended, the night didn't for the Jamaica Dogsled Team. They wandered down the street to a local bar. As they strolled in with their "Mush Mon" jackets and Newton in his yellow Jamaican soccer shirt the bar patrons whispered among themselves, glancing pointedly in the JDT's direction but not wanting to intrude on their exuberant mood.

When it came time to leave, Newton stood up and the patrons broke into spontaneous applause.

"This team has never been only about rescuing street dogs, racing overseas, promoting Jamaica and our sponsors," Danny mused in July, 2009. "It was also about young Jamaicans and giving them opportunity. I think Newton is a survivor and a wonderful human being. I think he is the essence of the Jamaican 'can-do' spirit. In other words, 'I will overcome any adversity to do well.' I am so proud of this kid you would never believe it.

"Who would have thought that Newton, who was an at-risk kid himself a couple of years ago, would ever become a role model for at-risk Jamaican boys. This part of our story should also be told."

Afterparty: (Clockwise) Susie, Moira, Newton, Carole, Danny and Hans.

Jamaican sports stars: Triple Olympic gold medalist Usain Bolt and Newton in New York, October, 2009.

Epilogue

In a photograph taken in New York City's Moka Night Club, triple Olympic gold medal winner and world sprint record holder Usain Bolt looks perplexed as he shakes hands with Newton. It might be because Newton is also a professional Jamaican athlete on the world stage, albeit in a sport that Bolt can't even start to fathom.

Usain Bolt enjoys a special place in society because he is an athlete of unusual ability and strength and he is the latest in an unending stream of great sprinters from the island nation. Speed is an obsession in Jamaica. So much so that many claim it is harder to qualify for the national team than it is to actually win the Olympic gold medal. Its champions more myth than mortal.

Since 1948, when Arthur Wint won the country's first gold in the 400 meters at the London Olympics, there has been a constant flow of Jamaican born speedsters whose exploits are golden and whose names are spoken

Newton and statue of Balto in Central Park, NYC.

with reverence. Britain's Linford Christie. Canada's Donovan Bailey and infamous Ben Johnson. Jamaica's own Herb McKenley, Shirley Fraser, Melaine Walker, Donald Quarrie, Veronica Campbell, Asafa Powell, Merlene Ottey, Lennox Miller and Juliet Cuthbert.

Their sport is a single explosive instant during which all is gained or lost. It is ferocious, almost cruel in its intensity, but brief in duration.

Given the brutal ferocity of his sport and the barren venues in which Usain Bolt competes the sprinter probably couldn't wrap his mind around a sport that consists of gliding through snow-covered wooded trails and over mountain paths for days on end. That embodies the synergy of man with beast with nature.

In a nation fixated on explosive acceleration it is almost unheard of for an athlete to compete in a discipline that emphasizes endurance over power and swiftness. Newton might as well be racing on a distant planet. Jamaicans can't visualize cold weather camping, long hours of hard work, working with dogs, intentionally making trips through remote places virtually devoid of civilization and waist deep in snow.

Like the disenfranchised elsewhere in the world, the poor and disadvantaged of Jamaica hunger for a better life. Seventy percent of the island's population lives at or below the poverty level.

For many of the island's young it is to music that they first turn to break the cycle. But the chance of becoming another Bob Marley, Burning Spear, Byron Lee or to amount to anything at all is virtually nil.

Their second choice is sports. To be the best at a sport can mean a ticket to a university education, travel, fame and financial security.

Jamaicans understand sport has the power to move society. What an athlete gains is far more intricate than just learning how to play a sport. What athletes really learn is the value of teamwork, perseverance, sportsmanship, the value of hard work and an ability to deal with adversity. It gives people a sense of their own strength.

Regardless of whether Bolt or Newton understand each other's respective sport, they both know how important their success is and how it reflects back upon their country. They are among the most celebrated in the world at what they do. Those who are designated as "stars" in Jamaica cease to be just athletes. They grow to be iconic figures and share the tremendous responsibility of becoming a part of their culture's collective consciousness.

Not only ambassadors of their nation to the world, they are spokesmen for the pursuit of excellence and emissaries of social change to their own countrymen. Both have a story to tell. A tale that is more than words. It has a soul. Its own heartbeat.

It concerns the way they live, how they perceive their world. It tells Jamaicans that what they are hearing has lessons from their past, value for their present and portents for their children's future.

Newton chats with children at risk while they visit the JDT museum.

Cove Hosts Special Boys

Nine grade-five boys from the St. Ann's Bay Primary School are still talking about their outing to Chukka Cove on Thursday, June 25, the day when Daniel Melville and his accommodating staff graciously hosted a special fun day for the boys who have been enrolled in a special instructional and mentorship program, Children of our Village, since October, 2007.

Children of our Village is the brainchild of Jamaican-born Herbert E. Murdock, an experienced English teacher and retired New York City high school principal who, because of the current, island-wide, academic underachievement of Jamaican males, is determined to do whatever he can to address a problem which he thinks is untenable. In collaboration with Miss Amy James, Principal of St. Ann's Bay Primary School, and the parents/guardians of the participating boys, the program seeks to address the pressing needs of at-risk, primary school boys in St. Ann's Bay and its environs. Children of our Village operates under the auspices of the St. Ann Homecoming and Heritage Foundation of which Mr. Murdock is the chairman.

Patron of the organization is Honourable Radcliffe O. Walters, Custos Rotulorum for St. Ann.

Assisted by a volunteer Foundation member, the Reverend Winston Walsh, Mr. Murdock visits the St. Ann's Bay Primary School on Tuesdays and Thursdays for one-hour language arts classes with the boys. In the 2007-2008 school year, when the boys were in Grade Four, instruction focused on preparation for the Grade Four Literacy

Test. Although not considered the brightest of last year's fourth graders, in May 2008, every boy passed the Grade Four Literacy Test; and some received perfect scores in more than one section of the test. In recognition of their efforts, the boys were treated at Dolphin Cove at the end of the school year.

This year, in a chance encounter with Mr. Melville, Mr. Murdock told him about the boys of Children of our Village and asked the affable Mr. Melville if he would provide the end-of-year entertainment for them.

Without a moment's hesitation, Mr. Melville agreed and began, on spot, to pave the way for the June 25 happening. That day, the boys, accompanied by Mr. Murdock and the Reverend Walsh, arrived at Chukka Cove at 8:45 a.m., and the fun immediately began when the visitors were met by the charming Miss Nicole Lynch who outlined the day's program and introduced Jamaica's celebrated dogsled musher, Oswald "Newton" Marshall, and his dogsled colleagues.

The boys had learnt only the week before that Jamaica had an official dogsled team and that one of that team, Oswald "Newton" Marshall, in March, 2009, had done Jamaica proud by placing thirteenth in a field of 27 international mushers in the Yukon Quest 1,000 Mile International Sled Dog Race. They were thrilled to meet Newton, whose ever-present smile and amiable disposition immediately made him a friend and big brother. Soon the boys were enjoying the screening of the *Sun Dog* documentary, which exposed them to the dangers and thrill of dogsledding and gave them a better understanding of Newton's remarkable achievement.

But the highlight of their visit was, without a doubt, the dry land ride on a sled pulled by fifteen harnessed dogs. That is the adventure that the boys cannot stop talking about. It rivaled the storybook magic carpet ride in its exhilarating, extraordinary flight through space and time. Not even the subsequent thrilling experience of running with the dogs on their leashes equaled the dogsled ride. After a hearty, hot lunch, each boy was presented with a bag of goodies including a tee-shirt, lunch bag, notebooks, pencils and a pen. Everyone wanted to know the date of the next visit.

June 25 will be long remembered by these nine boys, most of whom come from households headed by mothers and grandmothers who struggle daily to meet the financial and emotional needs of these youngsters. Some boys pass by Chukka Cove five days a week; others have passed by on several occasions. And each time they passed by, that site and what it offered, seemed as far removed from their lives as dining at Buckingham Palace still is. That is why they will not forget the day when a benevolent Jamaican, Daniel Melville, introduced them to another world, into a new, exciting realm of possibilities.

Herbert E. Murdock

July 1, 2009

"This alone makes the whole project worthwhile," Dick Watts, lunching at a restaurant in Whitehorse, had tears in his eyes as he read the press release about Chukka Cove and the special boys. "Of all the press clippings and PR generated in the last couple of years, this is the most special…but that really was the whole point of the thing wasn't it?"

He leaned back in his chair and thought back to a day in September, 2007. He permitted himself a smile and his emotions welled up again, "And the kid hanging around the gate was the one who ultimately brought it together, wasn't he?"

The JDT's ongoing legacy.

The JDT for the 2009-2010 season: Newton, Robb's trainer Ken Davis, Damion Robb, Lance Mackey, Danny.

Afterword

"We just want to finish this and then talk about the future," said Hans in Fairbanks after Newton completed the Quest. "I assume there is a future?"

"He (Newton) has earned the right to say, 'You know, I think I'll just stay warm for a couple of years and run the dogs on the beach' …and I wouldn't blame him if he did."

The decision to have Newton run the 2010 Iditarod was made shortly afterwards but questions had been raised concerning whether he would return to train with Hans.

Newton's conflict with Susie split the decision makers. Danny and Dick wanted him to stay with Hans. Everyone else thought they should switch to someone else. One of the names being debated was Lance Mackey's Comeback Kennel in Fairbanks, Alaska.

The turning point came when one of the handlers who worked for Hans and Susie during the winter of 2008-2009 visited Chukka in May, 2009. She told them that Newton and Susie's differences were irreconcilable. The decision to change to Comeback Kennels was made and announced on June 4, 2009.

When Newton arrived in Fairbanks at the beginning of December, 2009, Lance and Tonya Mackey knew as much about Newton as he knew about them. Other than brief encounters at the Copper Basin 300 and the Yukon Quest, nothing at all.

Lance had only two months to prepare Newton for the Iditarod. That was barely enough time to get him familiar with the dogs and into racing condition but not enough to turn him into a dog musher. Lance had to risk the assumption that Newton's training from Hans hadn't been eroded in the nine months he had been in Jamaica.

On Newton's first day in Alaska, Lance hooked Newton up to a team and sent him into the Arctic night for an 18-mile run. "He came back with a big smile on his face and the rest of the winter went one direction from there – up!!" enthused Lance.

Lance did have cause for concern a few times during the training. On one run, a 140-mile overnight trip near Manley, Alaska, Newton lost his team and got tangled in the trees three times in the first mile.

"There were three other teams. We had just left the dogyard. Everyone's impatient and the dogs are excited. Everything was chaos." Lance recalled. "I was starting to wonder what was going on. Can he not pay attention? Couldn't he hold on because the dogs were too powerful? Those were the things going through my head, but what was comforting to me was that he had a smile on his face through the whole thing.

"It was frustrating for me but he was enjoying the hell out of the whole thing! We got to where we were going and everything worked out fine in the end – it just took a little longer."

Lance smiled and shook his head as he remembered Newton's obvious embarrassment. "It was a good test of patience on my part. Finding out who Newton really was. I had to remain calm because it would have been very discouraging for him if I had yelled. But the dogs came out good and no sleds were torn up. The only thing hurt was his pride."

After a few initial problems the training went fairly smoothly. During one training run, when a group of mushers camped together around a massive bonfire on the side of the trail one cold night, Newton shocked them by huddling close to the flames and eating ice cream.

"Minus 45 isn't comfortable for people who are familiar with it." Lance laughed, "Far less for someone from Jamaica. We're trying to thaw out food and he's eating ice cream!"

(L to R) Tonya Mackey, Newton, Jason Mackey.

At 7:27 p.m. on March 20, 2010, just over 12 days after he left the Start line in Anchorage, Newton rode his sled runners across the Iditarod Finish line on Front Street in Nome, Alaska, waving a Jamaican flag and shouting, "Jamaica. I did it again!"

At the Finish Banquet, Newton had the opportunity to talk with both Hans Gatt and Susie Rogan. Newton thanked Hans and congratulated him on his 2010 Quest win. Newton and Susie were polite to each other but neither made any effort to make peace.

His relationship with Lance and Tonya had taken a different path.

"Newton has become a part of our family." Lance and Tonya had figured out how to communicate with Newton. They had the advantage of having raised a family. "Not just a Jamaican musher or a leased team. He is a true friend."

"Newton is a dog musher. He can proudly wear that title," concluded Lance, arguably the greatest long distance dog driver of all time. "He deeply loves the sport, the dogs and, given the opportunity, Newton has a great future in this sport.

"He has seen some really tough weather and hard trails. Running and completing middle and long distance races like the Copper Basin, the Yukon Quest and the Iditarod are not given to you – you have to earn them. That being said, I have no doubt there are still a few who still see Newton as a publicity stunt, but Newton has nothing to be ashamed of. He fits right into this insane sport as an athlete, a musher."

What Happened After...

- The building used to house the mushers at the McCabe Creek dog drop burned to the ground just hours after the final team departed. At the Finish Banquet Hugh Neff committed $5,000 of his winnings to assist the Kruse family in rebuilding.
- The jumble ice in front of and past Eagle, Alaska, that caused so much concern for the mushers before it was covered by snow, didn't go out easily when the river broke up in the spring of 2009. Too much of it jammed up on an island just downstream from Eagle, causing water levels to rapidly rise and flood the entire town site. Every building in the community was severely damaged or destroyed by the water.
- Residents of Dawson City showed true Northern community spirit when they were the first people to provide assistance and aid to the citizens of Eagle – arriving days before any support from the Alaska State government or U.S. government could get into the isolated town. Some Dawson residents continued to help in Eagle throughout the summer of 2009 as they rebuilt.

Lance Mackey, winner of the 2010 Iditarod.

- Sebastien Schnuelle competed in the 2009 Iditarod, finishing second behind Lance Mackey.

- Hans Gatt returned for the 2010 Yukon Quest and won his fourth championship, becoming the first musher in three years to defeat Lance Mackey in a long distance race. A month later, in the 2010 Iditarod, Lance triumphed with Hans coming second in the second-fastest Iditarod ever run.

- Acknowledgement of the JDT contribution to education and Jamaica's adult literacy problem came in 2010 when Cottey College, a liberal arts college founded in the 1880s for women, signed on to the JDT as an official sponsor. The privately operated educational institute in Nevada, Missouri, prepares students, men and women, from across the United States and 26 other nations, including Jamaica, for advancement to universities that provide a full degree curriculum.

- In 2010 Newton was presented with the Youth Musgrave Medal by the Institute of Jamaica. The institute has annually presented medals to Jamaicans since 1889 for achievements in the fields of literature, arts and science. The letter informing Newton of his award stated that it was for "exemplary courage and persistence."

Danny, Newton and Carole looking toward the future.

Glossary

A'right, Hike, Okay – commands used to get a team moving.

Basket – area in the sled where freight or passengers are carried.

Booties – a sock-like boot, usually made of fleece, which mushers put on a dog's feet to prevent snow and ice build-up between the toes.

Brake – heavy metal fork at the bottom back of the sled. When the prongs are forced into the snow the sled stops.

Brushbow – curved piece on the front of the dogsled.

Checkpoint – designated spot along the trail where the musher must "check in."

Dog Box – large wooden box fitted to the back of a truck and divided into individual sections for individual dogs. Used to transport the dogs.

Dropped dog – a dog the musher has dropped from his team at a checkpoint or other approved locations along the trail. The dog is cared for by veterinarians or handlers.

Dogsled – a sled on runners pulled by a dog team.

Dogyard – area where dogs are tied, chained or kenneled at the musher's home.

Driving bow/handlebar – top handle gripped by the musher while riding on the sled.

Drop chain – cable or chain that can be fastened temporarily between trees, posts or vehicles, with shorter leads attached to hold dogs while they are awaiting transport.

Gangline – central line running from the yoke at the front of the sled. Attaches the sled to all the dogs. The dogs are attached to the gangline via a tugline secured to the very back of each harness.

Gee – the command to go right.

Handler – the person who helps the musher train, transport and take care of the dogs.

Harness – diamond-shaped cloth strap webbing around the dog's chest, front legs and across its back. The harness attaches to the gangline and enables the dog to pull the sled.

Haw – the command to go left.

Holding area – staging area for the teams at the start of each race where the dogs are staked out, then hooked up for the race.

Ice hook – metal hook fastened by a line to the yoke at the front of the sled. It is jammed into the snow when the musher needs to hold the sled securely, usually when they are off the sled for some reason.

Kennel – a shelter or boarding area for dogs.

Lead dog(s) – the front dog or dogs in the team.

Litter – group of puppies born at one time to one female.

Neckline – line that attaches the dog's collar to the gangline.

On by – command used to direct the team past another team.

Pedaling – pushing the sled with one foot while the other one is riding on a sled runner.

Purse – the total amount of prize money that is split between the top finishers in a race.

Race marshal – the top official who ensures the race is run according to the rules.

Runner – the underside surface on which the sled slides.

Stakeout chain – used to tether a dog to a stake in the ground at the kennel. It is on a swivel enabling the dog to move freely.

Stanchions – upright pieces fencing in the side of a sled, running between the runner and top rail.

Swing dogs – pair of dogs directly behind the lead dogs.

Team dogs – any pair of dogs between the wheel dogs and swing dogs.

Tighten up – command to lead dog to keep the gangline taut.

Trail! – request for right of way on a trail.

Tugline – line that fastens the back loop of the harness to the gangline.

Wheel dogs – pair of dogs directly in front of the sled.

Whoa! Hold! Stop! – stop.

Metric Conversion Table

1 mile = 1.6 kilometers

1 kilometer = .62 miles

Yukon Quest 2009 Race Results

Total elapsed time

Musher	Days	Hours	Minutes
• Sebastien Schnuelle	9 days	23 hours	20 minutes
• Hugh Neff	9 days	23 hours	24 minutes
• Jon Little	10 days	0 hours	28 minutes
• Martin Buser	10 days	9 hours	40 minutes
• Michelle Phillips	10 days	9 hours	41 minutes
• William Kleedehn	10 days	11 hours	16 minutes
• Brent Sass	10 days	11 hours	54 minutes
• Dan Kaduce	10 days	12 hours	14 minutes
• Warren Palfrey	10 days	22 hours	26 minutes
• Normand Casavant	11 days	15 hours	2 minutes
• Mark Sleightholme	11 days	17 hours	34 minutes
• Colleen Robertia	11 days	17 hours	47 minutes
• Newton Marshall	11 days	19 hours	2 minutes
• Luc Tweddell	12 days	4 hours	35 minutes
• Wayne Hall	12 days	15 hours	9 minutes
• William Pinkham	12 days	18 hours	16 minutes
• Becca Moore	13 days	22 hours	49 minutes
• Iris Wood Sutton	13 days	23 hours	17 minutes

Scratched

Jean-Denis Britten
Josh Cadzow
Mike Ellis
Jason Mackey
Jerry Joinson
Didier Moggia
Kyla Boivin
Yuka Honda
Hans Gatt
David Dalton
Russ Bybee

Newton's Yukon Quest

Checkpoint	Rest time	Running time from previous checkpoint
Whitehorse		
Braeburn	6 hours 52 minutes	12 hours 59 minutes
Carmacks	6 hours 39 minutes	13 hours 1 minute
McCabe Creek (dog drop)	6 hours 47 minutes	5 hours 14 minutes
Pelly Crossing	9 hours 39 minutes	3 hours 18 minutes
Stepping Stone (hospitality)	7 hours 18 minutes	4 hours 12 minutes
Scroggie Creek (dog drop)	8 hours 25 minutes	14 hours 43 minutes
Dawson City	37 hours 7 minutes	17 hours 27 minutes
Forty Mile (hospitality)	4 hours 14 minutes	6 hours 11 minutes
Eagle	8 hours 17 minutes	15 hours 56 minutes
Slaven's (dog drop)	6 hours 19 minutes	19 hours 26 minutes
Circle City	8 hours 1 minute	8 hours 30 minutes
Central	6 hours 41 minutes	9 hours 41 minutes
Mile 101 (dog drop)	7 hours 38 minutes	5 hours 30 minutes
Twin Bears	8 hours 0 minutes	10 hours 15 minutes
Fairbanks		5 hours 48 minutes

Total running time:	6 days	8 hours	11 minutes
Total rest time:	5 days	11 hours	57 minutes
Average speed:	6.5 miles per hour (10.5 kilometers per hour)		
Total elapsed time:	11 days	19 hours	2 minutes

Acknowledgments

Without all of the following people, this book would not have been possible. They provided me with private and personal information that permitted me to venture into the heart of the JDT. My deepest appreciation to all of you and, if I have missed anyone, I apologize. I'm older than I was when I started writing this and don't have as good a memory anymore.

Jamaica
Danny Melville, Carole Melville, Newton Marshall, Devon Anderson, Shelley Kennedy, Brian Kennedy, Miss Penny, Pam Lawson, Damion Robb, Arnold Bertram, Daniel Melville Jr., Cyd Millar, Mr. Ridley, Miss Dorreen, Sergio, the staff at the JSPCA, the staff at Chukka Caribbean Adventures, Chris Blackwell

United States
Minnesota: Rick Johnson, Nettie Johnson, Dave Steele
Alaska: Lance Mackey, Tonya Mackey, John Schandelmeier, Bob Eley, Theresa Daily, Jeff Brady
Florida: Jimmy Buffett
New Mexico: Joe Runyan

Scotland
Alan Stewart, John Stewart

Canada
Yukon: Hans Gatt, Susie Rogan, Dick Watts, John Overell DVM, Dawn Dimond, Tom Firth, Stephen Reynolds, Moira Sauer, William Kleedehn, Sebastien Schnuelle, AV Action, Kurt Waddington, Joy Morgan, Yukon Quest International, Wynne Krangle, Brian Webb, Dee Enright, Harry Kern
British Columbia: Dr. Stanley Cohen, Erin McMullan, Sandy Reber and Reber Creative team, Barbara Schramm
Ontario: Andrea Stewart, Kevin Shackell, Maryanne Shackell, Rachel Manley, Tricia Ruddock, Kathy Avrich-Johnson
Alberta: Eppo Eerkes, Badland Buggies, Shaun Smith
Quebec: Yves Kirouac

Media
Print Publications: *Alaska Magazine, Alaska Science Forum, Dog and Driver, Dawson City News, Duluth News Tribune, Enroute Magazine, Encyclopedia Britannica, Evolution Home Library, Eye on the Trail: Official Iditarod Race News and Perspectives, Fairbanks Daily News - Miner, Haliburton Echo, Jamaica Gleaner, Jamaica Observer, Juneau Empire, Market Intelligence Report, McLean's Magazine, Mushing Magazine, New York Times, Ottawa Citizen, Pan Caribbean, Scottish Field Magazine, The Last Great Road Trip: Travel Guide, The Spectrum, Toronto Globe and Mail, Toronto Sun, The Tugline, The Tyee, Up Here Magazine, Variety Magazine, Westworld Magazine, Whitehorse Star Daily, Yukon News, Yukon Quest Annual*

Online: Caribbeannetnews.com, Gomush.com, marketwire.com, Petplace.com, OnlinePioneerPlus.com, Sleddogcentral.com, Wikipedia.com

TV and Film: *CBC News, The Mercer Report, Newswatch 12, SBS Sport, Sky News, Sun Dogs, Underdogs*

Organizations, Tourism, Businesses: Copper Basin 300, Elfstone Kennels, Jamaica Information Service, JSPCA, Margaritaville, Matthew Henson Center, Percy DeWolfe Memorial Mail Race, Provel Health Care, Royal Canin, Second Chance League, Sheep Mountain 150

Photo Credits (top-T, bottom-B, right-R, left-L, middle-M)
Chukka Caribbean: One Mush, iii, 21, 27, 30, 35, 69, 78, 86, 87, 92, 99, 105, 106 T, 146, 150 B, 153, 250, 279, 298, 314 second and third rows left
Eppo Eerkes: Foreword, 58, 102, 138-139, 165, 180, 191, 217, 232, 235 L, 243, 248, 254, 277, 281, 304-305, 306, 314 B
John Firth: 5, 28 T, 32, 73, 83, 128, 132, 150 T, 167, 172, 183, 190, 225, 227, 229, 231, 239, 240, 252, 270, 274, 282, 280
HarryKern.com: 10-11, 112-113, 120, 130-131
Newton Marshall: 44-45, 47, 49, 50, 77, 117, 118, 122, 145, 169, 192, 196, 202 (218, 266 provided by Newton Marshall)
Erin McMullan: 8, 9 B, 36, 135
Carole Melville: ii, vi, 3, 4, 7, 9 T, 13, 17, 20, 26, 28 B, 55, 56, 62, 70, 81, 85, 93, 94, 98, 148 TL, 158, 170, 195-195, 203, 209, 216, 221, 235 R, 265, 273, 284, 286, 289, 290, 291, 292, 293, 300, 301, 303, 314 TL and TR, 316 (294, 307 provided by Carole Melville)
Sun Dogs: v, 106 B, 147, 148 TR, BL and BR, 149, 151, 315 B
Tony Bursey: 2, 315 T; Double M Photography: 107
Angela Melville: 33; Danny Melville: 296; Ajamu Myrie: 295; Mark Ostazeski: 214
Stephen Reynolds: 206, 207, 211, 314 MR, 315 ML; Susie Rogan: 198; provided by Alan Stewart: 14, 63, 67, 68, 111; Dick Watts: 212; Erica Edghill: 315 MR

p. 40-41 Yukon Quest Trail Map provided by Yukon Quest International Association (Canada). Please note: The Mile 101 dog drop has since been changed to a checkpoint.

MUSH
MON!
JAMAICA DOGSLED